THE SECRET FILE ON
JOHN BIRCH

Captain John M. Birch
May 28, 1918 — August 25, 1945

Dedicated to the memory of

George and Ethel Birch,

devoted parents of Captain John M. Birch,

missionary and war hero

Table of Contents

INTRODUCTION

This is the biography of a Christian missionary and United States intelligence agent in China during World War II.

Government bureaucracy and political pressure served to keep many of the facts in the book secret for a number of years — particularly the truth about his murder by Chinese Communists. The complete story of his life can now be told for the first time, thanks to the declassification of essential documents.

In telling it we have followed a narrative form. Some scenes — always based on fact — have been created by the writers to flesh out certain events. Also, we have used a few fictitious names. This includes the nurse Jenny Campbell, a mechanic, a pilot and a few Chinese coolies. Except for Ms. Campbell, and Paul Daniel, all complete names in the book are the names of real persons involved in the life of John Birch.

This map of China shows in boldface areas in which John Birch operated as a missionary and intelligence officer.

Shanghai: This is where John Birch attended language school.

Hangchow: John served as missionary here.

Chungking: This was Chiang Kai-shek's wartime capital. Here John Birch was commissioned as a U.S. Army officer.

Kunming: The headquarters of the "Flying Tigers."

Kweilin: The field intelligence headquarters to which John Birch reported.

Changsha: Here John Birch was murdered by Chinese Communists.

Suchow: The burial place of John Birch.

1

The Message

*The word has just come over the radio that
Japan has unconditionally surrendered. Praise
God from whom all blessings flow. ... Liberty is
worth its price.*

—John Birch, in a letter to his parents, August
14, 1945

The telegram addressed to Mr. and Mrs. George Birch was received in Macon, Georgia, at 10:22 p.m., September 11, 1945. It was put in a stack of other messages for rural delivery the next morning. "With the war over, a lot of families are receiving good news," the clerk commented to the delivery woman who picked them up. "Sure is better than dispatching death notices."

"Isn't that the truth!" The delivery woman agreed. "I received word the other day that my son is on his way home. It's the happiest thing a mother can hear." She picked up the top message and glanced at the name. "Hey, this one's for George and Ethel. I know how excited she will be. She's a nice lady, Mrs. Birch is. I'll stop at her place first thing. No sense in keeping her waiting."

At six-thirty the next morning, Ethel Ellis Birch, a matronly woman of fifty, arose in the small two-story white clapboard house just off State Highway 87. She built a fire in the kitchen stove, put on water for coffee and sat down to read from her well-worn Scofield Reference Bible. She always enjoyed her quiet time alone with God. She began with a Scripture reading, and then spent time in prayer, asking individual blessings on family members. She was always conscientious, too, to thank Him for blessings received and for His daily care.

The house lay particularly still that day, nestled in the piney woods. Ethel's husband was away on a job for the Georgia Health Department, near the Alabama border. Four of their sons — Robert, Herbert, George Stanley and John — were still in the service. Daughter Betty had just begun the fall term at Bryan College in

Dayton, Tennessee. Douglas, the high schooler, was still at home, but sleeping, as was Ellis who held down an engineering job at nearby Warner Robbins Air Force Base, a job that kept Ellis out of the service.

Her lips moving silently, she prayed for her husband and daughter and each of the boys — especially for John, her first born, who had been in China for five years. He had been in combat and now would be on his way home. Perhaps there would be a telegram, or a phone call, saying, "I've landed in San Francisco."

She thanked God, as did so many others that morning, that the terrible war was over. The boys would be coming home. It might be a while before Robert, Herbert and George Stanley were released, since they had not been in the armed forces very long, but John was long overdue a furlough. "General Chennault keeps telling me to go home for a month's rest," he had written, "but I won't be coming until the last Jap is out of China."

With John, duty always came first. Just that week she had wondered how he would look. Would he act differently? It had been over five years since the family had hugged him a tearful goodbye on the railway platform at the Macon depot. At twenty-two he had gone away a boy, at least in his mother's mind, and now he would be returning a man of twenty-seven. A man who had seen the horrors of war and had fought to keep America free.

He had looked so handsome in his preaching suit when he stepped smartly into the railway car. Now she yearned to see him in his captain's uniform. Captain John Birch. She liked the sound of that. The girls at church would surely swarm around him. But first, the family would have him all to themselves.

They had always been proud of John. He was the smartest one, they all said, the one who must go to college, even if no one else did. He had been graduated *magna cum laude* from Mercer University and been nominated for a Rhodes Scholarship. Then, in barely a year, he was off to China as a Baptist missionary.

The letters had come regularly while he was in language school in Shanghai. When he completed the course with one of the highest marks ever recorded, the family had been pleased, but not surprised. "That's John," they all agreed. "He always did finish at the head of his class."

Ethel Birch had always felt confident the Lord would protect John out there in China as he biked and hiked across the rice paddies to preach in villages deep in Japanese-occupied territory. Before Pearl Harbor he had trekked 200 miles into Free China.

After that, the letters had come infrequently. They learned that General Claire Chennault, head of the famed Flying Tigers, had commissioned John as a second Lieutenant and put him in intelligence work. "The General said I could preach all I wanted," John had explained.

From 1942 on, John wrote only in the vaguest terms about his work. He never gave a location — his letters were just headed *China* — nor did he cite dates or the names of associates.

The family did know he had been awarded medals and was rapidly promoted to Captain. Then in mid-1944 the awards and promotions stopped, or at least John did not speak of them.

In one of his infrequent letters, he alluded to potential danger. In another, he mentioned occasional attacks of malaria. But he never discussed exactly what he did, making it difficult for the family to answer curious friends who wanted to know. "We think he does some kind of dangerous spy work," Ethel had usually replied. "He evidently travels around a lot."

Ethel was certain John had never faltered in his purpose for going to China. John had written, "If I survive the war, I shall never escape the call to serve Christ." His latest letter had been dated August 13, 1945, when he was waiting "at my little outpost for President Truman's final word concerning Japan's offer to surrender."

A month had passed since Japan had accepted Allied surrender terms, and every day reports were heard of military units being disbanded. Neighbors were getting telegrams that their sons were coming home. John's mail was being forwarded to Macon, but still there was no indication when he would arrive.

"Today, Lord, if it is Your will," the anxious mother prayed. "Let us hear today."

At seven-thirty, she fixed breakfast for Douglas and Ellis and they left for the day. She had cleared the dishes, done a few other chores and was making the bed when a car honked. She peered through the curtain at the vehicle making its way up the drive. *Telegram! Thank you, Lord!* Ethel Birch dropped the pillow she had been straightening and hurried down the stairs and out into the small yard.

"Telegram for you, Ethel," the woman announced. "Please sign here."

Ethel's heart fluttered. "Oh, I hope it says John has reached the States from overseas," she exclaimed as she signed for the message.

"There's nothing like a good telegram. I made yours my first stop of the day. We're all so proud of your John."

Ethel's heart fluttered. "Oh, I hope it says he has reached the States from overseas," she exclaimed as she signed for the message.

Her hands trembled as she opened the yellow envelope. It had to be from John.

> THE SECRETARY OF WAR HAS ASKED ME TO EXPRESS HIS DEEP REGRET THAT YOUR SON CAPT BIRCH JOHN M WAS KILLED IN CHINA 25 AUG 45 CONFIRMING LETTER FOLLOWS.
> EDWARD F WITSELL
> ACTING ADJUTANT GENERAL OF THE ARMY

John dead? Killed? A mistake. Yes, it has to be a mistake. The war is over. I refuse to believe this. God has always taken care of John. He's supposed to come home for a visit and then return to his missionary work. No, I can't. I won't believe it.

The next two days were a blur. John's father was notified. All his brothers and his sister were informed. Robert was in California preparing to join an occupational force in China. They all found it difficult to accept John's death since it supposedly happened after the war had ended.

The follow-up letter from Major General Edward F. Witsell came two days after the Western Union message.

> It is with deep regret that I confirm the telegram of recent date informing you of the death of your son, Captain John M. Birch, 0889028, Air Corps.
>
> The official casualty report states that your son was killed on 25 August 1945 en route to Suchow, China, on the Lunghai Railway, as the result of stray bullets ...
>
> I sincerely regret that this message must carry so much sorrow into your home and I hope that in time you may find sustaining comfort in knowing that he served his country honorably.

Ethel Birch showed the letter to her husband and sons Ellis and Douglas. "He just took this information from a report from China," she muttered. "It must be a mistake. The Lord is taking care of John."

She was alone again a week later when an Army jeep pulled into the drive. A young officer, carrying a clipboard, came to the door.

"I'm from the Chaplain's office at Warner Robbins," he informed her. "What information have you had concerning your son's death?"

Stoically, Ethel handed him the telegram from the War Department and the letter from General Witsell. The young man laid his clipboard on the dining table and turned aside to read the official communications.

While he was diverted, Ethel glanced at a photostat on top of the sheaf of papers on the clipbcard. She caught the name "Captain John Birch" and moved closer.

"Oh, my," she gasped, "this says he was killed by Communists!"

The officer whirled and snatched up the clipboard. "You ought not to have seen that, ma'am."

"Why not? He's *my* son," she protested.

"No, uh, well, yes," the white-faced soldier sputtered. "Ma'am, I made a terrible mistake. I was very careless. You weren't supposed to see this. Why, I could be court-martialed."

"But I want to know. He's my son!" she pleaded. "Please. Please let me read it."

"Okay," he sighed. "Read it. But I beg of you, don't say anything for at least three weeks. I'll be discharged by then."

He passed the clipboard to her. "Captain Birch was killed by Chinese Communists on the Lunghai Railroad, August 25, 1945," the report read.

"I've got to go, ma'am. Please don't say anything for three weeks. I don't want to be court-martialed for this."

The distressed mother promised. The officer left. She never saw or heard from him again.

The next official letter merely expanded on the telegram. Major General Charles B. Stone, commander of the Fourteenth Air Force which had absorbed Chennault's Flying Tigers, said:

> Captain Birch was en route to Suchow, China, on the Lunghai Railway on an official intelligence mission ... There was a clash between Chinese Central Government forces and irregular Chinese troops and your son was struck by a stray bullet. According to the reports received, his death was instantaneous and without pain. His body was interred outside the city of Suchow.

The Birches were confused. Were the "irregular Chinese troops" Communists? Had they killed John by accident or on purpose?

They had been hearing news broadcasts that the Chinese Nationalists, under Chiang Kai-shek, and Mao Tse Tung's Communists had stepped up fighting after the defeat of Japan. They had also heard the lonely voice of former President Herbert Hoover pleading for America to awake to the danger of communism which he said was already "sweeping across" Eastern Europe, while a "fifth column" of Communist spies and sympathizers were active in the U.S. government.

They knew that John, before leaving for China, had felt the greatest peril to world peace was international communism, not

Japan or Germany. A few weeks before the war ended he had written, "I believe that this war will set the stage for Antichrist. I'll have a lot to tell you when I get home. Things about the future of China and the world."

Had the Communists killed him because they felt he knew too much?

Early in November a letter came from Major General Claire L. Chennault, the commander of the Flying Tigers. He "had only just been advised of John's death. This news has indeed been as much of a blow to me as it must have been to you."

The mystery deepened. Chennault had left China just before the war ended. Some said he had been forced out by high level Army politics. In any case, why had he, John's former commander, not heard about John's death for over two months? "John," he assured the Birches, "was more than just a very good officer in my command. In fact, I have always felt toward him as a father might feel toward a son."

What was going on? Had Chennault seen the report that said John, an American army captain, had been killed by Communists ten days after the war ended? Had the press been told? Apparently not, since the Birches had seen nothing in the newspapers.

Later that month a neighbor brought over a small clipping from a California newspaper. "Our son Joe saw this when he came back from overseas," he explained. "Here the name is spelled B-u-r-c-h. He wondered if it was the John Birch we knew."

The troubled family read the news:

> Long dispatches are reaching Washington from Chungking and other tender spots in China. They are all marked top secret, although they deal with what is happening to the American soldiers and sailors in that area. No one has yet been officially informed about the murder of Capt. Burch by the Chinese Communists when that officer, after the Japanese surrender, was trying to make his way back to the American lines accompanied by four GIs. Incidents involving encounters between Americans and Yenan [Communist] forces are reported once in a while from China. But the reports are incomplete and do not give out the whole picture.

The article convinced the Birches that John had indeed been killed by Communists. But why the secrecy and who in the American government was responsible for withholding stories about such incidents?

A possible explanation came in a letter from a newspaper woman in Washington who had spent eight-and-a-half years in China. Adeline Gray wrote:

...Yesterday, I read of John Birch's death in the *Evening Star* and was very shocked. Your son was one of the finest men who ever came to China. He never drank, smoked, swore, or did an unkind thing to anyone. He believed wars were due and are due to lack of religion. He talked of this in most lofty and beautifully worded sentences.

He exerted a profound effect upon the thousands of people who came in contact with him. The American GIs he met were influenced to a better life and higher ideal and better modes of personal behavior by your son's own noble example. Tens of hundreds of Chinese loved him as dearly as though he were their own brother. Your son was truly one of the finest men it has ever been my fortune to meet. His loss is a great loss to not only China, but to America and the world. He loved China and the Chinese people dearly and planned to stay in China all his life.

During the war he performed many dangerous and heroic feats. As a member of the U.S. Army Intelligence, he often was parachuted out into Japanese areas and spent weeks and months behind the lines. He was an outstanding and beloved man of the U.S. Army in China; he was widely known all over China...

I understand that no news agency was allowed to send out the story of your son's death from China for fear of arousing Chinese Communist and American relations to a higher pitch of instability and ill-will. So his death was not mentioned in any news story from China. Otherwise, it would have been on the front page of every paper in the U.S. Perhaps the Chinese Reds killed him because they were afraid he would tell the U.S. Army and the Generalissimo's government something about the Reds' plans and activities for civil war in China. He knew so much about them and spoke the language.

Although your son's life was short, he achieved a great deal. In his few years, your son did more than most men do in a lifetime. I congratulate you upon having such a heroic and noble son.

Miss Gray enclosed the clipping to which she had referred from the *Washington Evening Star*. It repeated the California story and said John had been "murder[ed] by Communists."

Despite discrepancies in the description of John, the Birches felt certain the story was about their son. It was now plain to them that his murder by the Communists had been covered up by officials in the U.S. government.

This was difficult for George and Ethel Birch to accept. They were a patriotic, God-fearing, Baptist couple. They had raised seven children to reverence God and respect their country. They had not begrudged the service of four sons. They had sometimes wondered about their country's policies, especially in regard to communism. It was now clear their trust had been betrayed. Betrayed by giving them inaccurate information about the death of their oldest son and by withholding the true account of his murder from them and from the American public.

Their third son, George Stanley, was now in Guam. They were worried most about the next youngest, Robert, who was headed for China, presumably to join in the cleanup operations there after the Japanese surrender. "If he goes to China, the Communists might connect him with John and kill him too," Ethel lamented. They asked their congressman, Carl Vinson, to intervene. He explained the family's fears to Navy brass. Robert, who had been assigned to the very area where John had been killed, was quickly moved.

The arrival of John's personal effects was a bitter-sweet occasion. The box from the War Department contained his well-marked Scofield Bible, a *Cruden's Concordance*, his Flying Tigers' emblem, a 35 mm. camera, a small collapsible telescope, a Chinese Gold Air Hero medal (the highest that could be awarded to a foreigner), various articles of clothing, Chinese curios, his leather money belt, personal cashbook and a letter from sister Betty. But his diary that would provide details of his war service and his knowledge of Communists was missing.

One afternoon at Warner Robbins, Ellis was called to the property office. A pilot just returned from China was there. "Are you related to Captain John Birch?" he asked.

"I'm his brother."

"I heard you were, I met him in a hospital. There were four of us in a ward. Myself, a rabbi, a Catholic priest and John, who I think had malaria. I was the agitator. Not that I'm a religious type, though. I'd pose a question just to get them going. John would always quote the Bible. No matter what, he always had an answer from the Bible. Oh, what a brain your brother had. Brilliant. And a heart, too. We were there only thirty days or so and I came to love him like a brother."

It seemed everyone had loved John. Had admired and respected him. Yet no one had answers to the question plaguing his family: What had really happened to him?

"I won't give up," his mother declared. "I am going to find the truth of what happened to my son if it takes the rest of my life. The world is going to know about John Birch and how he lived and died for God and country."

2

The Investigation

*I have tried, as wholeheartedly as I could, to
serve the flag that had protected me all my life.*

—John Birch, letter to brother George Stanley,
August 13, 1945

The Birch family was not even told that there had been an official
investigation of John's death. But they were convinced that the
military-diplomatic establishment was giving them the runaround.
Mrs. Birch especially was haunted by the vision of the photostat she
had seen when the officer came to notify her of John's death by "stray
bullets." She kept telling her husband and children and anyone else
who would listen, "There's more to the story. I'm sure of it."

Four months after John's death, the family learned that General
Chennault was to speak in Atlanta. Mrs. Birch called his office in
Washington and obtained an appointment to see him at the
downtown Henry Grady Hotel where he would be staying.

When the parents and son Ellis walked into the lobby, a clerk
told them they couldn't see Chennault. "Just tell him the parents of
Captain John Birch are here," Mr. Birch insisted.

"Very well, but he isn't seeing visitors."

The response was immediate: "Send them right up."

The Big Tiger with the leathery face and jutting chin looked
tough, but his voice was soft. "I told you in my letter that I loved your
boy like a son," he said. "That's how I felt about him."

He described John's "rugged and dangerous work behind
Japanese lines." He said, "John wanted to take flight training, but I
wouldn't let him. I told him, 'You're more valuable to me than any
pilot I've got.'"

Mrs. Birch took down everything he said on a portable
typewriter. "John set up a system that enabled us to provide the
Chinese army with air support for the first time. Then I sent him out
to arrange for the rescue of American airmen shot down in remote

areas. I can't tell you how many pilots owe their lives to your boy. And missionaries. He got many of them out, too.

"This exposed John to a lot of disease. He was seriously ill many times. I kept telling him to take a furlough. He never would. Then he was transferred out of my command to OSS. That's the Office of Strategic Services. They took over all intelligence operations near the end of the war."

"Tell us how he died," the Birches requested. "Was he killed by stray bullets or Communists?"

"Communists!" the old war eagle snorted. "That's what friends have told me, although the War Department classified his file 'TOP SECRET.' His party was stopped on their mission by Communists. Being the officer in charge, John went to talk to them. They fired a volley in his face with no warning. They knew who he was. He walked straight toward them, and they killed him. They murdered one of the most loyal men I ever had."

Chennault was sobbing. "Forgive me for losing my composure. I'm not the tough old bird people make me out to be."

The next sentence came slowly, as if he were measuring every word. "I would never have sent John on that mission. That was a commando mission."

His chin thrust forward. "I'll tell you something else. If I'd been there when the report came that he had been killed, I'd have sent in bombers and blasted that Communist position to powder."

"Could you give us the names of some other men who knew John?" Ethel Birch asked. "I want to write them." Chennault passed along several names, but didn't know their stateside addresses.

When George and Ethel returned home they found a letter waiting from a young serviceman in California. He provided the names of the three Americans who had accompanied John on the fateful last mission.

Aunt May Cosman had been visiting from New Jersey for Christmas and wanted to return home. Mrs. Birch, Douglas and Ellis decided to drive her. Mr. Birch had to stay home and work.

"We'll stop in Washington," Ethel vowed. "We'll get John's file and the addresses of these men who knew him."

They left for New Jersey in the family's 1940 Chrysler and on the return trip stopped in Washington to see what they could learn at the Army Casualty Department.

They were ushered in to see a Major Sanders. He steered the conversation to the disposition of John's body.

"My husband has to be in on that," Ethel insisted impatiently. "Send the forms to our home."

She showed the major the list of names. "How long would it take to get their addresses?"

"Two or three weeks, madam."

"We can't wait that long. We're just here for one day."

"Well, two or three hours, if you want to wait."

"What is the shortest time?" she pressed. "We have some more places to go."

"Ten or fifteen minutes. Ellis can go ahead to the office which would have the addresses while we talk about the disposal of your son's body."

As he explained the procedure, she got the distinct impression that he was pressing for her decision. Again she insisted that the decision would have to be made jointly. "Douglas and I had better go see how Ellis is making out," she added.

"You can talk to him from here." The major dialed a number.

"Mother, Major Marshall says there are so many names in their file that they can't help us."

Major Sanders saw how distressed she was at this and declared, "You can get those addresses. Go on down and if you have any more trouble, let me know."

By the time Mrs. Birch and Douglas reached the other office, Major Marshall had left for lunch. The secretary told them the same thing the Major had told Ellis.

Ethel Birch appeared not to hear. "Here's one, Lieutenant Laird Ogle," she said, giving the name of one of the men with John on his last mission. "He served in China with the Office of Strategic Services."

The secretary shrugged and turned to her assistant. "Okay, see what you can do with it."

Within five minutes she returned with the address of Ogle. She then found a second address, but was unable to find a third.

The secretary called OSS headquarters. "I'm sending over a Mrs. George Birch. She's looking for the address of a Captain Grimes who was with your people in China."

At that point Major Marshall walked in and began explaining why they could not get the addresses.

"Oh, but I already have two," Ethel declared.

"You have! How did that happen?" he demanded loudly.

"We'll be going now. Come on, boys." The three were out the door before the major could get over his obvious shock.

Ellis drove the Chrysler to the address given by the secretary. He stopped in front of an imposing colonial structure. There was no identifying marker anywhere on the building.

"Mother, let's eat first," Ellis pleaded.

"No, I've got to get these addresses. You boys go find a place and come back and meet me here."

She began walking up the steps to the long porch. A young man in civilian clothes met her and asked politely if he could help. "I'm trying to find out something about my son who was killed in China just after the war was over," she told him.

"That would have been John Birch," he replied, to her surprise. "His death was so unnecessary."

"Did you know him?" she asked quickly.

"No, ma'am, but my best friend, a navy lieutenant, was sent on the official investigation."

"You mean there was an official investigation?"

"Oh, yes. Would you like my friend's address? His name is Thompson."

"I most certainly would," she responded, and followed him back to his office to get it.

His secretary wrote down the New York City address. "Your son's immediate commanding officer in OSS is in this building," she noted. "Colonel Paul Helliwell. Would you like to see him?"

Ethel nodded gratefully. She hadn't expected such good fortune.

An escort took the determined mother to Helliwell's office. "Who sent John on this mission?" she asked the officer immediately.

"I did," he replied a bit curtly.

"Why did you do it?" she demanded, remembering that General Chennault had called it a commando mission.

"Captain Birch was the best man for the job. He knew the language better than anyone else. He had always gotten along well with both national and Communist Chinese soldiers. And he volunteered."

"There was an official investigation," she mentioned matter-of-factly.

The Colonel's eyebrows raised. "You know about that?" Recovering quickly, he volunteered, "Would you like to have the address of the young man who handled it?"

When Ethel nodded, he excused himself. A few minutes later he returned looking a bit nonplussed. "I'm sorry, but the address is not in this building."

His obvious discomfort made her realize that she was not supposed to have that information. Indeed, she probably wasn't supposed to know there had been an official investigation. She decided not to press her advantage, yet.

"I do have another address for you," Colonel Helliwell offered. "Captain William Drummond wasn't with your son on his last mission, but they worked together before that. He lives right here in Washington."

She thanked him for the information.

After Ethel Birch and her boys had lunch they hunted up Captain Drummond and found him more than cooperative. He gave them stories about John that were more fascinating than any spy story Douglas or Ellis had ever read. But he could give them only hearsay evidence about John's death. He refused to speculate on why the official investigation had been classified top secret.

They left Drummond and went looking for Adeline Gray, the war correspondent who had written them earlier. When they started up the walk of her apartment building, a slim, attractive woman of about thirty-five walked out the door. "Shhhh," she cautioned. "Keep your voices down and come inside."

The newspaperwoman ushered them into her living room and pulled the shades. "If the wrong people saw me talking to you, I could be in trouble," she said mysteriously. "I might not be permitted to return to China."

"Why?" Ethel queried.

"Mrs. Birch, you don't realize it now, but twenty years from now you will."

It turned out that Miss Gray knew little that she hadn't already told them in her letter. She did tell about John helping her get aboard a refugee train fleeing the Japanese. "I was running and got caught in a crush of people. John saw me and reached down and pulled me up." She also reiterated that he had been killed by the Communists because he knew too much.

"That's just my opinion," she quickly added. "I can't prove it."

The Birches left the capital with more unanswered questions than when they had arrived. Ethel had a number of letters to write. She was more determined than ever to discover how and why John had died.

The letters she wrote drew immediate response from the officers who had known John. Each seemed eager to meet with her and talk about her tragic loss. While this correspondence was taking place, the attractive young nurse, Marjorie Tooker, came to visit. Marjorie glowed as she related details of her friendship with John in China. She told how he had gotten medicines and other supplies for her hospital. It was obvious that she had a deep affection for John.

Arrangements were made for Ethel and Marjorie to meet with the investigator, Lieutenant Thompson, and one of the men who had been with John on the last mission, Lieutenant Laird Ogle. They gathered in Thompson's New York City apartment.

"It was definitely murder," Lieutenant Ogle declared, "even though I didn't see it happen. It was definitely murder. See, John and his Chinese liaison, a Lieutenant Tung, left the main party to find the Communist commander. The rest of us were taken into custody after they left. Then we heard shots. It was a chilling sound. The war was over. There wasn't supposed to be any more bloodshed.

"I got the verbatim testimony of the Chinese officer," Lieutenant Thompson continued. "The Communists had left him for dead, but he survived to tell what happened. It seems John had antagonized the Communists by refusing to obey an order to disarm. It was murder all right, but they might not have killed him if he had complied with that order."

"I refuse to believe that," Ethel protested. "The killing must have been planned."

"Well, there is no way of knowing that," the intelligence officer responded kindly.

Ethel Birch was not satisfied. She felt he was holding back information, but he refused to tell her more. Undaunted, she returned to Washington to knock on more doors, ask more questions and pursue more leads.

Her tenacity paid off, and this time she actually saw John's casualty file. The cause of death still read, "Killed by stray bullets..."

She also ran into the cooperative young man who had given her Lieutenant Thompson's address. "I don't believe I ever met you before, madam," he said, averting her eyes. His embarrassment was so acute she realized he had gotten into trouble for giving her information that was not meant to fall into her hands. Not wanting to cause him more problems, she turned away.

They returned home to find that several interesting letters had arrived. General Charles B. Stone wrote, "I'm more enlightened about John's death now than when I wrote you previously. I have recommended John for the Distinguished Service Cross."

Colonel Wilfred Smith, John's immediate C.O. under General Chennault said, "I have recommended John for the Silver Star. He deserved every bit of it. He was the pioneer of our intelligence operations in China and more loyal to his God and his friends than any young man I ever knew."

Captain James Hart, who called John "the bravest man I ever knew," reported, "I have filed a recommendation for John to receive the Congressional Medal of Honor."

For some reason all these recommendations were lost in the military pipeline.

On subsequent trips to Washington Ethel Birch followed up every lead given her, trying to get a copy of John's top secret file and the report of the official investigation. She also endeavored to discover what had happened to the recommendations for medals, none of which John had ever been awarded.

It became quite evident some officers were dodging her, even after she had made personal appointments by telephone in advance. In one instance, a secretary claimed her Pentagon boss was out of town. A few minutes later Ethel surprised him in another office, where he sat on a desk, puffing a long cigar.

John's old associates were the most gracious and helpful. They related stories of her son's bravery and accomplishments that made her head spin in wonder. All praised him.

Lieutenant William Miller had been close to John during the last year of his life. "I'm a Catholic," he said, "and we argued about theology, but I came to know him as a dedicated man of God." Lieutenant Miller had taken charge of John's burial ceremony. "He was a legend in China and received a hero's burial," he assured her. After he finished describing the ceremony, she was glad they had decided to leave his body in China.

Lieutenant Arthur Hopkins, a Yale graduate and fellow intelligence agent, told her, "Your son was the most brilliant, the finest, the most able and the bravest officer I ever met."

Lieutenant Edwin James confessed, "I've only worshiped one man in my life. That was Captain John Birch."

All of John's wartime friends mentioned his concern about the Communists taking over China. Said Bill Miller: "John knew better perhaps than any other American about Communist activities in the region where we worked. He talked about communism by the hour."

Ethel Birch traveled around the country for five years, seeking to right the wrongs she felt had been done her son and endeavoring to bring his military records and the investigation of his death out of the dungeon of official secrecy. She did get a record of awards given him by General Chennault, but failed to get action on the higher medals for which she knew he had been recommended. Neither Congressman Vinson nor Georgia's Senator Richard Russell was able to help her. Once she asked Major General Witsell in frustration, "Couldn't you at least give him a Purple Heart?"

"No," he replied, "he wasn't killed by an enemy. The Chinese Communists were our allies."

Most frustrating of all was her inability to obtain or even see a copy of the investigation of John's death. It continued to be classified top secret.

Meanwhile during this period, 1945-50, the Communists made huge conquests. All of Eastern Europe fell behind the Iron Curtain, as well as Manchuria, Mongolia and China.

When China fell to the Communists, there was great breast-beating and finger-pointing in Washington. Accusations of disloyalty at worst and ignorance at best were hurled at high U.S. officials and political advisers who had been close to Presidents Roosevelt and Truman. They were responsible, it was charged, for the American policy that had resulted in, or at least hastened, the defeat of Chiang Kai-shek. They had dressed Mao Tse-tung's revolutionaries up as agrarian reformers and Chinese patriots, instead of full-blown Marxists who were bent on capturing, with Soviet aid, the world's most populous nation. They had influenced President Truman to insist that Chiang Kai-shek take Communists into a coalition government. And they had recommended policies giving the Soviets control of North Korea, and leading the Soviets and their North Korean puppets to believe that America would not fight for South Korea.

When the North Koreans invaded South Korea, June 25, 1950, an alarmed U.S. Senate was debating a bill to curb internal subversion and strengthen security at home. Ethel Birch noticed that California's Senator William Knowland was leading the fight for strong laws against American Communists and fellow travelers. She thought he ought to know about the cover-up of her son's murder and sent him her entire file. In her letter she suggested that he try to get the long-suppressed report of John's death.

Knowland asked the Senate Armed Services Committee to get the Birch file from the State Department, which sent over a folder containing only what Ethel Birch had already compiled. "I want the report on the murder investigation," Knowland demanded. "It's there."

The fifty-five page report was delivered, still marked TOP SECRET and for the eyes of the Senator alone.

The more he read, the angrier he got. On September 5, when American soldiers were dying by the hundreds in Korea, he stomped onto the Senate floor and at first chance demanded to be heard.

He began by reminding that previous reports by General A.C. Wedemeyer on China and Korea had been withheld "despite requests by members of the Senate ...

General Wedemeyer warned his government against the very things which have come to pass in Korea. Had this information been available to Congress and its committees, steps could have been taken ... that the last of our forces not be withdrawn in July of last year, or, if they were withdrawn, that the government of the Republic of Korea be properly equipped to meet the ultimate aggression which our own competent military advisers and the officials of the government of Korea saw in the offing.

There were other additional indications, Mr. President [of the Senate], which should have warned our government. One of the least known and most significant to me was the case of Captain John M. Birch of Macon, Georgia. I have asked that the Armed Services Committee get the file of Captain Birch and read the eyewitness account of his death in late August, 1945.

For the first time, five years after it happened, the U.S. Senate learned about the murder of an American officer by Communists after the war had ended.

A peculiar silence fell among the solons. The rustle of papers ceased. Whispered conferences across the aisles stopped. Even the pages paused to listen as Senator Knowland described the brutal killing.

All of this, Mr. President, was contained in the ... confidential file on Captain John M. Birch, United States Army, serial number 0889028.

If the Members of Congress had had this information in August or September of 1945, is there any person here who feels that they would have tolerated the subsequent activity of the State Department in trying to force a coalition between the government of the Republic of China and the same Communists represented by the man who shot Captain Birch in cold blood?

Is there any person here who does not believe that this simple story of a lone American officer, who was willing to sacrifice his life so that this nation might find out whether these Communists were friends or enemies, would not have warned us in time that these Chinese Communists were the same ruthless killers that Communists are the world over?

Does any person here think that if the story of Captain Birch had been known to the American people, that any American would have been taken in by the theory of fellow travelers that Chinese Communists were also agrarian liberals?

... Mr. President, if the Secretary of State and the President of the United States have not read the eyewitness account of the death of Captain Birch, I think it is unfortunate that it was not called to their attention as soon as it was available in 1945. If they had read it, I do not see how they could have approved the policies we followed in China subsequent to 1945.

The rules required that Senator Knowland return the secret file on John Birch to the State Department where it would remain classified and forbidden. Knowland dutifully complied.

But the Senator had revealed enough to confirm the belief of the Birches that the truth about the death of their son had indeed been covered up by government officials. They were left wiser and sadder. Officials of their country, for which John had died, had lied to them and to the American people.

Still the Birches were not without consolation. Sweet family memories could not be taken away. John's witness to his war buddies and the Chinese people would remain and survive the scourge of communism.

One war colleague told the Birches he could see John nowhere but in China: "I fancy him moving along the trails and dike paths, shoulders erect, pack on his back, singing, 'We Are Climbing Jacob's Ladder' and 'The Battle Hymn of the Republic.' I see him stop to give a Chinese farmer a tract and ask how his rice harvest is going. I hear him sigh, 'When this war is over, I'm going home for a rest and then come back and resume my missionary work. The Chinese people need to know about Jesus.' "

Half a century has elapsed since John's murder. In the ensuing years, he has been virtually forgotten. Most Americans think he is the founder and leader of the John Birch Society which was named in his memory. Among the few who know otherwise, only his family and a few surviving close associates know who he really was and what he accomplished.

This is his story. It is based upon recollections of his family and early friends, his associates in China, his letters that survive, public records and the now revealed top secret report of his death.

The evidence of the life and work of John M. Birch, American intelligence agent and missionary, reveals one of the most striking figures in American history.

3

The Budding Intellectual

*God has been very good to ... your children, in
giving us parents who love the right and the
truth ... rather than treasures of silver and gold.*

—John Birch, letter to parents,
May 7, 1944

L ook, John! This is America," young George Birch exclaimed to his
bewildered two-year-old. "This is your homeland." It was 1920,
and the Birch family stood on the deck of the *U.S.S. Monrovia*. They
huddled together for warmth against the biting spray and they
watched the bustling activity in Boston Harbor.

The Birches had left the United States less than three years
before to spread the gospel among the teeming millions of India. Now
they were forced by George's ill health to return to an America that
had changed dramatically during their absence.

The towheaded youngster gazed with serious blue eyes over the
rail of the steamship, and then glanced at his mother, who was
standing nearby with his infant brother in her arms. With both his
parents to protect him, he felt secure in this strange new place called
America. His parents exchanged encouraging smiles, each fighting
the sting of unshed tears.

George and Ethel Birch had traveled many miles together as a
couple. He had pursued his agricultural degree at the University of
Georgia and had offered himself for foreign missions. For practical
experience he accepted a position teaching agriculture at the Berry
Schools in North Georgia. It was there he met the vivacious Ethel
Ellis, a graduate of Wooster College in Ohio and also a foreign
missions volunteer.

They married September 12, 1917, the year the United States
declared war on Germany, and left for India immediately after their
honeymoon. John Morrison Birch was born the following May 28th,
within sight of the snow-capped Himalayas. Two years later, another
boy, Ellis, made his appearance.

Recurring bouts of malaria in George forced them to leave India. After having learned the difficult Hindustani language, both hated to quit. "I could help the Indian farmers so much," George had lamented. But there was no ignoring the missionary doctor's warning: "If you stay here, you won't live much longer."

They packed their meager belongings, took their two baby boys, and with heavy hearts left their adopted land. They looked forward to seeing their relatives in the U.S. again, and to showing off their remarkable children, but the thought of never returning to India was deeply disappointing.

On the Boston waterfront, the ship snuggled up to the dock, the anchors were dropped and the ramp put in place for departing passengers. A crowd awaited on the dock. John could see a number of upturned faces gathered there, some encircled by heavy wool, others by fur.

One of Ethel's uncles was there to greet them. He drove the travel-weary family on the eight hour journey to Vineland, in southern New Jersey, where Ethel's family lived.

Shortly after they arrived, one of her cousins turned to Ethel and remarked, "Too bad about little John."

"What do you mean?"

"Isn't he retarded?"

"Why no! Why do you ask?"

"I asked him a simple question. He didn't seem to comprehend it at all."

Ethel smiled knowingly. "Follow me," she said.

They found John sitting on the porch and inspecting what appeared to be an insect wing. He looked up at their approach. His mother asked him the aunt's question, but not in English. It was in Hindustani. "I like it here," John answered in halting English. But even at his young age there was no denying that British accent particular to India.

With the family settled, George went into the fruit-growing business with his father-in-law. A few months later their third son, George Stanley, was born. This called for a house of their own. Shortly after it was built, a daughter, Betty, joined the family.

At five, John was obviously a gifted child. But, with three younger children, his mother had precious little time to tutor him. Her Aunt May, a school teacher, became John's mentor. By the age of seven, he could read as well as most adults. He was enjoying **Pilgrim's Progress, Hurlburt's Story of the Bible,** and every *Saturday Evening Post* and *National Geographic* he could get his hands on. His memory was astounding. He could read a long paragraph and recite it back. If you told him the meaning of a long word, he never forgot it. And his imitations of his father, and of his grandfather's Italian customers, were hilarious.

John and Ellis attended the Spring Road Grammar School. The public school was adjacent to the Vineland Training School for the Feebleminded.When John was in the fifth grade, the educators from the Training School administered proficiency tests at Spring Road. John's score ran off the scale, which ended at a rating equivalent to the abilities of a fifteen-year-old. The Training School teachers recommended he be allowed to skip the sixth grade and go to junior high for the next term. This was done, and he was the head of his class.

One morning John decided he wanted to examine a dirigible. He and Ellis persuaded their mother to take them to Lakehurst, New Jersey, to see the *Los Angeles*. John, who was then nine, had already explained to Ellis how airplanes flew. But dirigibles remained a mystery. "What keeps the big bag up?" his little brother wanted to know.

"It isn't a bag. It's a blimp," John pontificated. "It's full of helium, a gas which is only one seventh as heavy as air. The helium makes the blimp rise until it reaches thinner and lighter air in the upper atmosphere. Understand?"

"I guess so," Ellis muttered.

When John didn't know the answer to a question, he went to the library and looked it up. The family could not afford a set of encyclopedias, but that was of no consequence to John. He enjoyed visiting the library—the treasure of accumulated knowledge, the smell of the wood, the crumble-edged pages of the older volumes. John was proud of the abilities God had given him, and was an enthusiastic and grateful steward of his gifts. However, he knew that real wisdom began with a healthy fear of the Lord.

During the Roaring Twenties, traditional moral values were crumbling. Still, the Birches went to the Presbyterian Sunday school and church every week. They read the Bible and prayed with their growing brood every evening after dinner. Instant obedience to a parent's command was demanded. The children were always to address elders, especially schoolteachers, with respect.

At that time, theological battles were raging in the big northern Protestant denominations. Modernists reduced biblical miracles to natural occurrences and ridiculed the infallibility of the Bible. They thought the Genesis account of creation had to be reconciled with the new theory of evolution, and that Jesus Christ was only a great teacher, who died a martyr's death. Fundamentalists maintained the Bible was above question. Miracles were supernatural events. Jesus was God in flesh, the spotless sacrificial lamb and the resurrected Lord who was coming again.

The Birches were stalwart Bible believers. As John's mentor, Aunt May, put it, "When there's a difference between God's Word and man's word, you always take the Bible."

When the Presbyterian church in Vineland got a modernist preacher, no one was surprised when the Birches and their relatives pulled out. They found their niche in the West Baptist Church. The pastor was a staunch conservative who believed that salvation was by the atonement of Christ, "plus nothing, minus nothing." Both George and Ethel became Baptists. It was soon afterwards that John made his profession of faith in Christ and was baptized.

He was only seven years old at the time, but nevertheless he felt "burdened" with sin. "I would go to bed at night scared to go to sleep," he testified later. "I would think, 'what if I should die before I wake?' I knew I was a sinner.

"Then one day the preacher gave an invitation and I felt moved to confess and believe on the Lord Jesus Christ as my Lord and Savior. I went down to the front and told the preacher I was trusting in Christ and his blood for the forgiveness of sin and that I believed with all my heart. For the first time I knew that I believed in the Lord Jesus Christ. I knew I was a saved person."

Fundamental Christians inside and outside the large Protestant denominations believed people were spiritually lost and headed for hell without Christ. They evangelized vigorously and their churches grew while churches under modernist leadership dwindled in numbers.

Leonard Livingston Legters came to West Baptist Church when John Birch was eleven years old. He told of a visit to the wild Nhambiquara Indians of southern Brazil. For young John it was *National Geographic* in a spiritual dimension.

"Two missionaries and I rode mules deep into the Amazon jungle where no outsiders had ever dared go.

"Suddenly we came face to face with a band of naked, bronze savages, ready to plunge their long spears into our hearts. Fortunately my missionary companion had learned a few words of their language from traders. 'We come in peace with the good news from the Maker of the world,' he said. My knees played 'Home Sweet Home.' My hair stood on end. They put down their spears and listened.

"That night we camped near their village. We were just getting to sleep when an awful wail pierced the forest. '*Awoieeeeee! Awoieeeeee!*' It pierced the marrow of my bones. 'What is it?' I asked Arthur Tylee.

" 'It's the death wail,' he answered. 'Someone has died and his spirit has been captured by the demons.' "

Legters paced along the platform, jabbing a forefinger at the adults and children in the pews.

"There are millions in Amazonia, Africa, and Asia who have never heard about Jesus. Can you hear their death wail? Will you take the gospel to them?"

The fiery preacher invited those willing to go as missionaries to make a public commitment. John Birch, who had listened spellbound, didn't go to the front of the auditorium, but a few days later his parents found a note on the living room table:

> The Lord is calling me to the mission field. I have the answer to the death wail of the lost.

The die was cast. John Birch would be a missionary preacher, carrying the message of the Bible to the heathen. For him, the Bible would be the final authority in life.

The nation was now in the grips of the Great Depression. Thousands of broke, homeless beggars roamed the countryside and cities, seeking food, clothing, shelter and a job. The most desperate scavenged in the garbage of the fortunate few.

In 1930 a letter came to George Birch from their old friend Miss Martha Berry of the Berry School in north Georgia. According to the letter, there was another job teaching agriculture there, if he wanted it. George was sure this was a provision from God. "The weather's warmer down there and it will be easier to raise a garden," he told Ethel. "Let's go back to the place where we met."

The indomitable Martha Berry welcomed them again with open arms. "My how you've multiplied since I last saw you," she exclaimed. "You were just two young people with stars in your eyes, on your way to India to serve the Lord. Now you have a congregation of your own." She smiled warmly at the children.

The Berry Schools had greatly changed in the fifteen years George and Ethel had been away. There were new buildings, more students and additional land for crops. Martha Berry's school had come a long way since 1902 when she had started a Sunday school for underprivileged mountain children. But her three-fold program of study, work and worship hadn't changed.

The Birches moved into a modest faculty house. The older children were accepted in the school for faculty children. The others of school age were enrolled in county schools. George was teaching agriculture for the first time since leaving India. John helped on campus by mowing lawns. Ethel was content in her full-time job of mothering.

Martha assigned the teachers to take turns at chaperoning dances. When it came their turn, George and Ethel balked. "It's just hugging set to music, and it's wrong," George declared.

Martha argued that dancing wouldn't corrupt anyone's morals and it would make the school more attractive to donors such as Henry Ford. George and Ethel declared that all the Ford millions couldn't make them do something they felt was wrong. George gave Martha his resignation.

George found a job as principal of a country grammar school for fifty dollars a month. They rented a house in tiny Crystal Springs, Georgia, close to his work, and enrolled all the children in local schools.

Ethel took a job teaching English at the local high school to help with the family income. The school was not accredited, and she wished John could attend an accredited one in an adjoining county, but they could not afford the added expense.

When Aunt May learned that John would graduate from an unaccredited high school, she wrote, "That boy must be able to get into a good college. Get him to a better school and I'll pay whatever it costs." So John transferred to Gore High School, where he excelled in debating, and he graduated a year later at the head of his class.

The three years at Crystal Springs were hard for the Birch family. Ethel's relatives in New Jersey and George's in Georgia kept the children in clothing. Ethel's and George's combined salaries barely paid for rent and groceries. But there was no complaining, not even when George became ill and couldn't work.

It started when a shin bruise developed into a nasty leg ulcer. When he discovered a red streak running up his leg, he went to a doctor. Fearing that George might die from blood poisoning or lose his leg, the doctor put him in the nearest hospital.

George recovered and went back to his job. He was unsettled about the future. With the seven children growing so fast, he felt it was time the family got a house of their own. Ethel agreed.

His parents had died, leaving George and his two sisters with five hundred acres of land north of Macon and along the Ocmulgee River. With Ethel's concurrence, he decided that they should move there, where John could attend Mercer University.

Of English ancestry, the Birches were long-time settlers in south-central Georgia. George's grandfather, John Birch, had died at twenty-nine during the Civil War, leaving a widow and three small boys. One became a lawyer, another an industrialist and the third, George's father, a surveyor and farmer. The grandfather and two of the uncles had attended Mercer. George and Ethel had named their oldest son after his industrialist uncle, John Neville Birch. Young John's middle name, Morrison, was the maiden name of George's Scottish mother.

There was no house on George's share of the land. Adjoining the property was an old abandoned mining town and rock quarry owned by a company. Access to the ninety-seven acres was through the Birch land.

The town was just a few old, ramshackle buildings, and some rusting mine machinery. The only place not in very poor condition was the superintendents' rock house. The company was eager to sell the land and the buildings at a very reasonable price. It took some scraping, but the Birches got the property.

The problem was that the land needed to be fenced and the superintendent's house made livable. George couldn't afford losing the time from work.

"I'll do the work," John said. "I'm only sixteen and can postpone going to college a year."

"And I'll help you," Ellis volunteered.

There was no arguing with the boys. They would go ahead and start work, and the family could follow.

4

The Student

I want to live slowly, to relax with my family
before a glowing fireplace, to welcome the visits
of my neighbors, to worship God, to enjoy a book,
to be on a shaded grassy bank and watch the
clouds sail across the blue.

—John Birch, from his essay, "War
Weary Farmer," April, 1945

During the last week of May, 1934, John and Ellis drove a Model-T
from northwest Georgia to Macon. They checked in with their
father's relatives and got directions to the land and the quarry place
some fifteen miles north of Macon.

They parked on the shoulder of State Highway 87 and followed
a rutted old road along a slope for about a mile. The first building
was the superintendent's stone house, now occupied by a squatter.
At John's behest, the "tenant" agreed to move to one of the workers
houses and, for a small wage, help with the cleaning. The boys looked
around before leaving. The old four-room house was in poor repair.
It needed paint and a lot of fixing up.

Some two hundred yards below the main house they came upon
some smaller houses, which had been built in a semicircle on a knoll.
The remaining old buildings were a little further on: a rickety old
dance hall, the post office and a dozen or so shacks in various states
of disrepair. The hill steepened here, and peering through the trees
the boys could see the Southern Railroad tracks and beyond, a
meadow leading to the bank of the slow-moving Ocmulgee River.

Suddenly an old black man wearing a floppy black hat peppered
with holes and one-gallus ragged overalls emerged from the
wilderness. "Iz you'uns lost?" he asked. "Kin I derect ye?"

John introduced himself and his fourteen-year-old brother and
announced that their family now owned the property. The old man
said he was Uncle Dan Gladden and in the next breath explained
how he got the name. "Before we coloreds got our freedom I wuz a

slave to a marster named Dan. He give me to a womern named Gladys. Since den, folks jist called me Dan Gladden.

"The mine bosses, dey kept me in grub and let me live in one of the shacks for helpin' out. When the mine closed down I moved into one of 'dese foremen houses. 'Hain't nobody to tell me I couldn't. 'Hain't nobody bothered me since. I hope you'uns will let me stay."

"Sure, Uncle Dan," John agreed. "We're not here to run you off. Could you show us around?"

The old man beamed and led them across the hill to a high cliff that overlooked the old quarry. "Down dere dey digged the granite. Hauled it out in railroad cars on a spur track. Den one day dey pulled out and left might near everything.

"Want to go mosey around in the quarry and see what we can find? Dar's some mighty interestin' caves down dere."

The suggestion was very tempting to the teen-aged boys, but there was work to do. With a sigh John replied, "Some other time, Uncle Dan. We'd better get busy."

Their first job was to clean up the big house and do some inside painting. They worked three days and didn't complete all the work, but at least the family could move in.

A white hired hand agreed to help build a corral. In one day they cut poles and strung three strands of barbed wire around a one-acre enclosure.

The next day Ethel Birch and the rest of the children arrived, followed by the trucks with the furniture and livestock — thirty cows and a bull.

Every day except Sunday, all summer and fall, John and Ellis worked. Every morning they had to let the cattle out to graze, then herd them back into the corral and go back to work on fencing 400 acres. It was hard work, but their hands soon toughened, their arm and shoulder muscles began to swell, and they slept well at night. Their father, who now worked at Carrollton for the Georgia Agricultural Extension Department, joined them whenever he could.

Their white helper moved on and Uncle Dan became the "hired hand." His pay included a rent-free building, free firewood, free transportation to and from Macon, free medical aid when needed, and $2.50 cash a week. "Dat's e-nuff to keep me in meat, syrup, and overalls," he said.

With Uncle Dan and other hired help, they got the land fenced, the meadow cleared, and some of the old houses patched up for hay barns. They dismantled the old dance hall and boarding house to get lumber for their stone residence.

It was a grand day when the commodious house, which they called Birchwood, was completed. The wide front door opened into a high-ceilinged hall. On one side were four bedrooms, each with its own granite fireplace. John and Ellis had the first one, the parents the second, then Betty, while the four younger boys, Herbert, George Stanley, Robert and Douglas bunked in the back bedroom. The living room, dining room, kitchen and breakfast room were across the hall. Out back, a Delco generator provided power for electric lighting and a well pump brought water into the house.

The following fall John enrolled at Mercer. He received a ministerial scholarship which paid most of his expenses. His Great Aunt May paid the rest.

He commuted to college, driving the Model-T to the campus in the morning and returning in the afternoon. With his father still away most of the time on work for the Georgia Extension Service, John was in charge of the farm.

The road to the highway had to be fixed, fences mended, hay cut and hauled from the meadows by the river and stored for the winter, row crops cultivated, cows milked and wood sawed and chopped. On top of all this, sparks from passing locomotives frequently started brush fires which called for the volunteer firemen — the Birch boys and Uncle Dan.

The Birches, like millions of other Depression families, could not afford to be sick. When Herbert, the third son, developed pneumonia, they had the doctor out only once. When Betty became ill there were only a few cents in the house. John, fortunately, had saved a few dollars toward the purchase of a bike. He gave this to buy medicine for his sister.

Each of the older children was allowed to have a calf to raise and sell. They had to care for it, however, and subtract any expense from the sale price. Every afternoon John picked up his calf in his arms, then set her gently down. "If I can lift her when she's a heifer, I can lift her when she's a cow," he predicted. But there came a time when he had to stay in town with a relative for a few days to attend classes. When he returned he was unable to lift the calf. It was one of his few failures in life.

John's storytelling ability always made work go faster. He had a well-cultivated sense of suspense. Just when the villain was ready to strike, he would switch to another sequence before returning to dramatize the hero's triumph. He acted his stories out, making up dialogue and sound effects as he went along. He seldom finished a story at quitting time, but left the action hanging. "Tune in tomorrow, same time, same station," he would say. This gave the brothers incentive to get back to work the next day.

His stories were almost always morality tales. His heroes were knights on white horses who always won or died as noble martyrs contending for the right. His favorite was King Arthur and the daring deeds of the Knights of the Round Table.

John's philosophy in storytelling meshed with the life view inherited from his parents. God and Satan and good and evil were real opposites and always in conflict. You were either on one side or the other. There was no middle ground, no foggy, gray never-never land.

He reflected the unfailing optimism of his mother who was fond of quoting Romans 8:28: " 'And we know that all things work together for good to them that love God, to them who are the called according to his purpose.' Nothing just happens to a true believer," she would say. "God has a plan in everything."

Another favorite verse acquired from his mother was, "In everything give thanks: for this is the will of God in Christ Jesus concerning you" (1 Thessalonians 5:18). Once when they were hauling hay up the hill from the river bottom the old truck quit. Leaving Ellis behind the wheel, John got out and turned the crank. The motor backfired. The crank jumped back, throwing him in the air, slamming his head against the radiator. Picking himself up from the ground, he rubbed his nose and grinned. "Thank the Lord, I didn't break my arm, but just skinned my nose."

Life at Birchwood wasn't all work. The Birch boys and their sister played cops and robbers amidst the tumble of boulders within the old granite quarry. They teased Uncle Dan about his "lady friend." The boys helped the old man with his correspondence, reading her letters to him, then taking dictation for his reply, for Uncle Dan was illiterate. Uncle Dan always insisted that the reader stuff his ears with cotton so he couldn't hear the letter.

On warm summer afternoons, when the chores were done, the boys fished and swam in the nearby river. John and Ellis made a cable swing and they swung and swam au natural, secure in the knowledge that neighbors were a mile away. Then after swimming they staked out "trot lines" for channel catfish.

Even without close neighbors, the Birches were never lonesome. Uncles and aunts and cousins from the extended Birch side of the family living in the Macon area came regularly. The cousins were intrigued with the mysteries of the old quarry and were charmed by Uncle Dan. The old black man taught them a quaint substitute for grace at the dinner table: "Twixt fingers, lip and gum; look out belly, here she comes." One of the cousins tried it at home and got a whipping. The Birchwood boys knew better.

Ethel Birch's mother and her Aunt May came for an occasional visit. Aunt May thought of the Birch kids as her own. She was still contributing to John's education.

John and Ellis sometimes drove the relatives back to New Jersey, with Aunt May paying their travel expense. Returning home, the boys always stopped in Washington, D.C. to visit the national shrines. John, especially, was enamored with the Revolutionary War and the founding of the nation. They spent a day in the Smithsonian, walked around the Washington Monument, climbed the steps of the Lincoln Memorial, looked at grave markers in Arlington Cemetery and walked the halls of Congress. On one occasion, when no guard was on duty, they climbed to the top of the Capitol dome because John wanted "to see what was up there and how far we can see from the top."

John was also vitally interested in the march of world events. The family had never subscribed to a Macon newspaper or owned a radio. The boys had mentioned a radio several times, but their father always said, "We can't afford it."

In 1935 Ellis traded for a crystal kit and an old one-tube set from a high school classmate. "How do they work?" John wondered. Ellis handed over some schematic diagrams. "You're the brain. You tell me."

John studied the diagrams, then remarked, "I'm going to find out how to build a better one." A couple of days later he brought home a book on radio theory from the Macon public library and stayed up all night reading. "I'll design it and you build it," he told Ellis.

They cannibalized the sets Ellis had bought, traded for some old tube bases and extra wire, and built a series of coils on cardboard cores from rolls of toilet paper. The completed set featured shortwave and longwave broadcast bands that could pull in stations from foreign countries with the aid of an outdoor aerial.

Mussolini's army had already invaded Ethiopia. Nightly, John heard Ethiopia's Hailie Selassie pleading for help from abroad. "The Italians are shooting Ethiopians in the streets from airplanes," John told Uncle Dan. "The Ethiopians are your cousins. Don't you think the world ought to help them?"

"I sho do," Uncle Dan replied, obviously appalled at the news. "Well, I do, too," John agreed.

John seldom missed the nightly news broadcasts. He was alarmed at the growing threat of Hitler and Mussolini, but took Franco's side after the Russians intervened in the Spanish Civil War. He felt communism would ultimately pose the greatest threat to freedom.

He was also concerned about the undeclared war between Japan and China, although as yet he had no plans of going to the Orient as a missionary. He felt America should brand the Shinto nation as the aggressor and stop selling strategic goods to Japan. In international affairs as well as in questions of personal morality he did not equivocate.

At Mercer University he was confronted with other issues that challenged his Christian beliefs and unbendable code of morality. Before enrolling, he had known little about his paternal grandfather's alma mater.

Mercer was one of about forty Southern Baptist colleges operated by the various Baptist state conventions. It was highly rated academically when John began classes in 1935. The law school was especially outstanding and included among its alumni a virtual "who's who" of Georgia's political leaders.

The religious aspect at Mercer was not so highly regarded in some Baptist ministerial circles. Undercurrents of criticism had circulated for years among conservative Southern Baptist pastors that Mercer tolerated "worldliness" in the student body and questionable teaching by some faculty members. Mercer, they said, was not living up to the ideals and beliefs of the church people who supported it and sent their sons and daughters. The strongest criticism came from some Macon Baptist pastors. Conversely, other pastors and Baptist laity praised Mercer for its liberal mindedness. By background and personal conviction John Birch stood solidly with the more conservative pastors.

If John had expected Mercer to be a fundamental Baptist school, he was sorely disappointed. Many students and even some faculty members smoked. All but a tiny minority patronized Macon theaters. Movie reviews ran in the student newspaper. Campus sororities and fraternities sponsored dances, then anathema to most Southern Baptists. Science professors lauded evolution as compatible with Christianity. The Bible professor appeared to ridicule certain cherished beliefs which John held dear.

The Birches had dutifully joined a Southern Baptist congregation, Dame's Ferry Baptist Church. It was near their home, and membership for John was also necessary for him to receive a ministerial partial-tuition scholarship at Mercer.

John took a major in religion, the standard pre-seminary route for a student planning on the ministry or a career in missions. He was automatically a member of the Ministerial Association. He also joined the Mercer Players and the debate team. He soon dropped out of the Mercer Players after playing a role in the stage play, "The Showoff." The student newspaper critic gave him a rave review.

As a debater, he could devastate an opponent with a calm, unemotional development of his argument. He had an uncanny way of making a decisive point for his side and inducing his opponent to nod in agreement. He could take one side of a subject and win, then take the contrary view and win again.

In class he might present a counter argument to a professor's view, but he was never known to raise his voice or lose control. Even when an opportunity presented itself, he was too much of a gentleman to show up the teacher before the class. After class, however, he would approach the professor and gently point out the discrepancy as he saw it.

John bought only one textbook. He made careful class notes, borrowed books from friends, and crammed by staying up all night before a big exam.

Chauncey Daley, John's chief competitor for grades, regarded him as a dynamic personality. "He had a personal magnetism, was a born leader, and was capable and gifted without measure," the classmate recalls. "John was a brilliant fellow who made As almost automatically."

John's writing talent was also apparent. "Birch, what are you planning on doing with your life?" his English Lit professor asked him after returning a short story with an "A" marked on it. "A missionary, sir," he replied. "Don't waste your life," the teacher counseled. "You should be a professional writer."

The editor of the student literary magazine, *Silhouette*, accepted John on his staff gladly. John's tenure was short-lived for he learned the editor wanted "nothing religious." In response, John subtly attacked the policies of the editor with satirical suggestions to prospective writers for *Silhouette*.

In the first piece he presented five satirical suggestions to prospective writers for *Silhouette*. "One does not write anything religious [or] moral," he wrote, "or anything branded as 'old-fashioned' by the younger generation... Sex is particularly popular" and "frequent grammatical and rhetorical stumbling... One should always be generous in the use of profanity; it adds a sophististicated air of nonchalance to otherwise amateurish writing. It is also an excellent substitute for missing links in chains of thought, and it serves wonderfully well as a cloak for the lack of language to convey forceful ideas."

Another article was in response to the editor's policy of rejecting religious articles. Why did he desire to write something religious? "My relationship to Jesus Christ, and through him to the Father, is by far the most important thing in my life. I firmly believe such a relationship to be the most important question in any human life; there I seek expression."

Despite the policy against religious material, his articles were published. Shortly thereafter John left the staff. This was during his junior year when he was held in high respect on the campus for his grades and debating skills.

He had never competed in high school sports, though he was in excellent physical condition. And though he cut a handsome figure, even in clothes bequeathed by relatives, and was friendly with girls, there is no indication that he ever thought seriously about romance while a student at Mercer.

The highlight of his junior year was his selection by a faculty committee as Mercer's nominee for the coveted Rhodes Scholarship. He was recommended for the honor by Dean John B. Clark, the faculty advisor to the debating team. Even though he lost to the candidate from another school in competition in Atlanta, representing Mercer was one of the highest honors the school could give.

5

The Contender

*I knew there was modernism at Mercer, that they
were teaching the Bible was not infallible. I knew I
ought to protest, but I kept my mouth shut.*

—John Birch, from a sermon,
November, 1939

While John Birch was still in college he began preaching in
Baptist churches. He cut a striking figure as he stood beside the
pulpit, holding his open Bible in his left hand and gesturing with his
right, looking people straight in the eye. He took a passage of
Scripture, explained it, pointing out shades of meaning in the
original Greek, then made pointed applications to daily life.
Invariably he got around to salvation, exhorting his listeners to
examine their hearts, to be sure they had experienced spiritual
rebirth and if not, to come forward acknowledging repentance of sin
and acceptance of Christ as Savior.

Southern Baptist leaders who knew him predicted that if he
didn't pursue a missionary career, he would one day hold a
prestigious pulpit. He had the speaking ability, courtliness, mind,
determination, and evangelistic drive to become great. He had a good
church-going family: his father served on the denomination's Foreign
Mission Board; his mother was a Sunday school teacher. He
continued to lead the Mercer student body in grades. Some thought
he was a bit too serious. They predicted a good wife would lighten his
disposition, although he still displayed no interest in any special girl.

Shortly before beginning his senior year at Mercer, John was
hired to fill the pulpit of a city church in Augusta, Georgia, until their
new pastor arrived. When his stint was finished there, he was called
to his first pastorate, a small church in the peach-and-cotton
community of Zenith, some thirty miles southwest of Macon.
Benevolence Baptist had long relied on Mercer seniors for student
pastors. It was a good trade-off. For about ten dollars per Sunday,
the church got a regular preacher to deliver a Sunday sermon, marry

their young and bury their dead. The student got a year's experience before going to seminary.

Getting a regular church meant John had to be ordained. A council of preachers and deacons queried him about his beliefs and pronounced him a loyal Southern Baptist. Then the brethren performed the ancient ceremony of the laying on of hands, each whispering a blessing in his ear as he knelt before them.

He no longer lived with his family, although he saw them often. At the beginning of his senior year he had moved in with Reed Larsen, a student from New York. Because of John's reputation as a brain, students began coming to him for help before exams.

Some complained they weren't getting the right kind of Bible teaching in the classroom. "Dr. Freeman is a liberal," they declared dogmatically. "We ought to expose him to the Georgia Baptist Convention."

John talked to his mother about Dr. John Freeman. "Remember, he's a teacher," she advised. "We should respect those who have authority over us." He decided not to join in any protest.

There was another reason that he didn't mention. He feared involvement in a protest might hurt his academic standing. He was determined to graduate with the highest grades in his class.

John did participate in a weekly Bible study with about twenty ministerial students. He also helped with the group's Saturday afternoon street meetings on Cherry Street. They would sow the downtown area with gospel tracts, invite shoppers to their sidewalk meeting, then hold a service with the cooperation of traffic police. John frequently preached.

After the service, the young evangelists filtered into the crowd, pressing hearers to accept Christ as Savior. Ernest Sheehan, a member of the group, remembers that John "never backed off from anyone. He wasn't a take-charge guy in a group, but he was dynamite one to one. He'd argue with a signpost until it turned blue."

The group called themselves the Bible Study Fellowship. Reid Lunsford, their leader, thought they should seek official recognition on the campus. John respected Lunsford because he was older and had sixteen years' experience in the pastorate. He agreed to go with him to President Spright Dowell.

Dowell, a heavy square-jawed man, had a secular school background and cared little about theology. His forte was institutional development. Under his leadership, Mercer had advanced dramatically in enrollment, classroom space and support.

Dowell was uneasy about the Bible Study Fellowship. He suspected links with certain Macon Baptist pastors who had been complaining for years about liberal teaching, dancing, drinking and gambling at Mercer. He was also worried that the south's most famous heresy hunter, J. Frank Norris of Fort Worth, Texas, might try to horn in.

Norris was then a topic of conversation wherever Southern Baptist leaders met. His weekly paper *The Fundamentalist* was read all over the south. Norris boasted of being pastor of the largest combined Baptist congregation in the world, 16,000 members. He commuted between First Baptist, Fort Worth and Temple Baptist, Detroit.

People either loved or hated Norris. Admirers called him a modern Savonarola, Luther and Moody rolled into the mightiest man of God in his generation. Opponents denounced him as a liar, reprobate, thief, perjurer, even murderer. Norris had once killed an enemy — "in self-defense" he claimed — and a jury believed him.

As President Dowell looked across his desk at John Birch and Reid Lunsford, he was thinking of the Macon preachers who had been such a thorn in the flesh and of the potential J. Frank Norris had for making trouble. He didn't want either to have a campus base. Yet he couldn't slight a student of John Birch's caliber.

"Well, you'll need a charter and a doctrinal statement," he told the two applicants. "Come back and see me when you have that."

John, respectful of authority, thanked him and they left. He knew of Norris as a fundamentalist leader, but was unaware of his tactics. Neither was he close to the Macon pastors who had been so critical of Mercer.

The two consulted with their group and returned with a typed list of beliefs to which the Fellowship subscribed. When Dowell pointed out some objectionable points. Lunsford smiled. "Dr. Dowell, I don't see how you can disagree. These were adopted by the Southern Baptist Convention in 1925."

The president reddened. They had tricked him. "Well . . . ahem . . . you'll have to obtain the signatures of the faculty members of the religion department."

Dr. John Freeman refused to sign. "That's his prerogative," Dowell said at their next meeting. "Your organization can't be certified."

Birch left, disgusted.

In January 1939, J. Frank Norris swept into south Georgia. John Birch was there when Norris preached about the revival on Mt. Carmel from 2 Kings 18. John sat transfixed as the Texas firehorse described the battle between the pagan prophets and Elijah. "And we can know the same kind of revival right here in Georgia," the revivalist promised, "if God's people will get on their knees and repent of their sin!"

The response was immediate as people crowded to the front of the auditorium, many of them weeping. John was so inspired by the challenge to put God first in his life that he returned for the next night's service.

This sermon centered on the work of missionaries in China. "The Fundamental Baptist Church in Shanghai is filled twice every Sunday," Norris informed his audience. "Our missionary, Fred Donnelson, wrote me he had sixty converts in the past month. There are thirty-six Chinese preachers laboring in the refugee camps, winning hundreds to Christ. Not since Morrison went to China over a hundred years ago has there been such opportunity."

Morrison was John Birch's middle name. John had long known about the daring English missionary linguist who had translated the Bible into the major Chinese language when it was a capital crime for a Chinese to teach a foreigner his language.

Norris continued. "Down in Hangchow, a great city that has been almost pulverized by Japanese bombers, we have dear 'Mother Sweet.' She and her husband went out as Northern Baptists. They left their denomination when it went over to modernism and came to us. Dr. Sweet went to be with the Lord in 1917, leaving Mother Sweet to carry on. She'll be seventy-five this year and is getting mighty feeble."

Rearing back and raising his voice, Norris cried, "I wish you could read her last letter. She said, 'I don't know how long these old hands can carry on. Please send me a young preacher, a soul-winner, one who will love the Chinese. The Chinese people here are so hungry for God, they'll receive him with open arms.'

Norris looked over the jammed church. "Is there a red-blooded young man here who loves God and is willing to go and help this dear saint? Is there one who counts not his life dear? One who will go, knowing that he might be killed by a Japanese bomb or die of disease before he is thirty? Is there one? Let him come forward tonight."

Norris had thrown out the challenge. For John Birch, there was nothing more important than preaching the gospel where the need was the greatest. Just the night before John had promised the Lord that he would be an Elijah for him, standing alone if need be, calling a sinful world to repentance. The pull on his heartstrings told him that God wanted him to take his stand in China.

He joined the stream of people moving to the front. "Sir, I'm willing to go," he told Norris. "Write me," Norris replied, not realizing the steely determination in the young man who stood before him.

At the next Fellowship meeting John made a confession to his friends. "I've been weak in my stand for the Lord. I knew there was modernism here at Mercer, but I was so concerned with my own reputation and making good grades that I was too much of a coward to speak out against it. I have recommitted myself to Christ and his kingdom, and if there is any way I can be used to bring revival to this campus, I'm willing. Even if I'm expelled, I am going to stand for righteousness."

"What we need to do is get an investigation of Dr. Freeman," Lunsford suggested. "The Georgia Baptist Convention has appointed a committee to check out the teaching in Baptist schools. If we could get them here, this heresy would be exposed once and for all. Let's write them! How many of you would be willing to sign the letter?"

John was one of those who agreed.

Their letter alleged Dr. Freeman and several other professors had said Adam and Eve were mythical, Christ's death was not necessary for salvation, the Bible contradicted itself and biblical writers were shackled by the superstitions of their time.

When the investigating committee received the students' letter, they did not respond to the charges directly. Instead, a member called on President Dowell who dismissed the complainants as irresponsible. "They belong to a secret society of heresy hunters," he claimed. "They don't represent our student body at all."

After the investigator left, Dowell called in John and the others who had signed the letter to the committee. He demanded that they dissolve their illegal Fellowship and never again go outside university channels to seek redress of grievances. "You come to me and the trustees," he ordered. "As for the complaints you sent to the committee, you're misinformed."

"No, sir," John replied adamantly. "We're trying to help Mercer. I've personally heard Dr. Freeman say there are contradictions in the Bible. He hasn't damaged me, I'm pretty solid. But he's undermining the faith of some of the students.

"Also, Mercer needs a revival, a cleansing from sin," John persisted. "There's drinking and gambling going on in the dormitories. And maybe immorality." He was referring to a current campaign by the Greek letter societies that all students be required to take the Wassermann blood test for diagnosis of syphilis.

"Calm down, young man," Dowell ordered. "There may be a little gambling and drinking, as there will be on any campus. We can't police the dormitories twenty-four hours a day, but you're not helping Mercer by spreading tales. I'm warning you and your friends to stop, or you could face dire consequences." John and his friends felt he meant expulsion.

Lunsford had told the Macon Baptist pastors about the letter to the investigating committee. When he and other Fellowship members reported their most recent run-in with Dowell, one of the pastors suggested they take their case directly to the Baptist preachers of the state.

John Birch and twelve other Fellowship members prepared allegations early in March. Before having them notarized and put in the mail, John and a few others felt Dr. Dowell should be given another chance. They went back to the president's office.

"Read your charges to me," Dowell requested somberly. Paragraph by paragraph, John read the statements, while the president sat shaking his head in dismay

"What are you going to do with these?" he asked apprehensively.

"Unless you act, we intend mailing them to all the Baptist pastors in the state," John declared.

"The trustees are the only one who can handle these complaints lawfully."

"Then convene the trustees," John pleaded.

"Yes, immediately," Reid Lunsford snapped in evident anger. "It's time to clean up the mess on this campus."

At Dowell's insistence, John promised to hold up the mailing until after the trustees met.

Dowell called the chairman of the Executive Committee of the trustees. They set up a meeting with a committee from the ministers' conference. The preachers pledged that if Dr. Freeman could be persuaded to resign, Birch and his friends would drop their charges. They also promised to raise money to support the professor in his retirement.

"You men present this to Dr. Freeman," Dowell said. "If he says yes, I'll accept his resignation." The preachers felt the president should talk to the professor, but Dowell would not and there the matter lay.

While the impasse continued, the thirteen students revised their statements, accepting some of the corrections President Dowell had given in his office. On March 9, they went before a notary public and swore that they were true. The papers were put in a safe to await Dr. Dowell's decision.

Thirteen days passed during which the president continued to dawdle. He was counting on a roly-poly double agent among the thirteen who had promised to keep the mailing from going out. The affidavits were mailed to eight hundred pastors on March 22.

John Birch returned to the campus the following Monday after preaching at his church and met a tide of hostility. The editor of *The Cluster*, the student newspaper, termed the action by the thirteen "crass, medieval bigotry, … sensational exhibitionism." Another student leader described the thirteen in print as "unadjusted … seeking not the welfare of the university but the intellectual and spiritual maiming of it." He further suggested that John Birch was J. Frank Norris' puppet.

Wherever John walked on campus, students refused to speak to him or hissed epithets such as "bigot." The following Saturday, his mother came into town and he remarked to her, "You may not want to walk down the street with me."

She put her arm around him and squeezed. "Son, you did what you felt was right. No one should ever be ashamed of doing that. I'm proud of you, and so is everyone else in our family."

Meanwhile, President Dowell was besieged by opponents and defenders of Dr. Freeman, while newspapers throughout the state headlined: **"Mercer Professors Charged with Heresy."** The story was picked up on the wire services and it ran in the New York City newspapers. Comparisons were made with the Scopes Trial over the teaching of evolution in Tennessee. Macon was dubbed another "monkey town."

Dowell feared the school was about to be torn apart. The situation had to be dealt with promptly. At his behest a special Committee of Inquiry of six trustees was elected to hold a hearing for the thirteen students and the five accused professors.

The hearing opened at 11 a.m., Thursday, March 30, 1939 in Roberts' Chapel. Only trustees, ordained ministers, faculty, the "Unholy Thirteen," as the affidavit signers were now being called, and a few select student leaders were admitted. Outside in a cold rain, a growing crowd of students and reporters waited. Some in the crowd circulated a petition calling for the expulsion of the thirteen.

Inside, Reverend Searborn Winn, the prosecutor assigned to the students, presented John Birch's three sworn-to affidavits against Dr. Freeman.

In the first, John claimed that Dr. Freeman had denied the reality of demon-possession as recorded in the Gospels. Second, he charged that the Bible professor had called atonement by the blood of Christ, farfetched. Third, he quoted Freeman from a class lecture, "When I say that my soul is saved I mean that my thinking is saved from error, that my will is saved from wrong willing and acting, that my emotion is saved from improper feeling."

The affair developed into a verbal slugfest between professor and student, with members of the audience loudly amening their respective champions. Finally John was excused and affidavits read against the other professors, two from the science department and two English teachers. Then attention swung back to Dr. Freeman when various preachers, students from past years, were called to give testimony about his teaching.

One former student claimed he had heard Professor Freeman call the biblical account of creation and the story of Job legends. A second prosecution witness charged Freeman had used a theological text written by a Unitarian.

Defense witnesses countered that Freeman was a loyal Baptist who believed in biblical inspiration and miracles.

Adjournment did not come until 9:15 p.m. It was still raining outside and the noisy crowd had grown to about 300.

As the first of the "Unholy Thirteen" emerged, shouts rang out, "Lynch Saint Birch!" "Get Lunsford, he's the ringleader!"

John stood near the front of the chapel. The fat double agent ventured out, then ducked back in when a big fraternity man threatened to take off his pants and throw him in the Ocmulgee river. "You've got to help me get out," he implored President Dowell.

Finally the Macon police arrived and dispersed the angry crowd that had become a mob.

Instead of condemning the violence, the student newspaper called for the expulsion of the thirteen "because they are neither in sympathy with Mercer's tolerant spirit or the spirit of the Crucified." The editor called them "a parochial, prejudiced group ... who should have thrived exceedingly well in any country before the Santa Maria sailed into the West Indies, and who should fare equally as well today crying 'Heil Hitler!' "

The Committee on Inquiry exonerated the science and English professors on all counts. Dr. Freeman had only made some mistakes, they announced. His personal faith ... in the fundamental truths of Christianity was convincing, and they recommended that the charges by John Birch be ignored.

Dowell and Freeman were lauded in the Macon newspapers while the thirteen were termed intolerant.

O.P. Gilbert, editor of the Georgia Baptist newspaper, *The Christian Index,* had a private discussion with President Dowell. Soon after, Dowell talked with Dr. Freeman who agreed to resign.

J. Frank Norris, whom Dowell and Gilbert had blamed for masterminding the affair, now entered the fracas. He wrote John Birch: "I congratulate you! You have stirred the whole nation. You and your fellow ministerial students will take rank with Martin Luther, Roger Williams and other worthies."

He asked John to rent the Macon auditorium for May 2, 3 and 4, and to be prepared to testify against the professors. "We will try these modernistic infidels ... and you can serve notice on that bunch of hyenas that they will not break up that meeting either."

When news got out that Norris was coming, Editor Gilbert wrote his friend Dowell in alarm: "If it is possible, some man of influence should see [the publisher] of the Macon papers and urge him, in confidence, not to feature the Norris meetings of May 2-4 ... Our leaders should get together and smother the Norris movement ..."

Whether Dowell or someone else of influence got to the Macon publisher is not known. What is certain is that Dowell tried to force John Birch to break with Norris and in so doing played right into Norris' hands.

First, Dowell talked to attorney James Estes, a trustee member of the Committee of Inquiry. The conversation reportedly ran like this: "I'm going to call in Birch and threaten to expel him unless he breaks with Norris. With a month before graduation, and a *magna cum laude* standing, that should make him think."

Estes looked aghast. "You can't fire that boy, Spright. He doesn't work for you, you work for him. He's a student."

"Well, if I can't, I'll make him think I can."

"Even if you could, it wouldn't be right," the lawyer persisted. "John Birch is a Baptist, clean and moral, and in the eyes of many people a better Christian than you are. How could you deny him what he has earned, when he has worked so hard to get the best grades in school? Even if you were justified in taking the action, think how it would look to the public if you let atheists, Jews and anybody else who meets the academic requirements graduate while you deny young Birch his diploma."

"Yes, but he's a Baptist. He's pressuring me from within."

"I don't care if he's a Buddhist. You can't keep him from graduating."

Nevertheless, Dowell summoned John to his office. "Call Norris and tell him not to come. Cancel the reservation at the auditorium for his meeting. Otherwise you won't graduate."

John's back stiffened. He looked straight at the president with steely eyes. "No, sir," he replied defiantly. "I gave Dr. Norris my word, and I'll keep it whether you give me my diploma or not. Is that all, sir?"

John told his parents about the threat. They were incensed. His father fired off a scalding letter to Dowell, sending copies to the Macon newspapers and also one to Norris with an accompanying note.

Norris wired George Birch: CHALLENGE THE UNIVERSITY TO EXPEL YOUR SON. IT WILL IMMORTALIZE HIM.

The flamboyant Texan wrote John, "This is the greatest opportunity of your life. If Dowell proceeds with this 'Haman act,' it will be his hanging. We'll unmask Mercer University to the Southern Baptist Convention."

Dowell repeated the threat again to John. Again the young man refused.

Tensions in the community began to mount as the date for the special meetings neared. Then, without explanation, Norris decided not to come. The decision seemed utterly out of character, but he never explained his change of mind.

Whatever Norris' reason for staying away, John Birch graduated *magna cum laude*. It was a bittersweet accomplishment because few students would offer congratulations. Most believed Birch and his friends had tried to wreck the school

Most of the graduating ministerial students were bound for Southern Baptist seminaries. John had transferred his allegiance to J. Frank Norris. Mercer's top scholar would be enrolling at Norris' newly formed Fundamental Baptist Bible Institute.

Norris realized he had a prize find in John Birch. He wanted to show him off in Detroit at his Temple Baptist Church. Early in June John rode to the Motor City with his parents, who were to continue on to New Jersey for a visit with relatives. While in Detroit John spoke about Mercer to the nine-day preachers' school which Norris conducted annually at the church.

"I knew there was modernism at Mercer, that they were teaching the Bible was not infallible. I knew I ought to protest, but I kept my mouth shut. Then I heard an old-fashioned, narrow-minded preacher. Oh, how the Lord did talk through Dr. Norris. The people got on their knees. I got on my knees and the Lord gave me courage to stand against evil."

Norris, who had been sitting there beaming, leaped up. "Let's sing, 'The Fight Is On.' Let the liberals and infidels in Baptist schools like Mercer University take notice: We're coming after you in the name of the Lord."

Many of the fundamental pastors wanted John to speak in their churches. One of the invitations he accepted was in West Oneonta, New York.

Before the meeting John rested at the parsonage. The pastor brought out his yearbook from the Moody Bible Institute. "That's John Stam, a missionary to China who was killed by the Communists. He was a top student and a great guy. Have you heard of him?"

John hadn't. "We were only told about Southern Baptist missionaries at Mercer."

"It's quite a story, his new friend told him. "He and his wife Betty and their little baby were kidnapped and held for ransom. When their mission wouldn't pay, the Communists cut off their heads. A Chinese doctor tried to intervene, but they killed him too. The baby miraculously survived and was brought to relatives in the States.

"A lot more missionaries have been killed by the Communists," the pastor cautioned, "and now China is at war with Japan."

"I know," John replied, "but the big enemy is communism."

"Have you considered that you might be killed like the Stams if you go to China?"

"Sure. But the Lord has called me and my life is in his hands. I'll not be turning back."

"I expected you to say that," the pastor ventured. "John Stam was just like that. He was selected to give the class address our graduation year, a great honor. I have a copy if you'd like to read it."

John read a paragraph from the martyred missionary's speech:

> Shall we beat a retreat, and turn back from our high calling in Christ Jesus; or dare we advance at God's command in face of the impossible? ... Let us remind ourselves that the Great Commission was never qualified by clauses calling for advance only if funds were plentiful and no hardship or self-denial involved. On the contrary, we are told to expect tribulation and even persecution, but with it victory in Christ.

"That expresses my sentiments exactly," John declared. "I hope I'll be worthy."

If John was disappointed in Norris' Fundamental Baptist Bible Institute in Fort Worth, he did not say so in letters home. Norris had touted the school as "the best training in the world for a young preacher. We have studied seminaries and Bible institutes of all kinds and found nothing that will approach our school. We expect two hundred to three hundred students the first semester." In reality the school was nonaccredited and unrecognized, and by academic standards a travesty in education. Only thirty students showed up and only three of them were college graduates; John, his roommate Oscar Wells, and Ralph Van Northwick. They met in a Sunday school room above the bookstore operated by the First Baptist Church of Fort Worth.

Norris also shared his time between two large churches and traveled extensively. He controlled every appointment and financial decision in both churches, the Bible Institute, and the small mission society which operated out of the Fort Worth church.

Any time Norris was in Fort Worth, he was liable to pop in on the boys at the Institute with whatever was burning on his mind. In September 1939, he came back from a round-the-world trip to warn that "ole Joe Stalin is up to something. Watch that mustache and long pipe."

Norris thought world disaster could only be headed off by the spread of fundamental Christianity. In line with this, he insisted that the boys in the Bible Institute spend as much time evangelizing and preaching as in the classroom.

John preached in churches all around Fort Worth and in Norris' pulpit as well — the highest honor he could receive from the colorful Texan. John's roommate, Oscar Wells, had a regular church at Monahans, Texas, and John preached a week's revival for him.

John and Oscar were too busy for serious romance. John's only dates consisted of buying a girl an occasional hamburger or taking her home from church.

One January morning in 1940 Norris burst excitedly into the classroom waving a letter. "This just came from the Donnelsons in Shanghai. Tens of thousands of refugees are crowding into the city and they don't have a church big enough for all the people who want to come. They've asked us to help them build the largest sanctuary on the foreign mission field. Let's pray the money in."

Afterward, John and Oscar told Norris, "We want to get going." Norris sent them to M.H. Wolfe, a former cotton broker he had appointed president of the World Fundamental Baptist Missionary Fellowship, which then had fifteen missionaries on the field.

"There's no money to send you," Wolfe told them bluntly.

"That may be," John replied, "but the Lord has called us and we mean to go as soon as this school term is out."

"Well, you boys better start praying and raising some money."

By April sufficient donations had come in to pay for their passage.

They graduated a month later. For this first commencement Norris brought thousands of fundamental Baptists to Fort Worth. John, Oscar and Van Northwick — the three graduates — all preached. John's subject was the inspiration of the Bible. Norris also preached, as did President Louis Entzinger, Wolfe and several others. As a grand finale the crowd gathered at nearby Lake Worth in the pouring rain to witness Norris baptizing over four hundred persons.

John took a short vacation at home, then his family accompanied him to the Macon train station for a last good-bye. Amid the hand shakes, back thumping and hugs there were many misty eyes. "We're all so proud of you, Son," Ethel Birch whispered in his ear when she held him in her arms for the last time. "You know we'll all be praying for you."

He jumped on the train propelled by the vim and vigor of his youthful zeal. His big adventure was about to begin. He gave his loved ones a big smile and a final wave and he was gone.

Then the tears began to flow. George handed Ethel his handkerchief and gave her a reassuring hug. "He'll be fine, Mother. The Lord is his protector."

"I know, George," she sniffled. "I wouldn't hold him back for anything. It's just that it's so hard not knowing when we'll see him again."

John stopped off in Fort Worth where there was a big send-off for him and Oscar Wells. The crowd of church members sang and offered words of encouragement to the two young recruits. Norris put his arms around them and cried, "God bless you, boys. We're behind you all the way. We'll be praying for you."

6

The Evangelist

For unto you it is given in the behalf of Christ,
not only to believe on him, but also to suffer for
his sake.

— Philippians 1:29, quoted by John Birch in a
sermon to the Christians in Wai Chang,
China, January 18, 1941

John Birch was barely twenty-two and Oscar Wells only two years older when they boarded the Japanese freighter, the S.S. *Teaimariau*, in Seattle. There were stopovers in Yokohama and Nagasaki which allowed the two Americans time to visit some tourist attractions before sailing on to Japanese-occupied Shanghai. For the first time, John was back in the hemisphere of his birth.

As they entered the customs building in Shanghai a balding, round-faced, smiling American in a flowered shirt waved at them from behind a glass partition. They recognized Fred Donnelson from photos published in *The Fundamentalist*. His letters had spurred them to hurry to China.

As Americans, they were given special treatment and hustled rapidly through health and passport checks. Donnelson greeted them warmly as they emerged, carrying their bags. "Glad you're here! Glad you're here!" he kept exclaiming.

The visits in Japan had been a preview of the crowded conditions in the Orient, but Shanghai was overwhelming to the newcomers. Here the throngs of people were greater, noisier and pushier. Peddlers and beggars closed around them. Men tugged at their coattails, offering rides to hotels. "Hang onto your wallets," Donnelson advised, "and follow me." He hurried them to rickshas and made sure their bags were loaded. Then leaping into the lead vehicle, he shouted a command and the sinewy, muscled runners pulled the rickshas into the maelstrom of humanity. How the Japanese soldiers stationed at regular intervals along the streets could control such mobs was more than John could imagine.

The lead ricksha coolie kept yelling in Chinese, "Get back! Get back! The foreign devils are coming." They darted between leather-faced *tio faos*, pairs of men carrying heavy loads on bamboo poles balanced on their shoulders and shouting "*ei-ho ei-ho*" in rhythm as they walked. Other Chinese on bikes zipped by, dodging pedestrians and an occasional automobile which seemed to move forward by sheer horn-power. Bouncing about on his ricksha, John was taking it all in.

It was the summer of 1939 and China had been at war with Japan for three years. It had fought the communist insurrection even longer than that. Chiang Kai-shek's Nationalist armies and Mao Tse-tung's Communist rebels were now biding an uneasy truce in face of their common enemy, Japan, which controlled the northern provinces and was tightening an armed noose around the nation's economy.

Thousands were dying every week from Japanese bullets and bombs and the famines that ravaged the countryside. Yet the war was undeclared and the missionaries hung grimly on, preaching to confused multitudes, feeding the starving and nursing the wounded in hospitals. They kept sending letters home, begging friends and relatives to talk to reporters, congressmen, anyone about America's seeming indifference to China.

John Birch was already aware of the problems. Since setting his heart on China he had read every available scrap of information about the world's most populous nation.

At Donnelson's signal the rickshas stopped before a building that looked like a small hotel. "This is the Missionary Home," he announced. "You'll stay here until we can fix up a room at the church." He took them inside to register. "Get a little rest and I'll be back to get you for dinner."

Donnelson was back before sundown. "We can walk to our apartment from here," the beaming midwesterner explained. They pushed along the crowded street and turned a corner. "We're on Yu Yuen Road between the foreign section in the north and the Chinese area in the south. When Lois and I had to leave Hangchow and come here, we were told no property was for rent anywhere. We wanted to start a church and a Bible school for Christian workers. Well, we've always believed God specializes in the impossible. We walked right down this lane where we're turning now and found workmen putting up that three-story brick building just ahead. We asked if it was already rented and they said we could have it for all of forty-five dollars a month. We signed the papers before it was finished and also leased a lot a few blocks away on which to build a church.

"The church building is packed out every Sunday. We have evangelistic meetings every night and about eighty home meetings each week. In addition, we send a team of evangelists into the country every weekend. We've baptized almost a thousand converts in three years and are winning more every week. These are not the kind of Christians you know at home. They've burned their idols, given up ancestor worship, and some have had their funerals preached by their families for following Jesus.

"Here's our place," he said, halting before the building. "We use part of it for the Bible school and part for living quarters. Come on up and meet the gang."

The "gang" consisted of Fred's smiling wife, Lois, and their teen-aged daughter and two elderly women, the fabled Mother Sweet and her long-time partner, Margaret Fitzgerald.

John approached Mother Sweet reverently and took the aged woman's hands in his. "God put China on my heart when I heard about your work in Hangchow," he told her with a voice choked with emotion. The lines on her face seemed to disappear as a broad smile lighted her countenance. Her eyes were brimming with tears as she gave him a motherly hug. "And you are God's answer to my prayers," she replied. "For years I have been pleading for him to send a young preacher who would be willing to serve those lovely people. And at last you are here."

John and Oscar were both made so very welcome that they immediately felt confirmed that this was indeed the place God had chosen for them to serve. As accepted members of the team, they were asked bluntly, "How do Americans in general feel about the war in China?" "And in Europe?" "Is our government going to fight?" The questions came flying at them.

"How do people feel about China?" Mother Sweet pressed.

"I'm afraid most Americans don't really think about China at all," John answered her gently, "except those who pray and support missionaries over here."

"They don't know about the Communist threat?" Donnelson exploded.

"We're told it's just a civil war between the Chinese," Oscar explained.

"But we've heard about missionaries killed by the Communists," John added, "like John and Betty Stam."

"There have been many others," Mother Sweet exclaimed. "You haven't heard the tenth of it. You will, though. You will."

John wanted to hear about Hangchow, the city God had laid on his heart.

"It's just a little over a hundred miles south of here," Mother Sweet began. "It was such a beautiful city and a great silk center. The Chinese have a proverb: 'Heaven above, Hangchow below.' " She paused. A warm smile spread across her face as her thoughts flew back to the Hangchow of her youth.

"My dear husband and I went there over forty years ago. The Lord enabled us to win many souls and to establish a boys' school and a girls' school. Then our great Northern Baptist Convention was corrupted by modernism. The precious old truths of God's Word were put aside. We resigned and came over to the Fundamental Baptists. We rented a little chapel on a narrow street. God began to bless. Souls were saved. The Lord miraculously provided money for our new Tai Ben Fang church.

"Then just when the work was prospering, my dear husband got sick and we had to return to Wisconsin. I buried him three weeks after our arrival. Everyone presumed I would stay in America after he went to be with the Lord."

"You came back alone?" John asked.

"I wasn't alone for long. Dear Margaret here and I took a house together. Two young ladies came out to help a while. Then the Lord sent us Fred and Lois. We started an orphans' home and a Bible school.

"This was in 1932, the depths of the Depression," Fred explained. "We couldn't find a single church to support us, so we sold our furniture, including the grand piano Lois had bought with money she earned giving piano lessons. That got us to Hangchow with just a few dollars left."

John and Oscar exchanged meaningful glances. They had traveled on a shoestring too.

"We spent five years in Hangchow, five of the most fruitful years of our lives. I could sit here all night telling you stories. We saw hundreds come to Jesus. Miracles like you wouldn't believe.

"Then the Japanese began bombing. They reduced so much of that beautiful city to rubble. So many people were killed. Yet the Lord protected us, didn't he, Mother Sweet?"

"Oh my, yes!" she exclaimed. "Why, one time we heard the planes and the Christian women and girls came running into our house. I led them into the yard with the Bible in one hand and the U.S. flag in the other and I knelt and prayed for God's protection. The planes turned at a right angle and went the other way."

"We stayed through all the bombing," Fred recalled. "But when the Japanese landed troops at the port and began attacking with big guns, we had to evacuate. It was a terribly difficult decision to make, but we'd have been killed if we'd stayed.

"We went home on furlough and then began work in Shanghai when we returned. We would have loved to return to Hangchow, but I didn't feel I should endanger my family. The city is really pitiful now. There are only about 200,000 people living where once there were a million."

"Well, I can't wait to get there," John blurted.

"I know you're in a hurry," the senior missionary nodded understandingly, "and we're anxious to have you go, and Oscar too if that's where the Lord should lead him, but you won't be much help until you learn the language. We've already reserved a place for the two of you at the Adventists' language school."

The next morning Fred accompanied John and Oscar to the school to enroll. "The course takes two years for most foreigners," the headmaster informed the fellows as they filled out some forms. "Some finish sooner and others never become fluent in a lifetime. It's one of the world's most difficult languages."

John was no stranger to languages. His childhood tongue in India had been Hindustani. He had studied French, Latin and Greek, and had an excellent grasp of English grammar. Chinese, however, was different from anything he had ever tackled.

Instead of having an alphabet, Chinese was based on picture writing. Memorizing thousands of different pictographic characters was only the beginning. A student had to learn numerous combinations, for the way characters are combined suggested an idea. A sun and a moon, for example, indicated brightness.

Chinese words were monosyllabic. The meaning and place in a sentence was determined by tones, and tones varied among different dialects. The word *ma* could mean mother, hemp, horse, or to scold, all depending on the tone. A single Chinese character could be written the same as a noun, verb, adjective, or adverb. Function depended on where it was placed in a sentence.

There were long hours of written work followed by private pronunciation sessions with a teacher. John's mentor was amazed at his ability to catch, repeat, and remember sounds. Not only did he have a near-photographic memory, but he was also a natural mimic. Within six weeks he could carry on a simple street conversation.

Reverend Beauchamp Vick, J. Frank Norris' associate in Detroit, arrived in August and wanted to visit Hangchow. John and Oscar were delighted when they were invited to accompany Vick and the Donnelsons to the war-ravaged city.

It was John's first opportunity to see the Chinese countryside. They caught the early morning train to the south and were soon speeding through lush green checkerboard rice fields. Picture-book verdant mountains, stair-stepped with terraces of tea plants, framed the background. Mulberry trees decorated yards around trim little houses.

"Everybody raises silkworms in this area," Fred Donnelson explained. "The silkworms feed on the mulberry leaves."

John kept spotting mounds and little brick houses in the fields. "What are they?" he asked.

"Graves," Donnelson explained. "The Chinese put their dead on top of the ground and pile on dirt. Some of those graves have been there for hundreds, perhaps thousands of years. Sometimes it seems China is one vast graveyard."

John fell silent in contemplation. So many millions of Chinese must have died without ever hearing the name of Jesus.

Except for the armed Japanese soldiers who paced the aisles of their railway car, war seemed faraway. Then as they neared Hangchow the countryside changed. The fields were overgrown with great gaping holes. Here and there John could see where entire villages had been burned to the ground.

"There are people out there," Donnelson said. "You just don't see them. This is where the battles have been fought."

As they clattered into the outskirts of Hangchow, John marveled at the beautiful surroundings and recalled Mother Sweet's descriptions. To the east was Hangchow Bay, barren except for a few fishing boats. Feeding into the bay was the wide Tsien Tang River, which banked the city on the south. Between Hangchow and the shimmering mountains to the west was an exquisite lake around which were built numerous pagodas. The bottom of the lake was said to be covered with ashes from the burning of incense.

As they pulled into the station John could see that the city itself was a wasteland. Rubble was heaped everywhere. Buildings gutted by fire and punctured by mortars looked as if they might collapse any moment. A long line of Chinese stretched along one street to a well-guarded building. Further along John saw people leaving with what appeared to be small bags of rice.

The train jolted to a stop. "Hangchow!" a voice called. They were directed by guards into a line of passengers shuffling slowly along the platform toward the station. As they came near the gate John saw hands dipping into a large washbowl full of a pink fluid. Closer up, he noticed hands that were covered with sores. When his turn came, he could almost feel the germs crawling over his hands as he dipped them in the antiseptic.

Beyond the gate they were forced to walk across mats soaked in disinfectant while two Japanese soldiers sprayed their clothing with more pink fluid, all a chilling reminder that China was a land of virulent diseases.

Off the platform it was Shanghai all over again, except the beggars, merchants and ricksha men here looked like living skeletons and none were smiling.

Then they heard voices. "Brother Fred, we are here!" John saw a smiling Chinese with thick, dark hair cut in western style.

"It's Pastor Du and some men from the church," Donnelson announced. The senior missionary led the Americans through the mob to where the Christians were waiting. They looked thin also, but were smiling.

They all jumped into waiting rickshas and were soon climbing the concrete steps of the large Tai Ben Fang Church. There wasn't a mark on the solid brick structure, although buildings nearby were smashed. "None of our property has been damaged. We praise the Lord," Pastor Du exclaimed.

It was a weekday and the late summer heat was stupefying, yet the sanctuary was jammed, the men on one side and the women on the other. As they entered, a children's choir sang a welcome. Then amidst many bows and salutations, they followed Pastor Du to the platform. Looking across the crowd of four or five hundred, John saw many faces glistening with tears, but behind the tears were friendly smiles.

Pastor Du opened the services with a welcoming address. He then presented Fred and Lois Donnelson. Fred followed with introductions of Reverend Vick and John and Oscar.

The visitors were all touched by the enthusiasm of the congregational singing. When offering baskets were passed, John wondered how these impoverished people could give anything, but the plates were piled high with coins and bills. Reverend Vick preached, with Donnelson interpreting. Then the people crowded around the visitors, smiling, talking, introducing themselves, sharing remembrances with the Donnelsons. John and Oscar stood to one side, nodding, offering only a few hesitant words, for the people here spoke the Mandarin dialect which was somewhat different from the dialect of Chinese they had been studying.

After leaving the building, Pastor Du took them to the orphanage and Bible school. A line of old people was waiting at the entrance. "We are feeding eighty-eight citizens," Du reported.

The girls at the orphanage sang a hymn and recited verses of Scripture they had learned. John recognized some of the youngsters from the children's choir. "They are from villages stricken by famine," Pastor Du explained. "Had our preacher boys not brought them here, they would have starved to death."

They met some of the student preachers and inspected the classrooms. Pastor Du looked at John. "They are eager for you to come and teach them."

They were all exhausted when the pastor and the deacons took them to the missionary residence where Mother Sweet and Miss Fitzgerald had once lived. The Chinese Christian family who now occupied the dwelling gave up their bedrooms for the visitors.

They entered the yard of the house through a gate in the side wall. "There is a reason for the gate being here instead of at the front," Pastor Du said. "You see, dragons and demons always follow straight lines; with the gate at the side they will miss this house. Of course, we Christians do not believe that," he laughed.

After dinner they returned to the church for another long service. Then back at the house Fred and Lois told stories until almost midnight.

"Let me tell you about Pastor Du," Fred said. "He comes from Sing Teng, a town of about 50,000 out in the country where we were the first to take the gospel.

"We had a car then and drove to where the town was about ten miles away, then walked the rest of the way. At the wide city wall the Chinese preachers and I knelt and asked the Lord to give us the city.

"We put up the tent and began nightly evangelistic meetings. Whole families came to the Lord. Hundreds gave up their idols to follow Jesus. We built a church right on the city wall. Four young men became preachers. Two of these were Paul Du and his brother Peter.

"We stayed with the new believers. One night I was sleeping in a loft when my host brought five men to me wanting to be saved. One was named Le Ting. 'Oh, how wicked I am,' he wailed. 'Can God save me?' I gave him God's promises from Scripture and he knelt and prayed the sinner's prayer. When he got up, he thanked me for not stopping in Shanghai or even Hangchow, but for coming all the way to Sing Teng to tell him about Jesus.

"Oh, I should tell you," the older missionary added as an afterthought, "Sing Teng is one of about 25 places where we established churches during our short stay in Hangchow. We have heard nothing from many in some time."

Despite the late hour, and the long exhausting day they had had, John was wide awake, listening intently to the tales of past triumphs. "I can't wait to get started," he declared.

They returned to Shanghai the next day with John more determined than ever to spend every available minute studying and practicing Chinese. He moved ahead rapidly, completing work in days that took other students weeks. In November the faculty agreed that he could continue his lessons in Hangchow with a private tutor and return periodically for exams. John thanked them profusely.

Since arriving, John and Oscar had each been receiving a steady fifty dollars a month from the mission office which Norris had relocated from Fort Worth to Chicago. This had been ample for living expenses and fees at the language school. John knew from letters received that churches and individuals were contributing more to his support. He assumed that Mr. Wolfe was saving the additional as a hedge against the future or giving it to other missionaries who needed it more. Still, it didn't seem quite right to withhold money that contributors thought was coming to him.

His primary concern was to get to Hangchow so he put money concerns out of his mind and settled down to his language studies.

Oscar was plodding along with the difficult language and was also directing the Bible school in Shanghai that was started by Fred Donnelson. For Oscar there was the added attraction of Miss Myrtle Huizenga, a young Christian Reformed Church missionary he intended to immerse. None of the single women John had met in Shanghai interested him. "They're all too old for me," he told anyone who queried about his marital prospects.

John remained for Thanksgiving with his colleagues in Shanghai. He enjoyed their company, but his thoughts were at Birchwood over 10,000 miles away. He was in almost the exact same latitude, so the seasons were the same for him as for his family, but this was the first time the entire family would not be together for Thanksgiving. He longed to see his beloved family, and yet he was at peace, content to be where he felt God wanted him.

With great anticipation John boarded the train to Hangchow. He prayed fervently during the trip. He so wanted God to do great things through him. There were about thirty missionaries of other groups there, but he would be the only Fundamental Baptist. Mother Sweet intended to die in China, but was too feeble to return to Hangchow. Miss Fitzgerald was ailing and would soon go on furlough.

Pastor Du and the deacons met him at the station and took him to the room in the Bible school that had been prepared for his sleeping quarters. Arrangements had been made for him to have his meals with Kepler and Pauline Van Evera, a Presbyterian missionary couple living close by.

The date was November 24, 1940. The war scene in Europe had worsened. All of western Europe was now under the heel of Hitler. Canada had entered the war but the U.S. was still holding out. From issues of *The Fundamentalist*, John knew that J. Frank Norris was still preaching isolationism.

Japan had tightened its economic stranglehold on China and was softening up the interior with bombing forays. Chiang Kai-shek's rag-tag armies were holding out and in some places counterattacking. They were only fifty miles from Hangchow and had announced they intended to recapture the city.

By December 1940, Hangchow was facing famine. The price of rice was beyond reach for poor people. Guerrillas, lurking outside the city wall, were constantly ambushing Japanese patrols. One guerrilla band crept into the city itself and wounded the puppet mayor. For each such incident, the Japanese response was brutal. A Chinese could be shot on mere suspicion of helping Chiang Kai-shek's army, and girls were raped at the convenience and desire of occupying soldiers.

At Christmastime people were dying daily. John often came across bodies on his way to breakfast with his Presbyterian friends. It was all he could do to swallow his food. Christmas Day, he preached his first sermon to the Tai Ben Fang congregation. The building was crowded and fifteen persons came forward to confess Christ as Savior and Lord. In the midst of terrible suffering, the Chinese could find no other hope.

Because of the tight security, news from churches in villages surrounding Hangchow was scarce. Some congregations, less than forty miles away, had not been heard from in over three years. They were in the no-man's land where Japanese soldiers patrolled by day and guerrillas ruled by night, caught between the Japanese and the Chinese army threatening to recapture Hangchow.

One of John's New Year's resolutions was to visit these churches, no matter what the risk. The third Saturday of January, 1941, he and Mr. Wu, one of the Chinese preachers, secured passes from the Japanese command post and biked into the countryside to check on the believers at Wang Shan and Wai Chang on the southwest side of Hangchow.

Every mile or two they encountered a Japanese patrol and had to stop and show their passes. Once a Japanese soldier became angry at Mr. Wu and threatened to tear up his pass. John gave the soldier a good lecture and he let them go on.

They passed burned-out villages and often heard gunfire. Peasants in tattered clothes tottered behind them begging for coins to buy food. They came upon hastily erected bamboo huts where emaciated children lay almost lifeless in the dirt.

Approaching Wang Shan, they caught sight of a new building. With thatched roof, mud walls and earthen floors, it wasn't much by western standards, but to John's eyes the new church was a beautiful symbol of faith. That evening the country folks packed every nook and cranny. They sang loud enough to drown out the guns crackling across the rice paddies. John and Wu preached until they were hoarse, and people came forward to accept Christ.

They slept in a bamboo hut and pressed on to Wai Chang the next morning. People along the way told them the Chinese army was just a mile beyond the village.

Wai Chang was gone, reduced to ashes, and the people scattered. That night John and Wu preached in a rural house to another overflow crowd. When John challenged them to burn their idols and trust in Christ, a large number responded.

The members of the Wai Chang church who were there begged John to return. "We have not had communion for four years," they said.

The next weekend John came back with Pastor Du from the Hangchow church. They administered the Lord's Supper in a tin plate and bamboo cups. As Pastor Du passed the cups of juice a machine gun opened up across the paddies. No one moved. When the minister said, "As Christ commanded, 'This do in remembrance of me,' " they lifted the cups to their lips and drank.

A message from the commanding officer of Chinese troops encamped across the river from Hangchow was waiting for Pastor Du and John when they returned. The officer was a member of the Hangchow church who had escaped to join Chiang's army. He was now asking his pastor and the missionary for help in starting evangelistic work among his men. Could they come and train his officers?

Under cover of darkness John and Pastor Du sneaked past Japanese sentries and slipped into a small boat at the river. It was a dark, stormy night and the waves kept dashing over the boat. They dared not flash a light to check their direction. This would have drawn instant fire from Japanese shore batteries.

A sleet and ice storm came on and they lost their way. Finally they foundered aground in cold mud and had to wade and drag the boat into a rice field.

"Who goes there?" a Chinese voice challenged.

"Pastor Du and the missionary," John replied, thinking they would be less likely to shoot at the voice of an American.

Dark figures advanced on them. "You are among friends," one called. "Come with us before you die in the weather."

They stayed the rest of the night in a cold grass hut with a squad of Chinese soldiers. Snow kept blowing through large holes, but John was warm as he shared the Good News. Before the night was over, three men in the squad knelt on the cold ground and made confessions of faith.

When morning came, one of the soldiers escorted them to the commander's tent. They spent that day instructing his Christian officers how to evangelize one to one. They dared not assemble a congregation within range of the Japanese guns. Then under the cover of darkness and the comfort of full stomachs, John and Du were taken back to their boat for the return crossing.

Letters had come from the homeland. One was from a boy John had once taught in Sunday school. "Do you like it over there?" he asked. John replied:

> Dear Bob:
> Yes sir! I do like it over here! There is war, starvation, disease, sin, idolatry, superstition, suffering, and death on every side, but our wonderful Savior keeps saving souls, answering prayers, and giving joy in the midst of sorrow.
> Two questions for you: First, has Jesus Christ saved you? Second, if he has, is he now using you to save other sinners? I trust the answer is "yes" both times.
> Yours in his love,
> John M. Birch

Another was from J. Frank Norris. He had asked Secretary of State Cordell Hull to instruct consular officials in Shanghai to keep a check on the welfare of Mother Sweet, the Donnelsons, Oscar and John. "I know you're in a dangerous position," he wrote John, "but you're serving the Lord where the battle is hottest. I have no pity for you whatever."

John thanked him and gave a full report of recent missionary journeys and growth of the church in Hangchow.

> One man, who walked sixteen miles into Hangchow to be baptized last fall, has since led six other men to a saving knowledge of Jesus Christ; another, recently saved, is thus reported by his neighbors to have "gone crazy." They say all he can do is "talk about this Jesus Christ and that book." God grant that many more may likewise "go crazy!"
> You are dead right, sir, when you say you feel no pity for my position. Why I'm having the time of my life!

John's letter to Norris containing reports of the dangerous trips was read by M.H. Wolfe, the mission's president. He wrote John to stay in Hangchow and not to so risk his life again.

For John it was once again human authority standing against what he felt to be God's clear leading. There was no doubt about what he would do. When fellow Christians were suffering and living in deadly danger every day, he could not cower in a place of safety. He had to follow the Lord's leading and trust himself to his care.

7

The Volunteer

*In these days of preparation for battle, what a
privilege it is to put on the whole armor of God
and prepare to defend the gospel of the King of
kings, until he comes!*

—John Birch, in a letter to Aunt May,
August 18, 1941

"Oscar! Oscar! Over here!" John yelled as he jumped and waved,
trying to get the attention of his friend who was gazing over the
crowd trying to find him. Oscar was nearly a head taller than most
Chinese and was easy to spot, but John was shorter and smaller of
stature and blended in with the throngs of Chinese milling about the
railroad station. "Here I am, Oscar!" John called again as he worked
his way toward the school chum he had not seen in months. With
great glee and much pounding on one another's backs the two
comrades were reunited, much to the amusement of the sedate
Orientals who watched the pale-faced young foreigners
patronistically.

"I've got so much to tell you," John chortled. "God has been so
good!"

"Well, I've got news myself," Oscar replied.

"Oh?" John's brows shot up, his curiosity pricked.

After a very effectual pause, Oscar announced, "Myrtle and I are
going to get married. Soon! So I thought I'd come spend a few weeks
with you on the firing line before settling down to wedded bliss and
the added responsibilities that entails."

"Well, congratulations! She's a fine girl. And if it's excitement
and adventure you are seeking, you've come to the right place."

John soon had raised Oscar's pulse with stories about his
excursions into no-man's land around Hangchow. "Pastor Du and I
intend to go all the way to Shangjao in Kiangsi Province," John
declared.

"That's across the lines into Free China, isn't it?" Oscar queried hesitantly. "It would be quite a trick getting back in there."

"Yes, there will be some danger getting up into those mountains," John agreed, "but you see, before the Japanese came into this area Fred Donnelson and the Chinese preachers started some churches back there. We've had no contact with them in years, and both Pastor Du and I feel it is important that we reassure them they have not been forgotten.

"There's no way to get permission from the Japanese for such a trip, so we'll have to be careful they don't discover our intentions. Want to go with us?"

Oscar grinned. "When do we leave?"

Three days later John, Oscar and Pastor Du biked through Hangchow's western gate. Oscar rode a woman's cycle that had been left behind by a missionary friend of Mother Sweet's. John and Pastor Du had been in and out so many times lately that the Japanese guards had taken to waving them by without checking for their passes. They assumed they were taking their friend to visit one of the nearby churches that night and would be returning in a day or two.

The fellows kept pedaling. Near sundown they stopped and ate with a Chinese family and hid their bikes. When darkness fell, they began moving up the trail again.

Three or four miles ahead they heard sounds of approaching marchers. They slipped into a clump of bamboo and watched breathlessly as a patrol of heavily armed troops passed. They weren't sure if they were Japanese or Chinese guerrillas, and they weren't about to investigate. As soon as it was safe they continued on their journey.

By midnight they were in the hills and climbing, but this was still no-man's land. Rounding a bank along a small stream, they heard a low whistle. Du whistled back. Two Chinese emerged from behind a boulder and greeted them warmly. The guerrillas gave them directions ahead and the location of a hut where they could sleep during the day. They reached the hut without further incident.

Traveling by night and sleeping by day, they reached a clear river and hired a boat for the last lap to Shangjao, a town of 10,000 set in the mountains like a jewel beside the fast flowing stream, almost two hundred miles from Hangchow.

They were now well within Free China where grim Japanese soldiers were not stationed on every street corner and where people could go as they pleased without passes. The food was better and cheaper here, the steps quicker, the smiles brighter.

"Welcome, Americans," passers-by on the street called out. "You, our friends. You come to help us fight Japanese? Soon, we hope."

By asking around they located the pastor of the Baptist church. "Yes, the Shangjao Church is still meeting," he reported happily. "Most of our men are away fighting the enemy, but I will spread the word of your presence and we will have a service this evening."

All three of the visitors preached to the forty or so people who congregated as soon as the amazing news got around that three men had come all the way from Hangchow to encourage them in their faith.

The next evening the Shangjao pastor took them to a village upstream where a second congregation welcomed them joyfully. "There are hundreds of places to the west where we could start churches," he said. "The people are so hungry for a message of hope. If only there were more messengers."

"We have to return to Hangchow, but we'll be back," John pledged.

They retraced their steps, arriving back in Hangchow a week later. Bicycling along as if they had been off on a picnic they rode casually back into town at midday. John waved jauntily to the Japanese gate guards who seemed unconcerned about their absence.

Oscar returned to Shanghai for his marriage to Myrtle on June 28th. For a honeymoon trip he brought her to Hangchow where their bridal suite was a room next to John's. All three took their meals with the hospitable Presbyterian missionaries.

Oscar took his bride back to Shanghai and then returned in August for another trip to Free China. They preached in new villages and met people who had never seen a Bible or heard the name Jesus. "This settles it," Oscar declared. "There are lots of missionaries in Shanghai. If I can get Myrtle back here, I want to take the gospel to every unevangelized town and village in Kiangsi."

In Hangchow another letter from M.H. Wolfe, president of the World Fundamental Baptist Mission Fellowship, was waiting for John. "Stay away from the fighting," he again demanded. "We need evangelists, not martyrs. You know how much Dr. Norris is against war."

John knew. Every issue of *The Fundamentalist* trumpeted a Norris lecture to President Roosevelt to stay out of the war in Europe. Since Hitler had broken his alliance with Stalin and invaded Russia, Norris had been saying, "Let the dictators destroy each other." Norris was now on a rampage against the newly passed Lend-Lease Act that empowered the President to provide arms, goods, and services to any nation whose defense he deemed vital to the U.S. He charged that Communists in the American government were behind Roosevelt's decision to send arms to the Russians. "We're arming our enemy," he thundered.

John agreed with Norris on the Communists, but was changing his mind about war. The U.S. couldn't sit by and let Hitler overrun England too, or allow Japan to subdue all of Asia. John felt that China could not hold out much longer unless America came to her aid.

There were still thirty missionaries remaining in Hangchow, mostly Presbyterian and Anglican social workers. John cooperated with them in relief projects and argued with them about doctrine. He had put the Mercer controversy behind him, but in fundamental beliefs he had not changed one whit. A major difference with the other missionaries was over eschatology. "Christianity will never reform the world," he maintained. "Conditions will get worse and worse. The hope of believers is the return of Christ to take us out of this evil world. Until he comes, we are commanded to evangelize the lost."

John's finances had improved though mail was erratic and some letters took four months. Besides the fifty dollars a month, he had received money from his parents, Aunt May, and several friends. He used the extra money to buy New Testaments for Chinese soldiers, food for starving Christians, and for expenses for the risky evangelistic expeditions.

One of the few luxuries he had allowed himself was a shortwave radio. Late at night when loneliness made him nostalgic for home, he would tune in KGEI in San Francisco and listen to messages broadcast as a public service for American families with loved ones in the Orient. One night he almost fell out of bed when he heard his mother being introduced.

"Hello, John, in Hangchow, China. We hope you are listening." He heard his mother's sweet, clear voice coming over the telephone relay. It was so sudden, so unexpected that he was choked with emotion. He listened intently, holding his breath lest he miss one precious syllable. "Mail has been slow lately, but we're all well. We miss you more than you can ever know, and we pray for you every day. They told us to keep our greeting brief, so here's each one to say, 'Hi.'" He recognized the voices of his father, brothers, and sister calling their greetings, and then the announcer came on to introduce the next family. They were gone.

The whole message had lasted only seconds and was over too quickly; yet the sound of their voices echoed in his ears. He had never fully realized just how much he missed them until hearing their voices had stirred old memories. Now the full impact of his loneliness hit him and he turned his face to the pillow, his eyes flooding with tears.

News reports indicated that U.S. – Japanese relations were worsening. Negotiations concerning the canceling of the embargo the U.S. had placed on shipment of vital oil and steel to Japan were deadlocked. The U.S. demanded that Japan give up captured Chinese territory and pull back troops from Indo-China. Japan was dependent on her conquered land for vital war supplies and so refused.

American pundits were speculating that Japan might launch a surprise attack on U.S. bases in the Pacific. They noted that German advances into Russia had freed Japan of fear that the Soviets might attack from the north. Now she was free to move in the Pacific to regain vital oil and other supplies that had been cut off by the American embargo.

The Japanese were aware that Roosevelt was now paying attention to Pacific bases, long neglected in favor of helping European allies. Bases in the Philippines, Hawaii, and on other islands were being strengthened. Japan also noted with anxiety that the American government had permitted General Claire Chennault, Chiang Kai-shek's foreign air adviser, to recruit an American Volunteer Group of pilots for service in China.

In late August Secretary of State Cordell Hull urged U.S. mission agencies to order their representatives out of Japanese-occupied China. M.H. Wolfe cabled the Fundamental Baptists in Shanghai and Hangchow to leave as a matter of life and death.

It was time for John to take another language exam. While in Shanghai he conferred with his colleagues about Wolfe's demand. Mother Sweet was adamant about staying. "Three years ago when I was in America my children begged me to remain with them. I told them then I would die in China, and the Lord hasn't given me any change in directions since."

"I'm with Mother Sweet," John declared.

Oscar and Myrtle Wells and Fred and Lois Donnelson made the decision unanimous. Miss Fitzgerald had already gone home.

Most members of the China Inland Mission, the largest group in the country, also decided to remain. The majority of missionaries affiliated with the large American denominations elected to go home until the situation improved.

"I'll be back one more time for my final exams in December. Then, I'll try and make it to Free China before war breaks out," John confided to his friends. "It'll be a little harder now, because I've been the only missionary working in the country outside Hangchow. The Japanese may be suspicious of me. I need your prayers."

"We'll keep the work going here," Fred Donnelson pledged. "We'll be praying for you, and you remember us too."

They prayed together; then the couples shook hands with John, and Mother Sweet embraced him. "God keep you, my boy. May he give you as many years in China as he has given me."

While John was catching the train back to Hangchow, J. Frank Norris was meeting with the British Prime Minister. Churchill turned on the charm and persuaded him that Western civilization was in grave danger and the time had come for the U.S. to enter the war. Norris immediately cabled President Roosevelt:

A FORMAL DECLARATION OF WAR IS THE ONLY THING THAT WILL FINISH HITLERISM. QUIT TEASING THE RATTLESNAKE AND CUT OFF HIS HEAD. A DECLARATION OF WAR WILL UNITE AMERICA AND ENCOURAGE NEUTRALS ... YOU HAVE DIVINE JUSTIFICATION ... NO ALTERNATIVE. ESTHER 4:14.

Announcement of the turnabout by the controversial and influential Texan made headline news in British newspapers and reached China. John wrote Norris that he supported him one hundred percent. Their letters probably crossed, for John soon received a letter from Norris praising the Fundamental Baptist missionaries for deciding to stay. Norris called them "brave and courageous." Wolfe regretted their decision and thought they were foolish.

An attack of dengue fever delayed John's plan for leaving on another trip to Shangjao until September 24th. That morning he and Evangelist Wu tied baggage to their bikes and rode through the west gate without incident. Outside the city they were met by a young guerrilla named Wang. "Travel is now very dangerous," he informed them. "I will escort you."

The three rested in the village of Hung Lung Tsuen. When they awakened, villagers told them, "The Japanese are thick about us. You must wait until we have the all-clear."

Thirty-two hours later the signal came and they left about midday, winding up a crooked trail toward a highway heavily used by the Japanese. A mile or so from the road they met a smuggler. "Wait up," he whispered. "Japanese are just ahead." John, Wu and Wang pushed their bikes up the hill to a thick pine and persimmon grove and waited. A few minutes later they heard gunshots. They guessed the soldiers had shot some travelers up ahead.

About four p.m. they were joined by more Chinese coming from the direction of Hung Lung Tsuen. The newcomers soon became impatient and took to the trail again. Soon, the trio heard gunshots and loud voices. The Japanese had apparently ambushed this party also.

Wang thought they should stay in the grove a while longer. John lunched on Chinese persimmons and read from the book of Ezekiel. About sundown they heard more people coming from the east. A long line of *tio fao* carriers, bulging loads swinging from their shoulder poles, emerged on the trail below. Their lips were moving, but the familiar *ei-ho* chant could not be heard.

Wang rolled a stone to attract their attention. When they looked up, he signaled danger ahead and waved them up the hill. They crowded into the grove with the three travelers and put down their heavy baggage — contraband for the Chinese army.

Darkness fell and a thin sliver of moon dimly marked the trail below. A guerilla came from the west and said it was safe now to cross the road. The *tio fao* men started first with John, Wu and Wang bringing up the rear.

The head of the line was near the road when the *tio fao* men began turning around, forcing the two preachers and the guerrilla backwards. A whispered warning explained the reverse: "The Japanese are at the head of the line."

"I know another path that crosses at a different place," Wu said. "Let's try it." John and Wang were game and off they went with the *tio fao* men following.

The moon had set, and they were now in darkness. Wang, who had been fighting back an attack of dengue fever, fell. "Leave me," he told his friends. John refused. "I'll push you on my bike." He and Wu lifted Wang onto the bike seat, and they began moving again.

The trail narrowed to eight or ten inches and wound down and through a marsh. The bike kept sliding off the raised path and into the muck. The men behind growled for John to go on. "Shut up," he yelled. "You might get sick yourself sometime." Fearing a fight, Wang slid off the bike and insisted he could walk. After what seemed like hours of stumbling through the darkness, they heard low voices and water splashing ahead. A boat was waiting in a canal. Strong arms grabbed Wang and lifted him aboard. Other men helped John and Wu get the bikes and baggage on. Then the oarsmen pushed the boat into the channel. When John asked why the rush, a man said that Japanese armored cars had crossed the highway and had been seen moving toward the canal. Later John learned that the Japanese killed seven men in the line behind them.

About midnight they were put ashore. They walked a few miles to a little Chinese inn and rented a room. The swarm of bugs which they disturbed didn't keep them from sleeping.

Around 2 a.m. John was awakened by the racket of a battle. Shells screamed overhead. Cannon boomed. Machine guns and rifles chattered from an uncomfortably close location. They crept out of the inn and ran for their bikes and baggage.

Ten miles further on they breakfasted with a Christian family that had escaped Hangchow. By nightfall they were at the home of a guerrilla chief, an old friend of John's from previous excursions. Several Chinese officers were there, along with a Japanese officer recently captured. The Japanese was sitting at the table eating and being treated with great courtesy. John knew what Japanese did to their prisoners and asked why this man was being treated so kindly. "It is the command of the Generalissimo," one of the Chinese explained. "He is a Christian, you know."

Another day's biking and another short jaunt by boat brought John and his party to a town that had electricity. John plugged in his radio and tuned in Chungking, the provisional Chinese capital. A big crowd gathered quickly. He let them listen a while, then turned the radio off and preached to them. Two young Chinese officers came up to say they wished to become Christians.

They spent the next night with China Inland Mission missionaries in the town of Lanchi, then took a train to Chinhwa, the provisional capital of Chekiang Province. There they ate with a Northern Baptist couple. The woman had once lived in Macon and knew some of John's relatives. The next day they reached Shangjao, after eight days of hard travel. The town had been bombed since John and Oscar had visited there in the spring. Many buildings had been destroyed. But the little church was still meeting, and John preached to a congregation of forty.

The believers could see that John and Wu had no place to stay. Wang had returned to his guerrilla unit. "We'll care for your needs," a leader in the group promised. "You can eat and sleep in our home."

After a few days Wu went back toward Hangchow, intending to visit churches along the way. John made Shangjao his base, biking to outlying villages to preach as he had done in the Hangchow area.

On one trip, John and two lay preachers from the Shangjao congregation, Chen and Hu, biked to Hwang Ho, the center community of three towns where no Christian herald had been for ten years. They preached to over a hundred. "The Holy Spirit led all the way through," John recorded. "Never before have I seen such earnest attention. Forty accepted Christ."

John heard of a noted anti-Christian town, Shia Chi, where a white-bearded elder had been waiting many years for baptism. He had cried out to the foreign Savior when about to be killed by a band of Communists. Ever since, he had stood alone against great persecution in his village, witnessing faithfully to relatives and neighbors.

On a Saturday John and Hu rode eighteen miles into the country and baptized the old man. From Shia Chi, they made a side trip to visit another lone believer in the town of Shi Chi. While John was preaching to about thirty of this man's neighbors, an aged storekeeper jumped to his feet. "I have never before believed in this Jesus," he announced. "I want to accept him right now."

John met an army officer who had been converted through reading a booklet by Chiang Kai-shek, *Why I Believe in Jesus Christ.* The officer invited the American, Hu, and Chen to preach to the men at his headquarters.

The three were received with many bows and inquiries about their health and families. Then they were taken to the drill field where three hundred soldiers sat in rows before the platform. John preached, then Chen, and last of all Hu. The men listened spellbound for over two hours. There was only one annoying interruption. A man appeared to be laughing at them from behind the fence surrounding the field.

Hu closed his sermon by asking, "Who wishes to accept Jesus Christ as Savior and follow him as Lord? Will he please stand?"

John stood looking over the ranks expectantly. There was a pause, then a man stood, another, then several others, until finally every enlisted man and officer was standing.

"They may not have understood you clearly," John whispered to Hu. Hu repeated his challenge, adding that becoming a Christian might bring persecution from relatives. This time when he said, "Stand," the whole company leaped to their feet as one man. John, who was a man not given to outbursts of emotion, shouted loudly, "Hallelujah! Praise the Lord! They all wanted to be saved!"

After counseling with the men and distributing some literature, John and his Chinese preacher companions returned to Shangjao. Two days later a man came to the house where John was staying. "I heard you and your friends at the drill field," he said. "One of the soldiers gave me a piece of paper on which I saw your address."

"Are you a soldier?"

"No, I was behind the fence."

"You were the man laughing at us?"

"Not laughing, but crying. I have not slept for two nights. Please tell me more."

After the man left, John wrote his family in Macon:

We read together from John's Gospel, Romans 10, and the book of 1 John. I wish you all could have seen his face light up and the tears of joy stream down his face as we read the precious promises of life eternal from the wonderful old book.

Free China is rightly named — what a glorious liberty to preach the gospel is mine! I can get on my bicycle and ride to Chungking, to Kunming, Rangoon, Burma, Siberia, Tibet, India, and Turkestan! But I don't need to go so far — within 100 miles of Shangjao there are hundreds of towns and villages without the gospel and hundreds of thousands of souls who have not even heard the message of salvation. With the exception of Tibet and a few other regions in the extreme west, *this is the least evangelized place in all China*! What a privilege is mine! May I use it rightly. I am enjoying excellent health, eating two meals of Chinese food a day, and the Holy Spirit has delivered me from some of the laziness of yore. He has given me enough Chinese to preach with and I am welcome anywhere because I am an American, and America is China's friend!

There was no telephone or telegraph office in Shangjao and John had the only radio. When he mentioned to a Chinese officer that he could pick up KGEI, San Francisco, from 9:30 to 11:30 at night the officer became excited. "We are so hungry for news from America," he sighed. "If you will permit, my men will string a telephone wire from my headquarters to here. When KGEI comes on, put the phone receiver by your radio. For this, I will be most grateful, and you may use the telephone to call anywhere in Free China."

John willingly consented and the wire was strung for nine miles. The telephone was a boon. With it he could get advance notice of Japanese planes approaching and warn the people of Shangjao to take shelter.

It was time now for his final language exam. Once more John slipped through the Japanese lines and back into Hangchow where he took the usual train to Shanghai. He was glad to see that his colleagues were still there. Mother Sweet was not strong, but her faith was as bright as ever. While in Shanghai John kept up by radio with the escalating war of words between Japan and the United States.

John completed his exams on a Friday and passed with an almost perfect grade. The headmaster wrote his parents:

> Never in teaching hundreds of foreigners to speak Chinese have we had a student as brilliant as your son. He not only understands and speaks the language, he is aware of subtleties and idioms which many foreigners never learn during a lifetime in China. I congratulate you on having such a son.

The next day, Saturday, John returned to Shangjao, and had supper with the Presbyterian missionaries. "If I don't show up for breakfast in the morning then you'll know I slipped through the Japanese lines," he told them.

"John, why don't you stay here and rest over the weekend," Mrs. Van Evera pleaded. He felt compelled to go, explaining, "I promised the Chinese soldiers I'd preach for them on Sunday."

John slipped out of Hangchow later that night and got through the lines just one day before the Japanese attack on Pearl Harbor. Had he taken the missionary's advice he would likely have been captured by the Japanese and been interned for the duration of the war.

On that infamous December Sunday in 1941 he preached for the Chinese soldiers then headed on toward Shangjao. The next day he heard the announcement of Pearl Harbor from Chinese soldiers along the way. "We are allies now," they told him joyfully. "We will defeat the enemy together."

John's first concern was for the Donnelsons, Wellses and Mother Sweet in Shanghai. There was no way he could telephone or send a telegram to them. He could only pray and wait.

In January a Chinese preacher from Shanghai suddenly appeared in Shangjao asking for John. He had sneaked through the lines. "Your friends are well, but in the custody of the Japanese," he reported. "They are without money and wish you to send this to Dr. Norris."

John read the message: *"To you and Mr. Wolfe. Please send all China funds via Birch in Free China ... The Shanghai work continues."*

John was running short himself. Since September he had received no money. He had only a few traveler's checks which the bank in Shangjao would not cash. He had already notified the American Embassy in Chungking of his location in Shangjao and asked how mission funds might be received. The Embassy advised that the office should transmit U.S. dollars to the Central Bank of China in Chungking which would then remit to the bank in Shangjao. Aided by Chinese army friends, John sent a radiogram and a telegram to Norris. He also mailed several air mail letters.

Three months passed while the Shanghai courier waited. John continued his itinerant ministry in the hills around Shangjao. A malaria attack put him to bed for a week, but upon regaining his strength he went right back to preaching.

Radio broadcasts brought discouraging news. The Japanese were marching across Malaysia, the Philippines and Burma. They had obviously caught the U.S. unprepared in the Pacific and were pushing the Americans back on every front. Reports from Europe were only a little less discouraging.

John was torn between his commission to preach and loyalty to his country and China. America, to his mind, was wielding the sword of the Lord against pagan invaders. As a citizen and a Christian, he was bound to serve his country. Yet as a clergyman he was exempt from the draft.

Should he volunteer? Perhaps he could go in as a chaplain. If not, he would fight. John was a peaceable man, but not opposed to violence in self-defense. He had no patience with pacifists.

There was also the matter of funds. If God wanted him to keep preaching to the Chinese, why didn't he send some money? On April 13 he wrote the American Military Mission in Chungking:

I am writing to enquire as to the present opportunities for and the need of volunteer service in the United States armed forces in this part of the world.

I am an American citizen (recently registered with the consulate in Kunming), twenty-three years old, able-bodied, and single. I was first honor man, Mercer University, (Ga.), '39, and an independent Baptist missionary in Jap-occupied Chekiang from July 1940 to the outbreak of war on December 8, 1941. Since that time I have been preaching here in Free Kiangsi, but am finding that increasingly hard to do on an empty stomach (no word or funds from home since November).

To continue my self-glorification, I can preach and pray, both in English and Chinese, can speak enough Mandarin to get by, can build and operate radio transmitters and receivers, can stand physical hardship. I believe in God, his Son, in America, and in freedom; I hold them all more precious than peace and more precious than my earthly life. I have lived for more than a year behind the Jap front lines, and what I have seen strengthens my belief in the worth of freedom and the need of destroying the Japanese army.

Why all this "I" stuff? Because I want to join the army. Why do I want to join the army? There are two reasons: first, I want to do my patriotic bit in pushing back the gang that is swarming on our boys in Bataan, P.I.; and second, the above-mentioned empty stomach.

I should like to be a chaplain — I am an ordained Baptist minister (I think that's what they wrote in the minutes of the Georgia Baptist Convention, 1937-39), but if there is no demand for chaplains I should cheerfully tote a rifle, run a shortwave set, or drive a truck, or be an interpreter, or whatever they tell me to do. What pay does a private draw a month? Twenty-one dollars? That's more than

enough for me. Please write me what my chances would be if I were to go to Chungking to volunteer, even if you have to write "Nil."
Yours for victory,
John M. Birch

Three days later the Chinese Army cashed the traveler's checks which the banks had rejected. John gave most of this money to the still-waiting messenger from Shanghai and borrowed a boat to escort him downriver to a point nearer Hangchow.

They crossed back into Chekiang Province and separated at Sing Teng where Chinese Christians assured John they would help the courier reach Hangchow, where he could board the train for Shanghai. Turning around, John set out to visit several of the country churches in the dangerous no-man's land before returning to Shangjao by boat.

On the evening of April 27, John stopped at a crowded Chinese inn in a small village on the river. He sat down at a rough wooden table and ordered a cheap meal of boiled red rice, green bamboo shoots and a meat scrap. A moment later a Chinese man came and sat down silently across from him. "You American?" he whispered.

John sensed a need for secrecy in the man's voice. Without looking up from his meal, he gave a barely perceptible nod.

"You finish. Follow me." The man took a drink, then a few more bites before adding, "Be very careful. Enemy eyes may be watching."

Nothing more was said. John ate slowly, allowing the Chinese to finish first. Then after he left, John paid for his meal and walked out casually. At the door he saw the man starting down the path beside the river. Shouldering his pack, John followed him.

The man came to a halt by a small enclosed sampan river boat that lay low in the water, obviously heavily loaded. The stranger jumped aboard and motioned for John to do the same. After looking all around to assure himself no one was watching, John followed, feeling more curious than frightened. The nervous little man John had been following rolled his eyes toward the door of the boat and announced mysteriously, "Americans!"

Americans? John thought incredulously. *Americans, out here? It couldn't be. If there were any Americans within a hundred miles I would know about it. They must be missionaries trying to escape from some place. What is going on?*

He walked over to the door and knocked softly. "Are any Americans in there?" he asked in his soft Georgia drawl.

Silence. Then a muffled voice saying, "No Japanese could make up an accent like that!" The door swung open and John entered the dark hold. He blinked a moment, adjusting his eyes to the faint light given off by a lantern that swung from the low ceiling. Then he shook his head, finding it hard to believe what he saw: five overgrown American flyers stuffed into the little hold, all grinning at him.

"Wha — what? Who? How?" he stammered.

The commanding officer gave him a little mock salute and introduced himself. "Colonel James H. Doolittle, United States Army Air Force. The boys and I just delivered a little present to Tojo, and we're having a bit of trouble getting back home."

8

The Rescuer

I should like to go home, but cannot find justification. This is no time to retreat.

—John Birch in letter to parents,
June 24, 1942

Jimmy Doolittle! John instantly recognized the name and grin of the aviation hero he and Ellis had admired as boys. Winner of numerous aviation trophies, Doolittle was famous as the first pilot to fly across the United States in less than twelve hours.

Recovering from his surprise, John stammered an introduction. "I — I'm John Birch, a Baptist missionary."

"Missionary or whatever, we're sure glad to see an American," Doolittle replied. "Let me introduce you to the boys. This is Dick Cole, our copilot from Ohio; Hank Potter, our navigator, from South Dakota; Paul Leonard, our gunner, from New Mexico; and Fred Braemer, from Seattle, the man who dropped the eggs on Tokyo."

"You really bombed Tokyo?" John asked, shaking his head in amazement. "I hadn't heard about any bombing mission on Japan, but then I've been back in the boondocks."

"Well, it was a super-secret mission," Doolittle explained. "Commissioned by the President. Can't tell you much except that we bombed Japan and had no place to land. Ran out of fuel and bailed out in a rain storm about 9:30 Saturday night. There were fifteen other planes in our group. Have you heard of any other Americans being found? We were all due to come down in this area."

"No sir. I hope they didn't drop behind Jap lines, or get picked up by Jap spies."

"How far is it to the lines?"

"Fifty, sixty miles. The Japanese hold Hangchow, where I used to work. They have spies all around here and they're probably looking for you to collect a reward."

"That's not a very encouraging thought. Do you suppose you could get us to the American military headquarters in Chungking?"

"I could take you as far as Lanchi," John proposed. "That's the nearest big town. I know some Chinese officers there who could get you to Chungking safely."

"Great! Let's get going."

"I'll make arrangements with the man who owns this boat and we can start immediately," John assured him.

Soon the old sampan was sloshing and groaning its way upstream as the disheveled looking crew munched on food John had picked up at the restaurant. Their hunger abated, Doolittle and his crew began swapping stories of their experiences since bailing out of their B-25.

"Potter and I landed close to one another," bombardier Braemer explained. "A bunch of Chinese soldiers found us and relieved us of all our valuables. Then they marched us off as if they were taking us to be executed. Luckily we ran into a Chinese who spoke English. He took us to his house and sent for their C.O. When the officer saw who we were, he bawled those characters out good and made them return our stuff. Then we went out looking for you guys and ran into Leonard."

"Yeah," the gunner broke in, "and man, was I glad to see them. I had hit on a mountainside and spent the night wrapped up in my parachute. The next morning I ran into four armed men. One motioned for me to put my hands up and the other three cocked their rifles. I pulled my .45 and fired into the air a couple of times and they took off like rabbits."

No one spoke for a minute. Finally Dick Cole confessed, "Well, I just don't have any exciting experience to relate. What happened to you, Colonel?"

"I hit in a rice paddy close to a lighted farmhouse," Doolittle explained. "I banged on a door and the farmer slammed the lock on the door and turned the lights out. I walked down a little road and saw a big box resting on two sawhorses. I thought it would make an adequate shelter, so I climbed in, only to find it occupied by a dead man.

"I figured I wasn't that desperate," Doolittle continued with a wry grin, "so I let him rest in peace and I foundered around in the dark until I discovered an old water mill. The next morning a farmer found me and took me to a Chinese military camp."

"The Lord must have been watching over all of you," John observed. "So many things could have happened."

Doolittle took a long look at the skinny young American who could make pious statements sound very natural. John was dressed in a long Chinese padded coat over creaseless trousers. After six months of living on cabbage and red rice while biking over rugged terrain, his strong muscles bulged beneath mahogany colored skin on his wiry frame. With his hair dyed black he could have passed for a Chinese coolie. He certainly didn't look like any cleric Doolittle had ever met.

"What kind of a missionary are you anyway?" the pilot asked quizzically.

"I'm with the World Fundamental Baptist Fellowship, sir."

"Never heard of them."

"Haven't heard from them myself for about six months," John cracked in dry humor.

"What have you been living on?" Doolittle asked so kindly that he made John feel very young.

"I've just been trusting the Lord to provide. Most of the provision has come from Chinese Christians who share their meager fare."

"They must think very highly of you to be willing to take you in like that, Johnny."

"Well, they're fine people. The Lord has given me a deep love and concern for the Chinese, and they seem to sense this."

"But with the war going on all around you, it's going to be hard to continue your work. What are your plans for the future?"

"I've written a letter to the American Military Mission in Chungking offering my services as a chaplain. If they don't want me, I guess I'll make my way to West China and start a new mission in virgin territory. Whatever doors the Lord opens, I plan to continue serving the Chinese people."

Doolittle mulled over that information a bit and then offered, "I'll put in a good word for you when I get to Chungking."

"I'd appreciate that, sir. And if it wouldn't be too much trouble, I'd sure appreciate it if you would contact my folks when you get back to the States. Let them know I'm okay."

"No problem. It would be my pleasure. I'll even contact those Fundamental Baptists of yours and give them a report on your condition."

"Oh, that would be great, sir. And tell them that word has come through the underground that our missionaries in Shanghai are in Japanese custody, but are all right."

"You just write down whatever messages you want me to deliver and I'll take care of it."

After the sampan finally reached its destination, John guided the crew through an area thick with Japanese-paid informers and puppets, and delivered them safely to the Chinese military headquarters at Lanchi.

"Ask if they've had reports of other fliers being found," Doolittle told John when they arrived.

John spoke to the officer in charge. He had heard of some and told John to assure Colonel Doolittle that the Chinese army was doing everything possible to keep the downed fliers out of enemy hands. "We congratulate the American fliers for their great victory over the enemy," John translated for the officer. "You have stung the dwarfs and have made them very angry. Our scouts tell us the enemy is searching everywhere for you."

While Doolittle and his men stood by, John made arrangements for hospitality and an escort to an airfield so they could be flown to Chungking. "It's all taken care of, Colonel," he assured the famous pilot. "Maybe I'll see you in Chungking."

He shook hands with all the crew and they thanked him profusely for guiding them to safety. Doolittle had been very impressed with John's skill at interpreting and the rapport he had with the Chinese officers, and again promised to recommend him at military headquarters in Chungking. They had only been together for a day and a night, but they were the only Americans John had had contact with for so long that it was hard to say good-bye.

After the Doolittle crew departed, John went on to Shangjao to check on the church there and his preacher friends, Hu and Chen. They reported that rumors were sweeping the town of an imminent Japanese offensive as punishment for the American bombing raid.

John went by the Shangjao Bank to see if any money had come from the mission office in Chicago and was pleasantly surprised to find that 3,000 Chinese dollars, about $300 in American value, had been telegraphed to him. It represented back pay for six months. He then stopped at the post office and was handed a telegram from the American Military Mission in Chungking ordering him to report to the nearest air base at Ch'u Hsien and await further orders.

He had planned to remain in Shangjao a while longer, but now hurried to say good-bye to Hu and Chen and the other members of the church. He gave the preachers most of his money to use for evacuation if the Japanese should threaten the town. After an emotional prayer meeting, he bade them good-bye.

John reached Ch'u Hsien to find two crews of Doolittle's Raiders there, desperate for an interpreter. While he was helping them get a flight to Chungking, a phone call came from a Canadian missionary friend, Reverend C.T. Paulson, at the town of Yang Kou. "Doolittle was just here on his way to Chungking and left some money and special instructions for you," Paulson informed him. "How soon can you come?"

John wanted to leave immediately, but another flight crew had arrived and pleaded with him to stay the night in Ch'u Hsien and help them get out to the capital the next day. John consented.

The next day the Canadian missionary handed him the $2,000 in Chinese money left by Colonel Doolittle with his orders: "You are to bury Corporal Leland D. Faktor and any others who may be brought in for burial, arrange medical aid for any injured, obtain all information possible on missing aviators, serve as secretary/translator to aviators stopping over at Ch'u Hsien, accompany the last crew to Chungking, and report to the Military Mission there."

This was a big assignment, and John hadn't even put on a uniform yet. Nevertheless, he was the only man for the job. No other Americans were available who knew the territory where the fliers had supposedly come down. John spoke the language and understood the people. He also had a network of dependable contacts among Chinese civilians and military, built up during preaching missions.

With sixteen B-25s on the daring raid, and five men to each crew, there were eighty men to account for. He checked off Doolittle's crew and the others he had sent on to Chungking. He telephoned Chinese officers at other bases, talked to friends who had contacts with occupied China, dispatched Chinese investigators to verify reports coming from remote villages. The task of finding all the men and getting them to safety was urgent. The Japanese had begun their attack and were sweeping through villages killing every inhabitant, even the children, in places where people were suspected of helping Doolittle's men.

At Ihwang in Kiangsi Province, the Japanese found the man who had given shelter to Lieutenant Harold F. Watson. They wrapped him in blankets, poured kerosene on him and forced his wife to set him afire. At this village they also threw hundreds of people into deep wells, destroyed American mission property in the vicinity and desecrated the graves in a missionary cemetery.

More Raiders kept arriving in Ch'u Hsien. John welcomed each one, debriefed them for information on missing crew members, arranged meals and lodging and scheduled medical treatment for the injured. As soon as possible he got them onto flights to Chungking.

From the time spent with Doolittle and his crew and from talking to other rescued fliers, John picked up many details of the super-secret mission that were not released to the American public until years after the war. The raid had been planned as a morale booster when the Allies were suffering staggering defeats and to show the Japanese that their homeland was vulnerable to American bombers. The sixteen B-25s had taken off from the carrier *Hornet* somewhere in the Pacific on a one-way flight. The course was set for the crews to bail out over southeastern China just as their fuel was running out. The men had dropped blindly through rain and clouds into mountainous terrain where no one was expecting them.

Every man John interviewed had a dramatic story to tell. Most fit into a general pattern. Soon after landing, they had been captured by Chinese guerrillas, who, upon learning their identity had taken them to the nearest headquarters. When the announcement came of their accomplishment, they were like royalty. Some were paraded through towns as conquering heroes before reaching Ch'u Hsien.

The grim news was that not all had been rescued. Of the eighty, John could account for sixty that had either bailed out or crash-landed in Free China. His Chinese underground contacts reported two crews had come down across the Japanese lines. Four of these were said to be dead, five captured, and one rumored to have escaped into Free China. This left two crews still unaccounted for.

From another source John learned that one of the missing crews had strayed off course and landed far to the north in Soviet Siberia. No information was available on their condition. This left only one crew whose whereabouts John was unable to discover.*

While aiding the living, John also set about to bury Corporal Faktor, the dead gunner whose body had been brought to Ch'u Hsien. Searchers had found him in the wreckage of his plane. His dog tag and other ID had been taken by scavengers, but his crew mates had been able to identify his body.

John asked the Chinese commander at Ch'u Hsien about purchasing a burial plot near the base. "We won't sell you one," he replied. "We will give it for a hundred years, or for as long as it is needed. And we'll also pay for the coffin and the stone." John understood the Chinese desire to express appreciation for the sacrifice the young American had made. He thanked them and scheduled the burial for May 5.

Daily air raids prevented the workmen from having the grave and stone ready, but John went ahead with a memorial service for young Faktor with thirteen of Doolittle's Raiders present. Two weeks later he conducted graveside services with the Chinese Air Force providing full military honors. That same day Doolittle, now a lieutenant general, was in the White House receiving the Congressional Medal of Honor from President Roosevelt. He and his men, each of whom received the Distinguished Service Cross, were the heroes of the hour.

Doolittle had contacted the Birch family with the news of John's safety and new address. John was flooded with mail — precious, beautiful letters from home. After over half a year with no contact from stateside loved ones, he felt so blessed to receive not only letters from his family but many friends also. Most touching was the $110 from his parents. He presumed that General Doolittle had given a pitiful account of how emaciated he was, but he was being well fed at the base.

Daily bombings continued at Ch'u Hsien and refugees were streaming past the base. Enemy ground troops were only a few miles away as John saw the last of the downed Raiders onto a plane. His assignment completed John was now ready and anxious to report to Chungking, but no more planes were available.

It was May 28, John's twenty-fourth birthday, and he was contemplating setting out on foot when some Chinese officers offered him a ride on a south-bound gasoline truck. Shortly after John's departure an enemy bomb hit the headquarters building where he had been living, killing four people. Upon learning of his narrow escape, he wrote his parents, "How wonderful to be under the protection and guidance of our all-seeing heavenly Father!"

By truck, boat and on foot, John finally reached Hengyang in southern Hunan Province. He hitched a ride in an ancient truck to the airfield, which was little more than a single 3,000-foot runway built by coolie labor from crushed rock and mud. Three P-40 fighter planes were parked over to the side. Each bore the shark's teeth insignia that symbolized the Flying Tigers. A Chinese and an American were working under the belly of one of the planes.

As John came closer, he rubbed his eyes in disbelief. Two of the planes were made of bamboo. The American noticed his incredulity and shouted, "That's the kind of stuff they're sending us."

John laughed and walked over to introduce himself to the mechanics. "I was just kiddin'," the American admitted. "Those dummy planes are General Chennault's idea. He had the coolies build 'em to fool the Japs. Make them think we have more planes than we really do."

"Good thinking," John grinned. "By the way, I've been helping Doolittle's fliers. Did he pass through here?"

---

*Final tally on the fate of the Doolittle Raiders showed five had come down in Siberia and were held by their Russian "allies" for almost a year before they escaped to Iran. Eight were captured by the Japanese, including the unaccounted for crew that had been forced to bail out over Japan. Three of these eight captives died from execution and one from starvation. The remaining four were brutally tortured. One of the four suvivors, Jacob DeShazer, returned to Japan after the war as a missionary and was influential in winning to Christianity Captain Mitsuo Fuchida, commander of the air armada that had attacked Pearl Harbor.

"Yeah, about a month ago. We got him out to Chungking on a DC-3. I hear he went on to Washington, D.C. and got the Congressional Medal of Honor."

"He deserved it," John replied. "I'm trying to get to Chungking myself to deliver my report. Any chance of getting a flight out of here?"

"Nope. When I get this baby patched up, I'm going back to Kunming. Then I'm shipping out, going home. Your best bet," the friendly mechanic continued, "is to catch the train tonight from Hengyang south to Kweilin. The Old Man, ah, General Chennault, is there and might give you a ride to Chungking."

"Okay, thanks. Mind if I stick around and watch until train time?"

"Suit yourself."

John moved in closer and saw that they were installing a bamboo container. "It's a reserve gas tank. Put together with fish glue. It gives the plane more range, when we can get gas."

"Another of Chennault's ideas?" John wondered.

"Yeah. That man's brilliant. Only the stupid higher-ups don't recognize it. If I'd been in his place I'd have quit long ago."

"Why are you leaving now?"

" 'Cause they're folding the AVG. That's the American Volunteer Group. We were recruited before Pearl Harbor by Chennault when he was the air adviser to the Chinese government. Now they've made the Old Man a general and have told us we *have* to go into the regular U.S. Army.

"Ever hear of General Clayton Bissell? Well, he's sitting over in Delhi, India, doling out our rations from flights over the Hump. The scuttlebutt is that he and Chennault haven't gotten along since they were in tactical school together back in the '30s. He came over to our base at Kunming and told us if we didn't make the transfer into the army he'd see that our draft boards were waiting for us when we landed on American soil. 'Bull,' we told him, 'you're not going to threaten us. We're going home.' At least nine out of ten of us are. I only know of five pilots that are staying and about twenty ground crew. Twenty-five guys and General Chennault. That's all they'll have to fight China's air battles."

The American, who had introduced himself as "Al," seemed anxious to sound off about his frustrations and he and John talked the rest of the afternoon. He told John of Chennault's problems with U.S. Army bureaucracy that had kept his Flying Tigers, as the AVG was called, pinched for fuel and other supplies. The business of dissolving the AVG and bringing the men into the regular Army, according to Al, was a means of controlling Chennault. He would be forced to take orders from General "Vinegar Joe" Stilwell, the supreme Allied Commander in the China-India-Burma war theater, and from General Bissell in India, who had been made a lieutenant general one day ahead of Chennault. "That was so he would have seniority over the Old Man," Al noted.

"But isn't winning the war the most important thing?"

"Doesn't look like it, the way they're goin'," Al grumbled. "They care more about spit and polish than whippin' the Japs. The Old Man isn't big on rules and regulations. Just so long as we do the main job."

The mechanic finished his work and he and John strolled over to the operations shack to get out of the sun. A radio operator was sitting before a transmitter, listening. When the staccato taps stopped, the operator wrote the message down, then turned to meet John.

After they got acquainted, John asked if the taps were some kind of code. "Yeah. It's no secret. That was one of our spotters reporting in. Nine taps, or nine o'clock, means he's sighted some Jap planes flying west. Six o'clock means south; twelve, north. There are other codes that indicate the altitude, type and number of planes. Are you familiar with the '*Jing-bao*' air alert system?"

"Yeah," John said, "The big black canvas balls that the Chinese run up on flat poles. I saw them in operation at Shangjao and Ch'u Hsien. One ball means enemy planes have been spotted coming in this direction. Two, they're heading straight for us and you should seek shelter. Three, they're coming closer. *Jing-bao* means 'to be alert' in Chinese."

"Ever hear of *Jing-bao* juice?" Al asked.

"I've heard it's a potent Chinese beverage," John smiled. "But I don't drink myself, so I've never tried it. I would like to know more about this warning system though."

"Chennault brought the idea to China," the radio man explained. "He learned it in tactical school. He made a deal with Chiang that if the Chinese would build us some airfields for our fighters, we would set up a warning net of observers and equip them with little crank radios.

"The Old Man built the net in three concentric circles around each air base and large town. The outer circle is 180 miles from the base, the middle one is 120 miles, and the inner circle only sixty miles away. The spotters are on mountaintops, in caves, anywhere they can sight planes. Not all have radios. Some phone in. Some just light fires and send smoke signals, but they're brave and dependable, even those behind Jap lines."

John was impressed. "What's this map with the little Japanse flags for?"

"That's tied in with the net. As the observers report in, we move the little flags around to show the location of the planes they've spotted. We can figure out numbers, courses and speeds by coordinates and estimate the direction of the enemy planes so our fighters can intercept."

"Brilliant."

"Yes, we think so. If Stilwell would only listen to the Old Man — but he won't."

Al pointed to his watch. "We'd better get you to the train station." Al barked a command to a Chinese to take John to the depot in a battered jeep that was parked nearby. The train was late leaving and didn't get into Kweilin until after daylight. Bone-tired, John hired a taxi for the trip to the airfield.

Kweilin was the southernmost base of a string of air bases down the middle of south central China. The ancient city marked the eastern corner of a triangle, with Kunming four hundred miles to the west and Chungking, the provisional capital, at the top.

The road to the airfield wound through a flat valley of rice paddies flanked by towering black limestone mountains shaped like inverted ice cream cones. The airstrip, similar to the one at Hengyang, ran parallel to the side of a mountain which was pocked by caves. No buildings were in evidence, but John spotted some men working around a bunch of planes and asked the driver to drop him off there. Another group of planes was parked nearer the mountain. As he walked nearer, he realized they were bamboo like the ones at Hengyang.

He announced himself and asked the whereabouts of General Chennault. One of the men pointed to one of the larger holes in the mountain. "He's in the operations cave."

John found the winding trail of stone steps that led upward and climbed to the dimly lit opening. As he climbed the trail, he tried to remember all he had heard about Chennault and his men: a controversial pilot with new ideas about air war who had been hired by Chiang Kai-shek as air adviser to train Chinese pilots, now heading up a motley bunch of flying mercenaries recruited in the U.S. before Pearl Harbor. John had heard that the "Flying Tigers" had defeated the Japanese in air battles when out-numbered ten to one. He had also heard that they were a wild-living, hell-raising bunch of daredevils who strutted in public like Texas gunfighters and drove their jeeps on sidewalks when the streets got too crowded. Nevertheless, the Tigers were fiercely admired by the Chinese, who almost revered Chennault. Many Americans, John had heard, couldn't stand Chennault because he was too much of a maverick and nonconformist.

John stepped hesitantly into the mouth of the cave where a Chinese sat playing with little Japanese flags on a plotting board. "Where can I find General Chennault?" he asked. The man pointed further back to a lean middle-aged man sitting with three or four other Americans.

The Big Tiger, as the Chinese called him, wore a leather flight jacket with the famous insignia — a winged tiger flying through a large V for victory — of the Flying Tigers. A flight cap bearing markings of the Chinese Air Force was perched jauntily on his head, shadowing a face lathered by years of flying in an open cockpit.

"General Chennault, sir?"

No response.

"You'll have to speak louder; he's hard of hearing," one of the men explained.

"SIR, GENERAL CHENNAULT!"

The Big Tiger turned and peered at John. There was a moment of silence as the two men sized each other up. John first noted the determination demonstrated in the jutting jaw of the older man. The leathery face, creased into a frown, gave the impression of severity and single-mindedness. Then they looked one another in the eye and John saw a tenderness, a deep sadness that told him this man had known much tragedy.

"I'm John Birch, sir. I've been helping the Doolittle fliers. Now I'm supposed to report to Chungking and was hoping to catch a flight there from here."

"Birch. Birch. Oh, yeah, you're the young missionary Jimmy Doolittle told me about. He gave you quite a recommendation. Liked the way you took control of the situation in a time of emergency."

"I was glad to be of service, sir."

"He said you had an excellent rapport with the Chinese military. That could be a valuable asset," Chennault mused. "Most Americans seem to think the Chinese are all a bunch of ignorant coolies." He spat out a curse, causing John to grimace. Chennault looked John over thoughtfully, took a long drag on his cigarette, blew the smoke through his nostrils, and asked, "Did you locate all of Doolittle's boys?"

John gave him the numbers in his report.

Chennault cursed again. "If Bissell had given me a day's notice, I could have talked down every one of the planes that made it to East China. There wouldn't have been a single casualty or a captive for the Japs. Could have saved every plane. We sure could use those B-25s," he sighed.

"If they'd asked me, I could have told them where to put their bombs. I've got better maps on Japan than the War Department." He swore again. "Fancy-pants think they know everything and don't know anything." He looked over at John. "What are you going to do after you turn in your report?"

"Well, the war has crippled our missionary work, so I've volunteered as a chaplain, but I don't know yet if they'll take me."

"Chaplain, eh?" Chennault rubbed his chin thoughtfully. "What's your denomination?"

"Baptist, sir. Fundamental Baptist."

"Well, what do you know, I'm a Baptist myself. Course I cuss and drink a little and give the Japs a little of their own medicine, but I'm a member of a Baptist church back in Louisiana. And you want to be a chaplain, huh?"

"Yes, sir," John replied firmly. "I want to serve God and my country."

"Well, I've got Paul Frillman already. Don't need another padre." The general paused long enough to light a new cigarette. "Maybe I could make you an assistant or something. I sure could use someone with your experience with the Chinese." When John made no comment he continued, "But you still have some time to make a final decision.

"In a couple of weeks my outfit's having to go into the regular Army. I don't like it, but I had no choice. They threatened to cut off my supplies if I didn't. I'd be glad to have you come in with us."

"I'll pray about it," John proposed.

"You do that, son, and while you're at it say a prayer for my pilots. They're risking their lives every day while the fancy-pants sit in their soft offices and dream up more regulations."

Chennault fell silent. John waited respectfully, then repeated his request for a ride to Chungking.

"Be at the plane at 1100," Chennault grunted. "You can stay at our hostel at the airfield in Chungking, if you'd like."

"Yes, sir. Thank you, sir," John replied politely, feeling as if he should salute or something. He wandered out of the cave and down to the field where he passed the time talking with some of the Chinese workmen.

Promptly at 11 a.m. they took off, with Chennault at the controls. Climbing to 10,000 feet he flew northwest over spectacular mountains before beginning his descent over the provisional capital. John looked down at the broad, fast-flowing Yangtze River which rose in Tibet and flowed 3,400 miles across the middle of China to the sea. The famous old city, with streets terracing the side of a hill, was visible across the river. Some streets were only rows of ruins, punctuated by skeletal hulks of houses that appeared ready to fall.

"The Japs almost destroyed Chungking before we taught them a lesson," Chennault muttered.

They passed over the city and set down smoothly at the airfield in a valley beyond the populated area. Unlike Hengyang and Kweilin there were hangars here and several barracks-like buildings. "You can stay in Hostel A with me and my pilots," Chennault said. "C'mon, I'll walk over with you."

After making arrangements for John's sleeping quarters, Chennault turned him over to a regular Army officer who seemed anxious to hear the report on Doolittle and his Raiders. John presented his written report and then handed in the $2,000 Doolittle had left to cover expenses.

"You didn't spend any of it?"

"No, sir. The Chinese Air Force paid all of Corporal Faktor's funeral expenses and gave me free lodging."

"Amazing. All the Chinese we know always have their hands out," the officer chuckled sarcastically.

John bristled with indignation at the slur, but kept his voice calm as he replied emphatically, "The Chinese have always been very good to me."

After the debriefing was completed, John mentioned his letter offering to volunteer. "If it's all right, I'd like to wait a few days. I'm considering joining General Chennault's group after they're inducted into the Army Air Force."

"Suit yourself. As a clergyman, you're not subject to the draft."

Weary from eighteen days of traveling, John enjoyed an early supper, followed by a good night's rest and a hearty breakfast. He then decided to go into the city and learn what he could about the war situation.

A sergeant delivering mail to the American Military Mission, the U.S. Embassy and the Office of War Information (OWI) gave him a ride for the thirty miles to the provisional capital which Chiang Kai-shek had established after the Japanese had occupied the Nationalist capital at Nanking.

John stopped by the head chaplain's office first. The pert young WAC at a typewriter said he was in a staff meeting, so John walked over to the OWI which had been established to promote a favorable image of the U.S. and to help America's allies with propaganda. No one was around, so he looked at some literature spread across a counter. To his amazement, he found a booklet praising Mao Tse-tung's revolutionaries.

A young, sallow-faced man suddenly appeared carrying a briefcase. "I don't believe we've met," he smiled pleasantly, putting forth a hand for John to shake. "My name's Paul Daniel."

"I'm John Birch, a Baptist missionary. I've volunteered as a chaplain, but don't know yet if they want me."

"Very interesting. I'm sure you'll make a fine chaplain. Unless my ears deceive me, you are from the southeastern part of the States."

A discussion ensued about the merits of growing up in the rural south as opposed to metropolitan living on the east coast. After a few minutes, John brought the conversation around to the pamphlet he had been reading. "I thought Mao's revolutionaries were bad guys, Communists. This seems to imply that they're the hope of China."

"You probably heard some right-winger call them Communists. They're not Marxists at all. We think of them as agrarian reformers. They're honest and idealistic, the kind of people we need to get behind." He glanced out the window and lowered his voice. "That's more than you can say for Chiang's generals."

"But isn't Chiang a Christian?" John protested.

"He pretends to be religious."

"But he's our ally."

"Yes, and he's losing the war while his generals get rich. Look, you don't have to accept my word. Ask the war correspondents who can't get their copy past Chiang's censors. They'll tell you about Chinese officers who keep dead men on payrolls and pocket their pay while living soldiers starve to death. About rich men's sons who buy their way out of the Army while poor peasants are kidnapped, roped together and dragged to conscription stations. You won't find Mao Tse-tung and Chou En-lai doing that."

John was confused. He'd certainly talk to some more people before drawing any conclusions.

John returned to the chaplain's office and found he was still tied up. The WAC/receptionist seemed too busy to talk, so he walked over to the USO for a sandwich and to visit with the hostesses. Not since leaving Hangchow had he talked to an American girl.

The mail sergeant had told him he was returning to the airfield at four o'clock, so John gave up on seeing the head chaplain so he could catch a ride back. He didn't want to be late for supper. After so many months on near starvation diet, it seemed he couldn't get enough to eat.

After wiping his plate clean with the last of his bread, John wandered into the day room and talked to a rangy pilot from Texas. His open, friendly personality and the fact that he had been one of Chennault's earliest volunteers, gave John confidence to ask him the question that had been haunting him all afternoon: "Is it true that the Generalissimo's government is corrupt?"

"Where did you hear that?"

"From a guy at the OWI."

"Yeah, that's the kind of stuff they're turning out. And I'll bet he said the Chinese Commies are pure and virtuous."

"He said they were agrarian democrats, sort of like the New Dealers at home."

"I'll level with you," the Texan replied seriously. "Everyone knows there's corruption and bribery in this country. A lot worse than at home. But the Gizmo himself is honest, although some of his generals are on the take. They seem to think that goes with the job."

"What about the revolutionaries?" John persisted.

"They're Marxists through and through, taking orders right out of Moscow. Ask Chennault. He's been here since '38 and knows the score."

"If that's true, then why are Americans like the man at the OWI promoting communism?"

"The Office of War Information is a rat's nest of left-wingers," came the bitter reply. "And their line is echoed by Stilwell's headquarters."

"General Stilwell is a left-winger?"

"Naw, but he listens to political advisers who feed him a lot of bull about Chiang and nothing but good stuff about Mao."

"Is that why Stilwell and General Chennault disagree?"

"That's part of it. The Old Man thinks the Gizmo's a great guy. He doesn't like the Commies, but he'll take their help or anybody's in fighting the Japs. The basic reason the Old Man and Vinegar Joe don't get along is they just don't think alike. Stilwell still thinks wars are won on the ground. The Old Man keeps trying to convince him that we've got to have air support.

"If you've kept up with the war, you know the Japs beat the pants off Stilwell in Burma. Now all he can think of is going back in there. The Old Man and all the Flying Tigers feel Stilwell had better wake up and defend China."

"But I thought the Generalissimo was the commander and that Stilwell was under his command."

"Well, the book says Stilwell is the Gizmo's chief-of-staff and commander of U.S. forces in the China-Burma-India war theater. But Stilwell has control of American Lend-Lease which the Gizmo could hardly live without. So he holds that as a club over the Gizmo's head."

"Pardon my ignorance," John said, shaking his head, "but where does General Bissell fit into this?"

"Bissell's head of the 10th Air Force. His headquarters are in Delhi, India. The guys in Chennault's old AVG who go into the Army Air Force will become the China Air Task Force, assigned to the 10th in India. To get anything done, Chennault will have to get clearance from Bissell, who doesn't like the Old Man anyway. Then Bissell will have to get it okayed from Stilwell, who has similar feelings. Can you imagine the stalling and the red tape?"

John gave a long sigh.

"If it was just General Chennault," the pilot continued, "we'd all stay and fight to the last man. But we're not going to get our tails blown out of the sky for Bissell and Stilwell. Well, most of us anyway. A few are staying."

The Texan stood up, stretched and flexed his muscles a bit. "Are you seriously considering joining this outfit?" he asked John with a cryptic smile.

"I was very impressed with General Chennault," John replied honestly. "I'd like to serve under him, but he already has a chaplain. I'm just going to wait and see what doors the Lord opens for me."

9

The Flying Tiger

*I get a better hearing and more respect from the
men when they know I'm not preaching for a
salary.*

—John Birch, letter to parents,
January 30, 1943

The next few days John kept busy visiting the American embassy, the USO and some American missionaries stationed in Chungking. He attended church services and talked with pilots at the hostel. He wrote letters home. And he waited. Waited for word about his commission into the chaplaincy.

"Has the Lord told you what to do yet, Birch?" General Chennault asked one morning as they passed on the steps of the hostel.

"No, sir," John grinned, "I still haven't had any word from military headquarters. Can't figure what's taking them so long to make up their minds."

"If you intend to join the Army, you might as well get used to it. War might be over before you hear." The General's jeep pulled up and Chennault asked, "Where are you headed? Want to ride into town with me?"

John hadn't planned on going to town that day, but jumped at the opportunity to have a talk with the General.

"You know, you could get into intelligence work and still preach on Sundays if you don't become a chaplain," the General suggested.

"Oh?" John replied noncommittally.

"I'll tell you what I need," Chennault confided. "I need some field intelligence officers who are old China hands. Men who lived in China before the war, speak the language, know the customs and can live in the field on Chinese food.

"The problem is, John, the enemy is throwing everything they have into taking China. They are totally dedicated, and they don't care what it costs them in terms of equipment or men. We don't have the luxury of endless supplies, and every time one of our boys goes down, I die a little." The Big Tiger swallowed hard and looked out at the passing scenery for a moment. John realized he was fighting to keep his composure. He found it deeply touching that the tough, hard-nosed General hurt so badly for the men he had lost.

"I'm not trying to talk you into anything, Birch," he continued.

"This would be dangerous, dirty work. There would be times of extreme danger, and also times of boredom, but it could save men's lives and make the difference in winning and losing this war. If you aren't sure you want to do this, if you aren't totally committed to the job, I don't want you. If you decide you want to serve your countrymen and protect your Chinese friends in this way, let me know. I'll give you a field commission and put you to work right away."

The conversation gave John a lot to think about, especially as the days passed and the hostel filled with Flying Tigers who had come to tell General Chennault good-bye. The *esprit de corps* among the men was contagious. It was evident they had great respect for the General, even though they were leaving his command for civilian life. Many had tears running down their cheeks as they left. John had never felt such devotion to any man, except his father.

Fifty-five pilots agreed to stay on a couple of weeks just in case the Japs tried to hit the Old Man's new outfit when it was weakest. On the evening of June 30 John was sitting with Chennault and some of the Tigers in the day room of Hostel A when Tokyo Rose came on the radio at her usual time.

"The bandits called the Flying Tigers have quit," she purred in her silky-smooth voice. "They are beaten, sick and tired. They are deserting their Chinese stooges. But don't feel sorry for them. They are taking home plenty of gold.

"The Imperial Japanese Government now gives warning. On the Fourth of July, the American Independence Day, it will utterly destroy the dregs that Chennault has left."

The General clicked off the shortwave radio and surveyed his group. "Well, boys, we don't want the Japs to think we've quit, do we? Let's prepare a little welcoming party."

The Old Man ordered every available P-40 to Kweilin. The planes were to come in by ones and twos from the other bases and taxi to camouflaged hiding places. In the slots beside the runway, where the P-40s usually parked, there would be bamboo dummies, spiked with gasoline. Then the pilots would go into town, make the round of the bars, and spread the line that the squadron had been sent to Kweilin to practice and would soon fly back to Chungking to defend the capital.

John was intrigued with the plan and itched to get into the action, but he had to remain an outsider, sitting in Chungking waiting anxiously for reports of the battle. On July 3 many of the daredevils returned to Chungking, crowing over their exploits, and mocking Tokyo Rose.

"We really gave it to 'em," one of them exclaimed as a group gathered around John, enjoying an appreciative audience. "See, the Chinese spotters started radioing in reports this morning that Jap planes had taken off from various bases. We all gathered into the operations cave at Kweilin with the Old Man so we could watch this Chinese officer move the little Jap flags across the plotting board. When all the flags came together in a straight line, pointing directly at Kweilin, Chennault gave the order for us to scramble."

"Yeah, what a scramble," another pilot interrupted. "Twenty-nine battered old P-40s roaring off the field to meet ninety-six Jap ships. We were ordered to climb to 21,000 feet and orbit west of the field, maintaining radio silence. We stayed up there, hiding in the sun, waiting for the order to attack."

The first pilot took over the narrative. "A little after 1300 a formation of Zeros appeared. We'd been hovering up there for nearly a half hour and were chomping at the bit, ready to get at 'em, but we had to wait 'til the Old Man gave the word. He played it cool, giving them plenty of time. First they peeled off, circling, diving, looping, strafing the fake planes. After all the dummies were afire they confidently formed back into a tight formation for the return flight."

" 'Take 'em, Tigers,' came the order, and we dove out of the sun, pouncing on the unsuspecting Zeros, spraying them with hot bursts of fire. They were flying so close and were so off guard, we couldn't miss! Twenty of them went spiraling down on the first pass, and the survivors ran in all directions. We pursued some as far as two hundred miles, and we shot down fourteen more."

"Yeah, we got thirty-four of their Zeros, and they burned a lot of bamboo. Wonder what ole Rosie is going to have to say about that?"

They tuned the radio for Tokyo Rose's evening broadcast. She bragged that the Imperial Japanese Air Force had destroyed forty-eight P-40s on the ground, but said nothing about the Zeros Chennault's men had brought down. John sat among the men listening to their catcalls, thinking how General Chennault must feel, happy for the victory while sad that these brave men were leaving China.

The next day a big Fourth of July barbecue party was given by Madame Chiang, the Honorary Commander of the AVG, and General Chennault. It would be the last time for the AVG to be together. Although John was not a member, he had received an engraved invitation to the affair, which was to be held at the home of China's revered President Lin Sen.

A sudden rainstorm canceled the lawn barbecue and they had to move inside the house. General Chennault stood in the receiving line with Madame Chiang and her sister, the widow of Sun Yat Sen, founder of the Chinese Republic. When John came by, General Chennault turned to the famous Soong sisters and introduced him. "I would like you to meet Reverend John Birch, a missionary who helped General Doolittle and his fliers."

John bowed stiffly. "I am honored to make the acquaintance of the First Lady of China and her esteemed sister. I believe we share a common interest. I am from Macon, Georgia, I understand you both attended Wesleyan College there."

The sisters were delighted with that information and immediately began sharing remembrances of their college days. John was enchanted to hear them speak English with the soft, lilting accent of his homeland. He found them both as charming and gracious as their reputations, and forgot all about being nervous over meeting such famous people.

Later they all played musical chairs, with the rough-and-tumble Tigers looking awkward in white suits and trying to maintain some degree of poise. The most memorable evening of John's life closed with Madame Sun Yat Sen presenting General Chennault with an oil painting of the Generalissimo, Madam Chiang and himself.

The next morning the General came over to John's table at breakfast. "Have you made a decision yet, Birch?"

"Not really. I talked with the head chaplain over at General Stilwell's American Military Mission headquarters and I think I know now what the delay is."

"What's that?"

"Well, the Army stipulates a chaplain must have ordination, a degree from an accredited seminary and pastoral experience before being commissioned. I've met the first and third requirements, but the Baptist Bible Institute I attended in Fort Worth is not accredited by the American Association of Theological Schools."

"So that means there's no chance of you being a chaplain?"

"Not if they go strictly according to the rules. However, I pointed out to them that I have had two years of experience in China and a personal recommendation from General Doolittle, which should count for something. The chaplain was very nice about it, said he would put in a request for a waiver, but you know how the Army is about rules. I really doubt if I get in."

"If you get tired of waiting around, I could give you a commission. Then if, by some miracle, the chaplaincy opens up somewhere else, you could transfer."

"I could?" John exclaimed eagerly. "Oh, yes sir. I would like that. I'm tired of being in limbo. I want to be useful, and I would be very honored to serve under you, even if it were only for a short time."

"Excellent, Lieutenant," Chennault grinned. "I'll get the paperwork done immediately."

A telegram was received by John's parents on July 10, 1942, reading:

NOW SECOND LIEUTENANT ADDRESS ARMY POST OFFICE 879 NEW YORK CITY REQUEST WOLFE STOP SALARY

LOVE JOHN

One of John's first decisions as a member of the 23rd was to offer his assistance to Chennault's chaplain, Paul Frillman. Frillman was a jovial ex-Lutheran missionary who was well-liked in the Chennault camp. John disagreed with him theologically and disapproved of his poker playing, social drinking and occasional strong language, and said so. Nevertheless, Frillman assigned John to preach in his absence and to help orient new inductees to the base.

The new pilots Stilwell had promised Chennault to replace the AVG men who quit were arriving daily. Chennault interviewed each one. He sent the first five packing when they confessed to fear of combat, and told several others they needed more flight training. The greenhorns he accepted for training cracked up eighteen P-40s in a seventeen-day period. He cussed Stilwell for sending him a bunch of rejects, but still the old master managed to develop some outstanding fliers from the bunch.

Most of the new men didn't stay around Chungking long. They were either rejected or quickly sent on to reinforce the skeleton crews of former Tigers at the other bases. John didn't get to know many of them well.

One he did make friends with was a young scholar named Arthur Hopkins who had volunteered to help Chennault with paperwork as a civilian. A Yale '41 man, Hopkins had won a two-year appointment to teach at the Yale-in-China Association's prestigious middle school at Changsha in central China where the Yale group also had a hospital and training school for nurses. The Japanese advance after the Doolittle raid had disrupted the school, and Hopkins came to Chungking offering his services. John found Hopkins' company stimulating and was disappointed when the Yale-in-China Association called him back to teach at the school which had been set up in refugee quarters. "I hope our paths cross again," John said sincerely as Hopkins bade good-bye.

The action around the base at Chungking increased, for now that the last of the Flying Tigers who had refused induction had left China, the Japanese were mounting an all-out onslaught on the eastern front. Particularly hard-hit was the northernmost base at Hengyang, which was bombed night after night. The Japs seemed determined to make the runway unusable, but after each attack coolies swarmed on the field and filled up the craters so the five remaining P-40s could take off for missions at dawn.

Toward the end of the month John heard that the chief of chaplains for the China-Burma-India theater was coming to Chungking. The timing seemed providential, for John had not yet taken off on a field trip for Chennault. He immediately requested that his file be reviewed, and this was arranged. Excited about the possibility of going over the heads of some of the nitpickers, John went to tell Chennault his good news.

He entered the Old Man's office to hear him laughing heartily. There hadn't been much to laugh about in recent weeks, so John was naturally curious, and the General seemed happy to share his glee. "That Tex Hill," he chuckled, shaking his head. "He just reported in. It seems the five guys left at Hengyang took off to hit Canton this morning, and on the way back their radios crackled with the warning that seventy Jap fighters were flying to head them off.

"As a flight leader, Ole Tex knew their only chance for survival was a big bluff. So that character grabbed his microphone and began barking orders for deployment of imaginary squadrons of planes. The other four caught on and would answer back using phony voices. And the Japs fell for it!" Chennault chortled. "They turned tail and ran! That Tex is my kind of man."

John's news seemed unimportant compared to that report, so he decided to tell the General about it later.

John confidently wrote his folks, "I suppose I shall be taking the wings and propeller off my collar soon and pinning on the cross."

When John shared his good news with the General, Chennault leaned back in his swivel chair and stroked his chin thoughtfully. "Do you think you could take a trip for me while you're waiting? I'm in desperate need of some accurate, up-to-date information about the condition of some of the small, out-of-the way airfields and the gas and ammo we hid there some time back."

"I'd be glad to, sir," John replied. "Make the time pass faster. I get quite frustrated just waiting around for the Army to make up its mind. I'd much rather be doing something useful."

"Great! Now let me explain the situation to you. It's no secret that Stilwell wants to keep the lion's share of men and supplies allotted to China to train Chinese soldiers for the recapture of

Burma. I guess it isn't all his fault," the General conceded with a sigh. "Some of the, ah, 'gentlemen' in Washington have written off China. They seem to forget that the Generalissimo has a million Jap soldiers tied down here — a million who would otherwise be in the Pacific fighting American boys.

"Okay, so we're unappreciated and neglected, but we're not about to quit! We're going to keep those sons of the Rising Sun busy no matter what. Now, this is the confidential part. I anticipated this problem, and a couple of years ago I had some Chinese friends cache ammo and gas at remote airfields in central and southeastern China. Here, I'll mark them off for you on this map." He drew circles at widely spaced locations on the map as he continued his discourse. "You can readily see the advantage of having gas and ammo at these fields. This gives our planes extra range, and in times of emergency they serve as optional landing places. We just might use them from time to time to surprise the Japs, but I've got to know if the stuff is still there and if the fields are in good condition. That's where you come in. I want you to take a Chinese operative and check out every one. Any questions?"

"Two, sir. May I preach to Chinese churches along the way?"

"John, I don't care if you preach to the devil, so long as you do your job. What's your other question?"

"If my chaplin's clearance comes through while I'm gone, will you still permit me to transfer?"

"And if it hasn't, you'll be my intelligence officer?"

"Agreed, sir," John replied, and accepted Chennault's outstretched hand. "When do we start?"

The General signed a special memorandum to "all concerned" for John to carry:

> The bearer, Lieutenant John M. Birch, is a trusted American officer in this command. He has been sent on a special mission. Any assistance, official or otherwise, that might be needed by Lieutenant Birch is hereby requested.

John and a Chinese companion, M.L. Wang, left in mid-September. Each took only what he could carry: canteen, first-aid kit, C-rations, a quilted Chinese coat, blankets, hunting knife, a holstered .45 and a money belt stuffed with Chinese currency. John also had a roll of maps, a list of contacts and a box of gospel tracts in Chinese.

During the next two months they covered over a thousand miles, walking, hitchhiking, flying short hops in Chinese Air Force planes, and chugging along rivers in launches. They traveled by day in safe territory and by night when near Japanese lines. They slept in the houses of contacts and on Sundays sought out churches where John was usually invited to preach.

At each airstrip John asked the contact to show them the cache. The supplies were entombed underground, hidden in corn bins, concealed under the floors of pagodas, suspended in wells and secreted in many other unlikely places. John meticulously examined every can of gas, bomb and box of bullets, noting them next to the name of the location on his list.

He then checked the condition of the runways and was pleased to find the villagers had maintained them all in meticulous condition. The peasants seemed to take great pride in doing their bit to help the war effort. Their eagerness reminded John of the many friends he had made during the six months after the fall of Hangchow. All of those people were now behind Japanese lines and there was no way he could get information concerning their condition. All he could do was pray that the Lord would sustain them during their hour of persecution.

John and Wang completed their assignment, confident they had done a good job. John reported back to the base near Chungking lean, tanned, and as one colleague put it, "hungry as a starved tomcat." He turned in his report to the General and then headed for the kitchen where he downed a stack of peanut butter sandwiches.

Chennault read John's report and promptly wrote a commendation for John's file with a recommendation for promotion. "Lieutenant Birch's invaluable secret mission for intelligence led him close to enemy territory," he wrote. "The successful accomplishment required fortitude, courage and devotion to duty."

The authorization for John to become a chaplain had not come through. Since he was a clergyman and had volunteered, he could resign his commission and go back to missionary work, but he was too patriotic for that. Besides, he had given his word to Chennault. He couldn't understand just why the Lord would want him in intelligence work, but it seemed that was the way he was leading. *Okay*, he thought, *I'll be a spy for God.*

John sensed a new confidence in Chennault. For one thing, some of the new pilots had proved their mettle. For another, the Army Air Force had coughed up a new batch of P-40s. He would have preferred the newer P-38s, which were equal to the new Jap Oscars, but P-40s beat sitting on the ground.

Then, in November Stilwell issued a directive that sent the Big Tiger into a rage. The caustic commander of the CBI theater ordered Chennault and his China Air Task Force (CATF) to move their headquarters from Chungking to Kunming in far western Yunnan

Province. Logistically it made no sense, unless Stilwell wanted them there to be in position to support an attack on Burma instead of giving air support to the front-line Chinese Army.

Kunming was almost in the Himalayas, on the China side of the Hump flying route, and about as next to nowhere as any place in Free China. "At Kunming," Stilwell further told Chennault, "you will be directly responsible to General Bissell in India. All communication with the Chinese command will be channeled through him."

Chennault cursed and growled and gnashed his teeth. It was the stupidest thing he could imagine Stilwell doing, but the reason seemed obvious. Stilwell, in his hatred for both Chennault and Chiang Kai-shek, wanted the two friends as far apart as possible.

Before Thanksgiving the CATF moved to the refugee-crowded frontier town. John was fascinated with Kunming, which was situated on a 6,000 foot plateau. Mingling among brown-skinned tribesmen who came to sell their pigs and skins, he could hear a score of exotic languages along the cobble-stoned streets. He envisioned himself going to some of these tribes after the war, perhaps to Tibet or Chinese Turkestan where the last missionary had recently been driven out. Perhaps to translate the Bible, develop indigenous churches and organize a string of agricultural cooperatives to boost their economy.

The bustling airfield was out beyond rice and poppy fields, between the town and a string of lakes. Thousands of coolies had carved the strip out of the raw red clay of Yunnan Province, then filled in the space with broken rocks. The strip could accommodate the heaviest bombers and the transports delivering supplies via the Hump route from India.

Chennault's operations "office" was down in a deep trench, roofed by tree trunks and a cushion of earth. From here he directed by microphone takeoffs and training maneuvers. His headquarters was an old tile-roof mud house that looked as if it might collapse at any moment. He lived in a rented bungalow just off the base with his dachshund, Joe; the CATF medic, Dr. Tom Gentry; and a Chinese cook.

John was ensconced in a shack within shouting distance of the General's headquarters. "You are my intelligence department and will answer directly to me," Chennault informed him. "Your first duty is to correct our aerial maps, based on what you learned on your recent mission. You'll debrief the pilots when they come in. Get everything they saw. You'll handle the intelligence from Chungking and Navy ships off the coast and keep me up-to-date on what the enemy is doing."

John spread the maps on a table and started to work. Fortunately he had helped in the U.S. Agriculture Department's land survey program around Macon one summer and knew how to read aerial maps. He was constantly interrupted by radio reports and by incoming pilots who got impatient when he wasn't on hand to debrief them.

Talking to the pilots was interesting and he enjoyed it, except for the cursing. John could be blunt. "Look, do you have to take the Lord's name in vain in every sentence?" he asked one. To another he said, "Just tell me what you saw, never mind the profanity." Some of the pilots didn't appreciate his comments and said so, but when they were headed for a dangerous mission they never complained when he called out, "I'll be praying for you."

At Chennault's request, John bunked with the senior officers though he was still only a second lieutenant. "I've already recommended you three times for promotion since your mission," Chennault told him, "But it has to be approved by Bissell."

Besides the prestige of associating with the top brass, John liked the informality of Chennault's command. The Old Man wore a tie only when a top dog like Stilwell or an official from Washington was coming. He didn't care for saluting and didn't mind what his men wore on ordinary occasions. Nor was he much on rules for community living. The Flying Tigers had democratically decided when they wanted lights out in their barracks and what penalties were to be assessed for base infractions. "You're grown men," he told the CATF guys, "and don't have to be told when to go to bed and when to get up. Just watch it when Stilwell, Bissell, or some boot-lickin' inspector comes around from Washington."

When it came to the main business of fighting the Japs, John saw that the Old Man was a perfectionist. He could be merciless to those whose careless actions put the lives of others in danger. Sloppy dress and unshined shoes might be of no consequence, but disobedience to orders in battle could not be tolerated. "Just remember," Chennault kept reminding, "we're here to do a job. If you're not willing to break your tail for victory, then take the next plane out."

Despite his crudeness and profanity, John's admiration for Claire Chennault was growing every day.

In personnel and planes the CATF was looking better. Stilwell had sent a few crackerjacks. Twenty seasoned fliers had come in from Panama. Chennault lured a squadron over from India, where operations had been bogged down by monsoon rains. They were at Kunming for "flying experience," but he did not intend to let them go back. He had recently received six B-25 bombers and another covey of P-40s.

Getting supplies was as bad as ever. Transports flying the Himalayan Hump landed regularly. Most refueled and then flew their cargo on to Chungking. Chennault taught his men to eat Chinese food and live off the land, but fuel, ammo, warm clothing, razor blades and soap could not be bought locally. It was galling to see the tons of American canned food, beer, cigarettes and auto gas bound for Stilwell's staff and the American embassy in Chungking — especially when there was not enough gas to get all the CATF planes off the ground for bombing missions.

Mail calls were two and three weeks apart. Once when no mail was delivered for three weeks, Chennault sent a DC-3 over the Hump to India with orders to fill it with mail bags that he knew were stacked in a storage shed at Bissell's headquarters. The plane came back filled with tennis shoes for the Chinese Army. Following it came a second plane carrying a field team of inspectors from Bissell's headquarters in Delhi. They did a quick walk-around, noted muddy floors in the barracks, men with unshined shoes and a noticeable lack of saluting. When they handed Chennault a copy of their report, he muttered to one of his pilots, "Bissell, I think, would rather have a clean salute than a Jap plane knocked down."

To add to the frustration, Bissell's staff held up CATF promotions and recommendations for six months. The promotions, they claimed, were being worked into a new table of organization. General Bissell would be the judge of who deserved decorations. Most actions cited by Chennault, he said, were done only "in the line of duty" and deserved no special recognition. Such response maddened Chennault, for he knew his men were out every day, when gas and weather permitted, risking their lives while Bissell's staff did their paperwork in comfortable offices.

Chennault's men vented their anger by teaching unwitting Chinese coolies to greet each arriving plane crew and passengers with "nuts to Bissell." "It's an old American welcome," they assured the Chinese. One afternoon General Bissell himself stepped off a DC-3 and was greeted by the grinning coolies, bowing and shouting, "Nuts to Bissell!" He was not amused.

On December 10, when resentment was running high against General Bissell and his staff, two new officers arrived and asked for General Chennault.

"Lieutenant Colonel Jesse Williams and Captain Wilfred Smith reporting, sir."

"Who sent you birds?" Chennault asked grumpily.

"General Bissell, sir," Williams replied. "I'm your new A-2 (chief of intelligence) and Captain Smith here is my assistant."

"I don't appreciate Bissell picking my staff. I've got an intelligence man, Lieutenant Birch." Chennault glared at them a few seconds, then, thinking better, said, "Well, as long as you're here, go get yourselves a room and some chow."

Williams and Smith hung around ten days while Chennault kept ignoring them. Both were highly qualified and were disgusted at being caught between two feuding generals. Williams had been an oil company executive in Shanghai for eighteen years before Pearl Harbor. Smith, the son of Christian & Missionary Alliance missionaries, had been raised on the Yangtze River and held a PhD in Oriental History from the University of Michigan.

They finally decided to bypass Chennault and start to work. Walking into the intelligence shack, they introduced themselves to John. It was an awkward moment. John had been reporting directly to General Chennault. Now he had two bosses to go through.

"General Bissell sent us," Williams said.

"General Bissell isn't very popular around here, sir," John muttered.

"We can't help that," Smith declared. "We're just here to do a job and we'll expect to have your cooperation."

As disgusted as he was with the Army's talent for snafus, John was not one to rebel in ranks. "At your service, gentlemen," he replied dutifully. "If you'll take chairs, I'll show you what I'm doing."

Despite the awkward meeting, the three soon developed a good rapport and could laugh at the break-down in communications. John came to respect both officers as patriots with a deep understanding of the situation in China.

John had now adjusted himself to the fact that he would not be a professional chaplain. The opportunities he had as a lay officer were proving to be deeply satisfying. Christmas week he preached at Kunming for Chaplain Frillman, then flew to another base and led the first Christmas service ever held there for Americans. "I had a good opportunity to preach the old gospel in telling why Christ came," John wrote his parents. "I get a better hearing and more respect from the men when they know that I am not preaching for a salary."

The realization that this was true had been quite a revelation for John. He wanted to serve God and country, and had thought the way to do this was through the chaplaincy. When those doors were closed to him, he found it difficult to understand why God didn't override the circumstances for him. Now he knew the Lord's way was better. Not only did he have more acceptance from the servicemen, but he also was free to preach to the Chinese as opportunities presented themselves.

10

The Warrior

The eternal Word, the sword of the Spirit, is even now more important than the thunder of guns and the crash of bombs.

—John Birch, letter to parents,
January 30, 1943

The New Year of 1943 brought good news from the Chinese underground in occupied Shanghai. Oscar and Myrtle Wells and Fred and Lois Donnelson were alive and in reasonably good health, as of November. They did not know the whereabouts of Mother Sweet and John could only hope and pray she had been sent home on a neutral mercy ship.

He also received word from his family that twenty-two-year-old George Stanley had taken a "strong stand for Christ" and was receiving flight instruction as an Army Air Force cadet. John responded:

> Tell George Stanley that I congratulate and admire him for his Christian stand. ... I would not have him a pacifist or anything approaching one, and I hope he soon gets his wings and uses them for Uncle Sam, but I am thrilled to think that my little brother realized that the eternal Word, the sword of the Spirit, is even now more important than the thunder of guns and the crash of bombs ... "Those things which cannot be shaken may remain" (Hebrews 12:27).

John's message to his younger brother reflected his own philosophy about participation in war. Winning the war was for him only the prelude to the greater battle which he intended to wage in China after victory was secured. Quoting from Judges 15:8, he told Captain Smith one evening, "God has told me that I am to smite them hip and thigh."

The problem was, the Japanese had been doing most of the smiting. MacArthur was losing hundreds of men every day against determined Japanese resistance in the Pacific. The bloody battle for

Guadalcanal was five months old and the island was still not in Allied hands. Chennault believed his air force could give them support by hitting the Japanese merchant vessels moving raw materials from China, but he couldn't convince Stilwell.

Chinese morale was at its lowest ebb since the war began. The Japanese realized this and were pushing a propaganda campaign under the motto: "Asia for the Asiatics." Meanwhile, General Bissell's staff in Delhi worked on their tables of organization, and Stilwell sat in Chungking, listening to his State Department advisers extol Mao's Communists and denigrate Chiang's Nationalists, and brooding over a return to Burma.

Chennault had urged Stilwell to forward a message to General George C. Marshall, chairman of the U.S. Joint Chiefs of Staff and General Hap Arnold, head of the U.S. Army Air Force:

> Situation in Orient appears extremely critical ... Action of a small effective U.S. air force in China ... could destroy much of the war materials flowing through and around Formosa to southern islands for use against MacArthur. Inspire Chinese ground forces to action against Japanese occupied areas. Neutralize Jap air efforts in Burma and Indo-China. Relieve immediate Jap threat to India. Safeguard our air transport line to China and supply a successful offensive to inspire all Allied Powers.

He asked for 500 bombers and fighters plus 100 transports.

> Give me complete authority in the theater. I will accept full responsibility for attainment of objectives listed. Urge this be forwarded immediately for decision and necessary action.

Stilwell pigeonholed the plea.

Colonel Merrian Cooper, Chennault's chief of staff, wrote a letter to his friend Major General "Wild Bill" Donovan, chief of the new Office of Strategic Services (OSS). When Donovan circulated the letter around Washington, the War Department, where Stilwell had staunch friends, initiated immediate action — to transfer Cooper from China "for medical reasons."

Meanwhile, Wendell Wilkie, the Republican presidential candidate in 1940, stopped in China on his "One World" tour and demanded of Stilwell that he be permitted to talk with Chennault. Knowing Wilkie was a powerful political figure, Stilwell gave his consent.

When Wilkie heard Chennault's story he was shocked. "Put it in a letter and I'll deliver it personally to President Roosevelt," he pledged.

After Wilkie left, Stilwell sent word he was cutting CATF's gas deliveries by 50 percent. Chennault countered that he would have to ground all his planes. Stilwell backed down.

Chennault intended to be ready when the reinforcements came. He called in Jesse Williams and Wilfred Smith and told them, "We've got to do something about intelligence on the coast." He explained the problem. " 'Wild Bill' Donovan has OSS operatives working behind enemy lines in Europe, but in China we have to depend on Stilwell's headquarters in Chungking. We all know that it's sometimes a week late. We've got to have information within the hour if we're going to hit enemy ships along the coast.

"This is your department, gentlemen. What do you suggest?"

"General, we don't have an organization like the OSS," Captain Smith protested.

Chennault glared back. "You've got Birch! Send him out to the coast with some radios. He can enlist some patriotic Chinese operatives who will report back to us here."

Smith found John in the intelligence shack filing the latest radio reports from Chungking. He presented the assignment and added, "You'll be working behind enemy lines. It will be extremely dangerous."

"I only have one question," John responded.

"What's that, Birch?"

"General Chennault allowed me to preach to the Chinese churches on Sundays. Would I be allowed to do that on this mission also?"

"I don't care if you preach on Mondays, so long as you get the job done." Smith included a choice expletive for added effect.

"Captain, I don't appreciate your language."

"Birch, you tend to your business and I'll tend to mine," Smith snapped back. "Now start drawing up a list of what you will need to take with you."

Late in January John was flown to CATF's easternmost airfield. He unloaded his baggage of survival gear, tracts, and radios and hired a coolie. Since he would be operating behind Japanese lines it was necessary to disguise himself as Chinese. He died his hair black, donned a peasant's blue cotton jacket and trousers, put on sandals and began the most daring adventure in his life.

His first destination was a coastal village in Fukien Province across from Formosa, over three hundred miles away and deep in Japanese territory. As he marched up a mountain trail he taught his coolie an old spiritual he had learned at the Berry Schools:

We are climbing Jacob's ladder.
We are climbing Jacob's ladder.
We are climbing Jacob's ladder.
Soldiers of the cross.

They crossed through a pass and descended to a river where John secured a sampan from a guerrilla. He discharged his coolie and sailed down river to a market town where he turned in the boat to another guerrilla and engaged a new coolie.

After a quick lunch in an open-air Chinese restaurant, in plain view of Japanese soldiers, he and his new assistant pushed along a country road where they would take another boat. Before reaching this river, however, he edged into a secluded grove at the top of a small hill and checked in by radio with Captain Smith at Kunming. It was understood that Smith would be listening at 2 and 4 p.m. each day. At other times John could call on the emergency channel which was monitored twenty-four hours a day.

The eight-day journey brought him into a Christian area near the city of Nanking. Here he was among good friends. Chinese believers greeted him with incredulous smiles and loving embraces. Dismissing the coolie, he accepted the hospitality of the believers to spend the night and preach at their church the next day, Sunday. They met in a farmer's home, far off the nearest road. While John preached, two deacons manned a lookout for Japanese patrols.

"The enemy has burned all the churches in this vicinity," a venerable elder told John. "But they cannot destroy our faith."

For the rest of the way to the coast John carried greetings from one Christian group to another. Several times he passed close by Japanese soldiers. Once he and a new coolie were stopped and asked what was in the boxes. "Goods for the coast," John replied in the local dialect and was waved on. John took this as just one more indication of God's protection. "God is with us. We are serving a righteous cause," he assured the coolie.

Emerging from a village near the coast, he sighted an enemy checkpoint a half mile ahead. Knowing it would be impossible to avoid the guards, and fearful of being stopped, he prayed for wisdom.

He spotted a large wooden "honey bucket" beside the edge of a field. Familiar with the Chinese practice of dumping human excrement — "night fertilizer" — into newly cultivated land, he knew instantly what to do. He identified himself and his coolie to the farmer working nearby and asked to borrow the bucket and a pole. Consent gained, he stuffed his incriminating gear into the bucket and slammed the lid on top. He took one end of the pole and the coolie the other and they started toward the checkpoint with the bucket swaying between them.

Minutes later they reached the Japanese soldiers. John looked at the bucket and grimaced. The soldiers looked away and held their noses as they passed through. They walked on until they were out of sight. When they found a secure place near a stream they stopped and cleaned the pungent residue of dung from their gear.

John finally reached a fishing village overlooking a bay. From here, in good weather, one could see for miles out to sea. Ships would be passing close to shore to avoid detection by Allied submarines. It was the perfect place for spotters.

Quietly, discreetly, John visited in the village until he found a Christian he was sure could be trusted. At John's request the believer took him to the leaders of the church and he explained the mission.

"I need two fishermen willing to risk their lives for China," John said.

One of the church leaders, a deacon, said he was a fisherman and would volunteer. He could also enlist a friend. A time was set for John to meet with them. He questioned them intensely about their attitude toward the war effort. Satisfied they were true patriots, he produced a radio set and taught them how to work the crank and transmit messages. "You will rotate on watches," John told them.

"We realize you are doing this to win the victory and drive back the enemy to his homeland, but we will pay you ten dollars a month for your expenses and to recompense you for the time you lose from your fishing. For as long as you send us reports we will get the money to you."

John gave each a copy of the standard telegraph code book which matched Chinese characters to English words by numbers. To confuse the Japanese, who would certainly intercept some of the messages, he had devised a system of mixing up pages on various days. On Monday page one became page ten, on Tuesday page two became page five, and so on. It was a simple way of coding, but one the Japanese never broke.

After instructing the Chinese operatives to keep the radio well hidden and to transmit from different locations, John moved down the coast and set up two more stations at intervals of about a hundred miles. He then slipped back to an airfield in Free China for pickup and flight back to Kunming.

Meanwhile, Captain Smith had set up other stations in Free China to relay reports from the coastal spotters. Transmitting range of the crank radios was seldom more than two hundred miles. When John arrived back, Captain Smith was already receiving fifty to sixty ship sightings a day.

"Alpha two at eleven-oh-two a.m., proceeding north," meant two Jap vessels were passing Alpha station at this time. The messages were deceptively simple and easily decodable. To save even more time, Chennault installed a teletype system on the base. A sighting could be sent within a minute to Operations, which kept tabs on all available planes at the eastern airfields. Often planes were in the air within ten minutes after the spotter radioed his report and by estimating a ship's speed could be over the target within little more than an hour. Nothing like this had happened in the China war theater before.

There were not enough CATF planes to take advantage of all the sightings, and sometimes all were fogged in. Captain Smith had the radioman compile a "book" of each day's reports for evening transmission to U.S. Navy personnel at Stilwell's headquarters in Chungking. From there the information went to subs and destroyers at sea, and they moved in for the kill.

For setting up the spotter net, John and Captain Smith received commendations from General Chennault, who sent recommendations for promotion to Bissell's headquarters in India. Nothing happened for the moment, although this marked the third time John had been so named by Chennault.

Chennault was both elated and frustrated. Elated by the success of the intelligence operation. Frustrated by the lack of planes.

However, Wendell Wilkie had delivered his letter to President Roosevelt. He sent a copy on to the War Department where it caused a major blowup. Enemies of Chennault were already on the defensive, because magazine writers and filmmakers had been busy exploiting the Chennault legend. He and his men were being popularized by Milton Caniff's "Terry and the Pirates." The creator of the popular comic strip was a friend of Casey Vincent's, Chennault's eastern wing commander, and he used real names.

At the same time Madame Chiang was touring the U.S., pleading China's cause and praising Chennault's small air force. She had just addressed a joint session of Congress, provoking a major uproar against the Stilwell policy that had hamstrung Chennault.

When Roosevelt, Churchill and Stalin met at Casablanca, Madame Chiang conveyed her husband's alarm that so little was being done to help China. She wondered how much longer the country could withstand the Japanese, noting that soldiers were starving and freezing to death for lack of supplies, and many CATF planes were grounded because of empty gas tanks. Those who had been blaming all of China's troubles on Chiang's corrupt generals were unable to counter her persuasion. The alarmed Allied leaders dispatched a commission, led by General Hap Arnold, to talk with the Generalissimo.

They found him in no mood for pleasantries. China, he told them, had been fighting the Japanese since 1937 and had sacrificed hundreds of thousands of lives. China had kept a million Japanese troops tied down who would otherwise be fighting in the Pacific. China's internal threat of takeover by Communists was not taken seriously by China's British and American Allies. Indeed, General Stilwell's advisors actually seemed to favor the Communists. Only General Chennault and his brave men were trying to save China. For them, Chiang wanted five hundred planes, a 10,000-ton monthly Hump lift and a separate command. Immediately.

General Arnold was a personal friend of Stilwell's and had not liked Chennault since tactical school when Chennault had rebutted his belief that fighter planes would be ineffective in war. Arnold had also been responsible for General Bissell's famous one-day seniority over Chennault. However, Arnold's patriotism overrode personal feelings, and he acted in Chiang's and Chennault's favor.

On March 10, 1943, Chennault's command was made independent of Bissell and enlarged to become the 14th Air Force, with a promise of five hundred planes and personnel to keep them flying. Chennault was promoted to major general and his key men were elevated proportionately. John received his first lieutenant's silver bar and Captain Smith the silver oak leaf of a lieutenant colonel.

Two weeks later Stilwell was ordered by Arnold, at President Roosevelt's request, to transfer control of the Hump airlift from Bissell to Chennault. Because Roosevelt failed to issue an executive command, trusting Arnold to see the order carried out, Stilwell never executed the directive. Stilwell intended to keep on diverting a large proportion of Hump tonnage to his Burma project.

The following month Stilwell and Chennault were summoned to Washington for the British-American Trident war strategy talks. When discussion switched to Asia, the battle began between the two generals from China.

Stilwell had no confidence in Chiang and thought him a "vacillating, tricky, undependable old scoundrel, who never keeps his word." Stilwell pushed his idea of invading Burma and opening a land route to China. "The war will be won by men in the trenches," he declared.

Chennault called the Generalissimo "one of the two or three greatest military and political leaders in the world today. He has never broken a commitment or promise to me."

Roosevelt was greatly distressed over heavy American casualties in the Pacific. "What help can you give MacArthur?" he asked Chennault.

"Mr. President, give us the planes and the men and supplies to keep them flying and we'll sink a million tons of enemy shipping in a year. Most of that will be going to the Pacific."

Roosevelt banged his fist on the desk. "If you can sink a million tons, we'll break their back!"

Neither Roosevelt nor Chennault knew then that Stilwell would refuse to carry out the order putting the Hump operation under Chennault. Nor did Roosevelt know of the subtle forces in Stilwell's Chungking headquarters and in key U.S. Government agencies who were echoing a secret "party line" from Moscow for the defeat of Chiang Kai-shek's Nationalist government by Chinese Communists.

The Japanese were not unaware of the sudden shift in American war policy. While Chennault was still in Washington, they launched two new offensives. Jap bombers, based in Burma and Indo-China, began hitting Kunming and other air bases in Yunnan Province, trying to cut the Hump supply line into China. On a second front in central China, Japanese ground troops on the Yangtze began driving for Chungking.

The planes of the new 14th Air Force, still sporting the old sharktooth insignia of the Flying Tigers, shuttled from one front to another, tangling with Jap fighters and bombers in the southwest one day, and supporting Chinese defenders on the Yangtze the next. Though running desperately low on gas, they beat off the attacks in Yunnan. The Yangtze assistance was more difficult and called for aid from John Birch.

"Your mission," Colonel Smith told him, "is to serve as liaison between the 14th Air Force and Marshal Hsueh Yo's army in the Ninth War Area. Your primary responsibility will be to coordinate air support for Marshal Yo's armies. We hope you will set a pattern for liaisons in other war areas."

Yo was as much a legend in China as General Chennault. Stilwell, in a rare tribute, called him "the only tough guy in the Chinese Army." The Japanese respected and feared him more than any other Chinese commander. His code name "Little Tiger" indicated what Chennault's men thought of him. Soft-spoken and almost engulfed by the long black hip boots he usually wore, Yo looked more like a scholar than a fighter. Inside he was as hard as steel, and like Chennault, he had the ability to draw the fiercest loyalty from his ill-equipped farmboy soldiers.

Colonel Smith and other headquarters personnel at Kunming discussed the new challenge with John. Pilots had been relying on

Chinese army intelligence, sent through Stilwell's staff, or visual sighting. Some terrible mistakes had been made. In one instance an entire friendly village had been wiped out. Until Chinese coordinators could be trained and reliable communication established, an American was needed to search out the most critical targets and then "talk" pilots in for direct hits. The liaison would also set up an air rescue procedure for crews that might be shot down. Such an American had to have the confidence of the Chinese commander and work closely with him. "That's why we chose you to be the pioneer, John," Colonel Smith said. "While you're in the field," he added, "we'll be preparing others to take your place."

The Colonel set up the 14th's field intelligence operation in Kweilin and dispatched John to Changsha where Marshall Yo had his headquarters. The historic old walled city lay due south of the Yangtze Bulge from which enemy troops were mounting a westward advance toward Chungking.

Changsha lay in the fertile rice basket of central China. To get there, John had to go by train to Siangtan, then take a sampan twenty miles down the Siangsiang River to the old walled city. When he arrived, the city looked worse than Hangchow. It had been burned once by fleeing Chinese defenders and occupied twice by the Japanese. It was now back in the hands of the Chinese, but the rubble-strewn streets were practically deserted. Homes and other facilities had been looted and stripped by Japanese soldiers.

The Little Tiger had drawn the Japanese south into Changsha the year before and allowed them to occupy the city a short time. Then he drew the net and his barefooted soldiers suddenly appeared out of the brush, severed the enemy's supply lines, and decimated the Jap flanks. The survivors fled north to the Yangtze Bulge to lick their wounds, with the Japanese generals vowing not to be fooled by Marshall Yo again.

The Little Tiger and John got along famously. Yo gave John a house next door to his headquarters and invited him to sit in on his general staff meetings. They pored over maps of the area around Icheng, west of the Bulge, where the enemy troops were pushing westward. John got the locations of key guerrillas behind Japanese lines and took off with a detachment of Yo's soldiers.

John's escorts were barefooted farm boys, clad in flimsy cheesecloth, and poorly armed with a rifle for every third or fourth man. Disguised again as a coolie, John walked with them on the three hundred-mile hike to the battlefront, sharing the red rice and cabbage cooked in their field kitchens, which were only black iron kettles carried on bamboo poles.

On one difficult stretch John rode a Mongol pony for sixty miles through a snowstorm. As they neared the front lines, the escorts turned John over to a band of guerrillas who foraged deep into enemy territory. A day's walk took them close to an enemy supply depot housed in an abandoned pagoda.

John crept back to a high spot, raised his antenna, and radioed Colonel Smith, using the prearranged code words. "I've got the table laid for a banquet. When can I spread the cloth?"

"Roger. Tuesday at 10 a.m. Repeat. Tuesday at 10 a.m. Look for White Pontiac."

Monday night John and his guerrilla friends spread white strips of cloth on the ground with an arrow pointing to the target. At ten the next morning John waited in a clump of bushes uphill from the pagoda. When he heard a plane's motor, he raised his antenna. With the plane almost overhead, he clicked on the transmitter. "White Pontiac, this is John. Do you see my white panels?"

"Not yet. I'll make another pass."

The pilot circled and came back. "Okay, I see your cloth. Is it the pagoda?"

"Roger, the pagoda."

"Roger. I'll take care of it."

The P-40 banked and came in low with guns blazing. The explosion shook the ground for hundreds of yards around. John and the guerrillas were almost knocked over.

"You made a clean hit, White Pontiac. Now don't go 'way. There's a howitzer in a clump of bushes across the rice paddy, uh, about a half mile due north from the pagoda. He's firing at you. Can you take him?"

"Can do." The pilot dove toward the spot John had indicated. John kept watch with field glasses. "You're headed in the right direction, White Pontiac. Now a little to the left. Watch him. He's trying to get you in his sights. See him in the bushes there? Okay, start squirting."

The deadly ack-ack poured from the plane. The pilot made a second pass. "Looks like you got him. See ya' again."

John and the guerrillas quickly scuttled across the hill to look for another target. This time they crawled under cover of darkness to a Jap camp and located the fuel depot. With guards walking within hearing distance John laid his "table" for the next morning, then moved out of earshot and radioed Colonel Smith. Near sunup, before the camp was fully awake, two fat Liberator bombers roared in and hit the fuel tanks dead center. Bodies flew in all directions. Flames roared across the camp with men screaming and running for their lives. Having been hidden at a safe distance, John and the guerrillas slipped away before their presence was ever discovered.

For the next month, John roamed the battlefront, setting up more targets, hiding in caves, living with the guerrillas, backtracking at times through the lines to consult with Marshall Yo, aiding Chinese personnel in the rescue of downed airmen and performing other duties as need arose. Backed by perfectly coordinated air support, the Little Tiger's army quelled the offensive and sent the Japs retreating back into their Bulge defenses.

John was full of praise for the Chinese soldiers when he came upon Marshall Yo at an advance base. "I saw men go into battle unarmed and take rifles from dead Jap soldiers," he reported.

"They're instructed to do that," Yo replied. "We have only one rifle for every three men."

Yo was in awe of John. "Give me fifty men like Lieutenant Birch," he radioed Colonel Smith, "and I'll whip the whole dwarf army with one hand tied behind my back."

With the lull in the fighting, John returned to Changsha where he dropped in at the battered Yale-in-China Association hospital for some medication to ward off another attack of malaria. He ran into Arthur Hopkins, his old acquaintance from the previous summer at Chungking.

"My term is about up with Yale-in-China," Arthur told him. "I'm going to enlist with the 14th."

"What will you do?" John asked.

"I'd like to help you in intelligence. You're getting to be quite a legend in China, you know."

John was genuinely embarrassed. "I've just done my duty. Besides, you can hardly compare my work with the risks the pilots take almost every day. I sure would be glad to have you on the team, though."

"Let me introduce you to the American staff at the hospital." Arthur grinned and led him to an office just off the corridor.

A smiling brown-haired young woman wearing a nurse's uniform came from behind the desk to greet him. "This is the American staff," Arthur explained. "Marjorie Tooker."

"I just happen to be the only American here at the moment," the nurse smiled. "Dr. Win Pettus is home on sick leave and Dr. Phil Greene is on furlough."

Marj looked at her watch. "It's almost noon and my house is just across the street. Why don't you fellows come over and have lunch with me?"

John felt a strange sensation of contentment the moment he stepped into the small house that nestled into the landscape across from the hospital. As he glanced around, he realized the smiling American nurse had managed to turn the place into a home. Nostalgia overwhelmed him. It had been so long since he had had a home. Marjorie put some classical records on her victrola and the three sat down before steaming bowls of noodle soup. With the soft strains of violins playing in the background and warm, friendly Americans to talk to, the conversation just naturally turned to childhood memories of home.

John told them about his family and was in the middle of a long story about Uncle Dan before he realized he was doing most of the talking. Embarrassed by his uncharacteristic chatter, he started questioning his hostess. "How did you wind up in such an outpost as this?"

"My dad knew some people on the board of the Yale-in-China Association. I came out here as a nurse before the war, then went home and got my master's in nursing from Western Reserve University. I already knew the doctors here and applied for the job of director of nursing. We have a Chinese superintendent and some fine Chinese doctors."

"Is Yale-in-China a mission organization?" John wondered.

"Well, sort of. The idea was born out of missionary zeal in 1901, after the Boxer Rebellion when almost two hundred Protestant missionaries and children were killed in China. I presume you've heard about that?"

"Oh, yes," John replied, nodding his head. "I've heard stories from some of the China Inland Mission missionaries about people who were beheaded, burned to death in their homes, or stoned by mobs. I'd say that the Boxer Rebellion marked a turning point for Christian work in China."

"I'm sure it did," Marj agreed. "Christian young people in the universities in the States were stirred by the sacrifice of the martyrs. Oxford and Cambridge launched their own mission; so some of the Yale men felt Yale should have one also. The first school opened in 1906: the hospital and nursing and medical schools came about eight years later."

Time had slipped away and Marj had to return to the hospital. As John and Arthur walked her back, John asked, "How are you fixed for medicine and equipment?"

"We lost our X-ray machine when the Japs were last here," Marj recalled. "We're always short of medicines."

"You treat many 14th Air Force People?"

"Not many of your guys get up here. I did bury one who crashed right down the street. We get a few British and Australian soldiers.

Mostly it's Chinese soldiers from Marshall Yo's army. Our hundred beds are usually full."

"Well, you deserve a little help from the 14th," John said. "Tell me your most critical need, and I'll try and pick it up the next time I'm in Kunming."

"That would be great," Marj smiled. "Say, I'm having a little get-together at my place Friday night for the British nurses who are stationed here with the Red Cross. Would you like to come?"

"I wish I could," he replied sincerely, "but I have to attend a Chinese military dinner with Colonel Smith that night. He's flying up from Kweilin. Maybe another night?"

She assured him there would be other occasions, but Friday night as he sat wearing his one dress uniform at the impressive dinner Marshall Yo's staff was giving he found his mind drifting to the peaceful little cottage near the hospital.

During the second course of the meal Colonel Smith rose to his feet and offered a toast to their host. "To your good health, sir," he said in impeccable Chinese. "Bottoms up!"

"I beg your understanding," the Chinese officer replied, "but an old war wound makes it impossible for me to respond. Therefore I choose three of my men as substitutes." He nodded to three Chinese colonels, each of whom rose to toast Colonel Smith. This meant that Smith was drinking three cups of rice wine for each toast. John knew it would be an insulting breach of Chinese custom for Smith to fail to drink each cup, but after more than a dozen drinks he began to worry about his C.O. It would be humiliating if the Colonel passed out drunk. John knew the only honorable way out was for the Colonel to have a substitute, and that he was the only available candidate.

The toasting continued, and John grew more and more worried. Finally his sense of duty won the battle that had raged in his conscience. Leaping to his feet he called out, "I'm Colonel Smith's substitute. Bottoms up!"

Smith's eyebrows flew up and a look of shock came over his face, for he knew what a strict teetotaler John was. Then he realized John was trying to protect him and he had to smile, for what John didn't know was that the Colonel had whispered to his waiter to serve him tea when he realized his predicament. He was in no danger of getting drunk, but found it very amusing to watch the straightlaced young Birch drink the rest of his toasts.

As they were leaving the dinner, Smith contemplated what a deep sense of loyalty John had for him, to have bent his own rules about drinking. "Come on, son," he said, placing an arm around John.

"We'd better get home. You've got quite a buzz on." The incident marked a deepening of the relationship between the two men.

11

The Spy

I'm so happy you have a Christian girl.
Sometimes I wish I had one, then I look at the
messed up world and am glad I don't.

—John Birch, letter to brother George Stanley,
December 30, 1943

In July of 1943, John was called back to Kunming for a new intelligence briefing and to be part of the commissioning of some new intelligence officers. The trip was made more pleasant by the presence of his good friend, Arthur Hopkins, who was to be one of the new members of the 14th.

On their arrival John led him toward the old mud house that had served as headquarters for the 14th Air Force. He remembered its walls with patches on top of patches, the result of many bombings. The tile roof leaked copiously and the walls were pockmarked from flying shrapnel. General Chennault had requested a new headquarters building, but General Stilwell adamantly refused. To John's great surprise he found a new brick edifice had been erected in his absence. "Stilwell wouldn't build me one, so the Chinese did," Chennault explained.

They assembled in the war room with Colonel Smith and Colonel Williams, who introduced Hopkins and the other new intelligence operatives: Malcolm Rosholt, a journalist from Wisconsin who had lived in China before the war; William Drummond, a former art dealer in Peking; Hamilton Freeman, a brooding intellectual and son of the famous historian of the U.S. South, Douglas Freeman; Tom West, a cosmetics salesman with an engineering degree; Dr. Robert Lynn, a former medical missionary in China; and Paul Frillman, the Lutheran ex-missionary who had transferred from the chaplaincy.

"Gentlemen, meet John Birch, who is also a former missionary. He's your forerunner, the pioneer. John will give us a short report about his recent mission to the Icheng front."

John talked matter-of-factly about his experiences as a liaison with Chinese soldiers. He praised the accomplishments of Marshall Yo and his barefoot army.

"What John did was unique in this war," Colonel Williams observed. "He proved that an American can live and work with a Chinese army. For the first time Chinese foot soldiers received coordinated American air support against the enemy.

"We hope to assign each one of you as a liaison officer to a Chinese general. You'll call in air strikes on appropriate targets. You'll train Chinese communications officers. You'll build bridges between the 14th Air Force and the Chinese army."

Colonel Smith then gave them an orientation in communication with his field intelligence headquarters at Kweilin, periodically calling on John to explain something from his point of view. The new agents asked questions revealing their astuteness and interest in the work. John was confident they could do the job.

John now felt the time had come to launch out in a new direction. He went to General Chennault and asked for permission to apply for training to become a fighter pilot.

Flying had interested John since he had watched barnstormers do their spins and rolls as a youngster back in New Jersey. Joining the Flying Tigers where he spent much of his free time around planes, querying mechanics and pilots, climbing in and out of cockpits and occasionally taking up one of the small ships used in training Chinese pilots had heightened his desire to fly. He enjoyed the elation of leaving the ground, skimming over the countryside, bouncing amidst air currents. He had watched Chennault's top fliers peeling off from formation, diving, strafing, outwitting enemy fighters. At such times he felt a mixture of admiration and guilt: admiration at the skill and bravery of these men — guilt that they were risking their lives while he watched from a "safe" position. Some of them, he knew, had wives and children at home.

He was also thinking that flying would help in missionary work after the war. Lately he had been eyeing Chinese Turkestan, where there was not a single missionary for over four million people. Or perhaps equally uncharted mountainous Tibet. A plane would speed the gospel to those who had never heard.

"Sir, you now have other men for my work," he told Chennault. "I think I can help the 14th more as a fighter pilot. My health is good. I have the stamina and coordination. I'd like to be considered."

The sagacious Chennault did not try to talk him out of it, but only said, "I know you'd make a good flier, John, but I'm not the one to make that decision. I'll have to send your application through channels. We'll see what becomes of it."

John said he understood and reported back to Colonel Smith. "You did a great job on the coast," his C.O. congratulated him. "Your operatives keep sending in sightings every day. What our pilots don't get, the Navy subs do."

"Glad to hear that, sir. By the way, I've put in for flight training, but the General says that might take a while."

"Oh?"

"Yes, sir. I don't think it's right for me to be on the ground while the pilots are laying their lives on the line every day."

"Well, right now the Old Man wants you to go along the Yangtze River and set up a lookout network there as you did on the coast. You can also arrange some air strikes while you're up there. If we can interdict the shipping on the Yangtze River as well as along the coast, we'll make a big contribution to winning the war and save many American lives in the process.

"We'll give you a couple of Chinese radio men and a bunch of radios to carry into the Bulge north of Changsha where the enemy is concentrated. You'll make contact with General Heuen Yoh, who commands the Second Guerrilla Brigade. He'll give you all the help you need."

"What about a liaison for Marshall Yo?"

"We're sending Hopkins and Sergeant Leroy Eichenberry to that post. Hopkins will be your radio backup. You can fly up to Changsha together. Hopkins and Eichenberry will stay there. You and two Chinese assistants will strike out for the Yangtze. Hire whatever coolies you need. Think you can handle it?"

John stiffened. "Of course I can. The Lord is with me."

"I don't doubt that the Lord is with you, John, and I wasn't questioning your courage. Now you'd better get moving."

John rounded up Hopkins, Eichenberry and the two Chinese radio men. They got a flight to Hengyang the next morning, then waited at the base until time for the north-south train that night.

John and the two Americans wandered around, stopping to chat with Chinese workmen and a few pilots. Around noon they were kibitzing with a pilot when a Chinese lookout ran up the *jing bao* ball on the flag pole. This meant enemy planes were headed in the direction of Hengyang. Noon wasn't their usual time.

They ran to the operations shack where a radio operator was taking messages from spotters: fourteen Jap bombers escorted by sixteen Zeros.

Forty-five minutes later the lookout ran up a second ball, meaning they were definitely headed for Hengyang. The pilots raced for four battered and patched old P-40s parked behind a covey of decoys. Four against thirty. They roared into the sun to wait the arrival of the "guests."

Peering from a shelter, Birch, Hopkins and Eichenberry saw the enemy ships appear as dots in the eastern sky. As they drew nearer, John nudged Hopkins. "They're going to bomb the railroad station in the middle of the day. They'll massacre a thousand civilians!"

"Hey, here come our boys!" Hopkins cheered. The four P-40s came hurtling out of the sun, their shark's teeth gleaming in the clear air. The enemy planes were caught completely by surprise. They had apparently thought Hengyang was unprotected.

The Americans broke up the smooth Japanese formation on the first pass, sending two bombers spinning to earth. The others turned and headed for home. Only a few bombs had been dropped, and none had hit the railroad station.

Pulling out of their dives, the P-40s swooped back to take on the sixteen Zeros. Birch and Hopkins saw a Zero plummet toward the earth, followed by a P-40. The enemy plane hit the ground in a burst of flame. At the last second the American pilot pulled up and wobbled to a crash landing in a rice paddy.

The three remaining P-40s continued the dogfight, bagging two more Zeros before the other thirteen headed for safety. Two of the P-40s chased the fleeing Zeros for a hundred miles before returning to base. The third one, crippled, came down hard just short of the runway.

This pilot and the one who had come down in the rice paddy walked in on their own power, cursing the Zeros that had escaped. It seemed miraculous that they were unhurt. John pumped their hands, ignoring the strong language, and exclaiming, "I was sure praying for you guys. I just wish I could have been up there with you."

In the darkness before dawn John and his companions caught the night train to Changsha. John talked expectantly about flight training. "When I get back from this assignment," he assured Hopkins, "the authorization should be waiting. General Chennault has a lot more clout now."

John spent a couple of weeks in Changsha before departing for enemy territory on the Yangtze. He first introduced Hopkins and Eichenberry to Marshall Yo and helped them set up their small radio station. He then hiked over to the Yale-in-China hospital where he presented Marjorie Tooker with the box of medicines he had begged from the 14th's medic at Kunming.

Marj seemed delighted. Both with the medicine and with seeing John again. "Kinda strange you should show up just in time for lunch again," she kidded.

"Yeah, isn't that unusual?" he grinned.

130

As they walked over to her house she extended an invitation for Saturday evening. "I'll be here," he promised. He found himself drawn to this bright, attractive Yankee brunette. He had met a number of pretty military nurses at Chungking and Kunming, but none appeared to have the depth of Marj. She really loved the Chinese people. She enjoyed talking about things that mattered, not just the latest hit songs and movies from the States. She was an excellent listener and John found it easy to confide in her. She would make someone a good wife.

Saturday night John showed up with Hopkins and Eichenberry in tow. They joined the three British nurses, two doctors and a couple of Australian officers who had already gathered around the fireplace in Marj's livingroom. It was fun for John to be in a group of singles his age, but the air was blue with smoke. It bothered John to see Marjorie smoking, but then everyone except John did. He thought it was a nasty habit.

Marj had a stack of fragile 78 rpm swing records she put on for dancing. The dancing also bothered John. He felt embarrassed and thought of leaving. He had never danced in his life and as a pastor had preached against the practice.

"Come on, Lieutenant," a blonde British nurse called gaily to him. "Let me show you how we do it in London."

John smiled and shook his head, turning back to the girl he was talking to beside the fireplace. Marj invited him to join in. Again, he declined.

Around ten the group began leaving. John stayed around and helped Marj straighten up. Then they enjoyed a cup of tea by the fire. When he rose to leave at eleven, she suggested he stay at the bachelor's quarters next to the hospital.

"No," he responded, "I'd rather stay in the house General Yo has provided."

"You might have trouble finding a ricksha at this time of night."

"That's okay. It's only a couple of miles. I'll walk."

Marj stood for a minute in the doorway and watched as the slim young figure marched jauntily into the night. John was an enigma to her. He liked to joke and laugh, had a delightful sense of humor, and yet there was this intense seriousness about him. He seemed free and open and willing to talk about anything, except his war experiences. The carnage he had seen in the line of duty was a memory he kept walled in some secret compartment of his mind. His dedication to God was not an appendage to his life; it was the essence of his being. He was strong, and yet tender, a kind, considerate, completely captivating southern gentleman. She hoped to see more of him.

On duty or off, John was always on the go. When not having anything specific to do, he would walk around and talk to the local Chinese. Occasionally he dropped into a bar with some of the pilots. The intelligence group was suspicious of the prostitutes, so John would chat with the bar girls about their home villages and families in an effort to detect enemy informants. Occasionally he would talk a soldier out of consorting with a girl. If he thought security was involved, he would pass a warning along to the man's commanding officer.

Early in August John said good-bye to Arthur Hopkins. "You know something of the danger involved in this mission, Art, so I was wondering if you'd do me a favor."

"Name it."

"If — if I don't come back, would you write my folks for me? Tell them how much I love them, and that I deeply appreciate my Christian home and upbringing."

"You can depend on me," his friend promised.

Fully confident Hopkins would keep his word, John set off with the two Chinese radio operators and six coolies he had hired to carry several boxes of heavy equipment. Some of the boxes contained radios, others held "clams" — plastic explosives inside small magnetized metal boxes with built-in timers. These were ideal for clamping on the steel hulls of small Japanese cargo boats. By the time they exploded, the person who had set them could be far from the scene.

John could have ridden in a rented sedan chair, as most Westerners customarily did on long trips but he wanted to disprove the Chinese belief that Americans were too soft for battle.

Trudging in scorching heat over green hills and sloshing through mosquito-infested swamps, John and his party reached the Yangtze in ten days. A band of guerrillas met them at a secret spot and took them to their general. John brought greetings from Marshall Yo and General Chennault, but the biggest encouragement to the tired fighters was his own presence. He was the first American most had seen since the Japanese occupation of the area.

The guerrillas spirited John and the radio operators down the river in a series of Chinese junks. He set up five watch stations at hundred-mile intervals, putting one on an island barely a stone's throw from where enemy ships were passing. The agents gladly accepted the usual ten-dollars-a-month stipend for "expenses" and began transmitting immediately. From that time not a Japanese ship moved on the Yangtze without being observed by one of John's secret Chinese agents.

While on the river, John learned that the enemy was drawing more materials from the nearby Shihweiyao iron mines and smelter than the Allies had believed. He radioed coded information on the location of blast furnaces and docks. Fourteenth Air Force bombers began hitting them within hours.

When the planes first came over, some of the guerrillas thought they were Japanese. "No, Americans," John whispered. Instead of berating the Chinese for their ignorance, he taught them aircraft markings. He also set up a system for rescuing downed American fliers and transporting them to the nearest American base. From this time the 14th did not lose a single American flier who survived a plane crash in the area.

While with the guerrillas John almost lost his life during an unexpected skirmish with a Japanese patrol. "I came rather close to death, but I never felt more safe or secure," he wrote his folks. He never mentioned the incident again.

In another instance the guerrillas led him to a suburb of Hangkow. Under the very noses of Japanese soldiers, they determined that the enemy had driven residents out and had stored explosives in their houses. The area was too crowded to risk "setting a table" and directing planes in with cloth panels. John radioed directions. Planes came over, but were unable to distinguish the houses containing war materials from others occupied by Chinese civilians. John made a detailed map of the targets, then sneaked back through the lines to an advance landing field for pickup. He rode in the nose of the lead bomber to direct the planes to the targets. The first bombs set off a chain of explosions that roared through the suburb like a string of giant firecrackers. Dense smoke engulfed the area for miles around. It was one of the most destructive raids of the war. Tons and tons of ammo and gasoline were destroyed. Guerrillas reported seeing truckloads of Japanese bodies being hauled away.

The bomber flew John back to a base south of Changsha, and he caught another plane from there to Kunming. Another high-level intelligence meeting ensued. John gave his report with a prediction: "The Japs are mobilizing. They will soon launch a drive on Changsha." Everyone knew that from Changsha the way was clear for the enemy to capture Hengyang, Kweilin and other vital 14th Air Force bases. Only Marshall Yo's rag-tag army stood in the way of the enemy advance. "He'll need all the support we can give him," the tight-lipped, grim-faced Chennault stated matter-of-factly.

John was ordered back to Changsha with personnel and equipment to set up a more powerful radio station. Paul Frillman had joined Arthur Hopkins in the Little Tiger's headquarters. When the enemy attacked, as John had predicted, Malcolm Rosholt took command of the Changsha station, freeing John to move to the front lines and coordinate air support during the fighting.

Supported by heavy air cover, 40,000 Japanese troops, backed by 20,000 Korean, Mongol and Chinese puppet fighters, poured out of the Bulge and moved south along the west shore of Tung Ting Lake. At Changteh, only 110 miles north of Changsha, they were met by 14,000 Chinese soldiers under the command of Marshall Yo. With John in the front lines, calling in air strikes on enemy fortifications, the battle raged eight weeks.

A fierce air battle took care of the enemy air cover. After that 14th planes enjoyed open season on enemy fortifications, supply lines and troop concentrations. John worked twenty hours a day, dashing through heavy artillery fire to mark targets and keep the planes from hitting friendly troops.

He grew tired and short-tempered. When planes didn't arrive as requested or supplies weren't dropped as promised, he would get on the radio to Colonel Smith in Kweilin. "What's wrong with you, Colonel? Don't you want to win this war? Men are dying like flies up here while you're messing around. Let's get some planes up here."

It wasn't the best way for a man to talk to his commanding officer, who was doing the best he could. "All right, John, I'm trying," Smith replied. "Keep your shirt on and have a little patience. Remember we've got problems on this end, too."

The biggest problem remained Joe Stilwell, who was still sitting on President Roosevelt's order to give Chennault control of Hump flights. Stilwell was rationing gas and spare plane parts to the 14th while hoarding supplies for his Burma invasion. Also, Chennault wasn't receiving all the planes and pilots he had been promised.

In some of the fiercest fighting of the war, the enemy captured Changteh. John radioed for air strikes and this time the squat Liberator bombers roared in on schedule and blasted the city to rubble. Behind them came a wave of P-40s that caught thousands of Japanese trying to flee the city. Paul Frillman, who had come up to help John, reported a hillside covered with bodies.

Though he had suffered grievous losses, Marshall Yo ordered his tired troops to take the offensive. They chased the enemy up the lakeshore, often firing at point-blank range, grabbing rifles and ammo from corpses, while the American planes roared overhead, spewing streams of fire at fleeing Japanese. By the end of December they had driven the Japs back into their Bulge sanctuary

John had been sickened by the carnage, but he was still no pacifist. All he wanted to do was get the war over in a hurry.

Returning to Kunming, he received his promotion to Captain and was given opportunity to rest a while. He ate voraciously, two meals at a sitting, downing stacks of peanut butter sandwiches in between. He gained back most of the weight he had lost, but the hardness cemented in his face from walking through fields strewn with dead soldiers remained. He felt old and tired and war-weary.

Letters came from home bringing both good news and bad. Birchwood had burned. While his family was in church, sparks from a passing Southern Railroad locomotive had ignited the grazing meadow. A high wind had whipped the flames up the hill, destroying fences, barns, everything. With the fences down, four cows had wandered onto the railroad tracks and been killed by another train. Other cows ruined a neighbor's garden. All their household belongings were lost, including pictures and valuable papers.

The loss was all the greater because of being uninsured. Their application for protection had been turned down, presumably because of other house fires caused by engine sparks and their meadow had caught fire from sparks previously.

"We're going to sue if we can get a lawyer," John's mother vowed. Meanwhile, they had found a temporary house. Neighbors, church friends, and relatives were donating clothing, kitchenware, bedding and used furniture.

Sorrowing over his family's loss helped John forget the burdens of war. He wished he "could fly home and help rebuild Birchwood." He reminded them again from the Book of Hebrews, " 'Those things which cannot be shaken remain.' " He had been sending home $100 each month for his folks to buy land. "Any land or money that is mine I here and now give to you, Father and Mother. Please sell anything else before your own land!"

The good news was that George Stanley, who intended to enter the ministry, had announced his engagement to a fine young woman. John sent heartfelt congratulations to his younger brother. "I'm so happy you have a Christian girl. Sometimes I wish I had one. Then I look at the messed up world and am glad I don't.

"As for me, chances of transfer home for flight training are diminishing as the importance of my job here is increasing."

He didn't mention what Chennault had told him about his application for flight training. "John, I just can't let you go to flight school. You're worth more to me than any ten pilots."

12

The Romantic

I longed for sympathy, understanding, and
counsel from Father — from a man — from any
man who might have known what it is to want a
woman, yet to be unable to have her without
surrendering too much of one's principles and
plans.

— John Birch, letter to parents,
May 21, 1944

Captain John Birch was back in Changsha conducting a training school for Chinese army radio operators and cryptographers. Malcolm Rosholt was running the radio station at Changsha. Arthur Hopkins was in North China on a secret assignment behind enemy lines. Paul Frillman, the ex-chaplain, was in southeast China extending the net of Chinese agents John had established along the coast. Freeman, West and Drummond were assigned as liaisons to Chinese armies in other areas.

Marshal Yo was eager to get John's students into the field. "We're losing men every day because of poor communications," he told John. "Please hurry."

There was no way John could speed up the process because he lacked basic equipment. There were less than a dozen radio sets for a hundred student operators.

He had already asked Colonel Smith for additional sets, but he put in another call to his C.O. in Kweilin.

"We've requisitioned them, John," Smith replied. "They should be in any day now."

"Any day, any day. I've heard that song before," John griped. "Don't you want to win the war?"

Smith was tired of hearing that from John. "Of course I want to win the war. You've got to realize, I'm doing all I can."

"Well, have somebody pull some strings. The Little Tiger is getting impatient."

"Tell him our strings are limited. And try to understand our problems here."

Smith felt like hauling John in for a reprimand. *He might be the best intelligence agent in China, but he is one of the world's worst diplomats,* Smith thought. *Second only to General Chennault. Maybe that's why the Old Man took to Birch so readily. They're both so brutally frank and absolutely fearless.*

Smith knew John was aware of the supply problem. Everybody in the 14th Air Force was. Bull-headed Vinegar Joe Stilwell seemed at times to be doing all he could to keep the 14th from functioning. Back in the summer Stilwell had turned down an offer of field radios from "Wild Bill" Donovan, commander of the Office of Strategic Services, on grounds that they weren't needed. The real reason was he didn't want Wild Bill packing any influence in China.

Getting radios was even more difficult now, for Stilwell was trying to reopen the Burma Road with a small American infantry force and the Chinese troops he had been training in India. He was determined to open a land route into Free China and avenge his previous defeat, even if there wasn't a Free China left when he got back.

While John fretted and fumed in Changsha, the 14th kept hitting enemy shipping on the Yangtze and along the coast. Because of Stilwell's decisions and the demands of his staff in Chungking, gas for the 14th was still limited. Nevertheless, Chennault's pilots sank 65,000 tons of Japanese shipping in February of 1944, one-third of all enemy tonnage destroyed in the Pacific that month.

In desperation Chennault bypassed army channels and wrote President Roosevelt that the supplies weren't coming through. "Give us 10,000 Hump tons a month and we'll sink 200,000 tons of enemy shipping the next month," he pleaded.

"You'll get it," F.D.R. pledged. "You are the doctor and I approve your treatment." But not even the President could clear the bureaucratic pipeline that was choking the China war effort.

While waiting for the radios and his next assignment, John was spending more time with the nurses in Changsha. He already liked Marj Tooker as a friend and admired her immensely, but he also enjoyed meeting others. He met a "charming" Air Evac nurse, but she wasn't the one. Then in early February Marj casually introduced him to a dark-haired Scotch lassie at one of her gatherings. "John, this is Jenny Campbell. She's with the British Red Cross."

Jenny flashed him a big smile and his heart skipped a beat. For the first time in his life he was swept off his feet. "I'm so happy to meet you," she said in her lilting Scottish accent. He felt like asking,

"Where have you been all my life?" but settled for, "How long have you been in Changsha?"

"Several months. It's rather strange we haven't met before."

"Strange?" John mimicked her burr, smiling. "I think a better word would be tragic. I've been in and out of Changsha so many times the past few months, I'd have enjoyed it so much more if I'd known you were here. Tell me about yourself. I must make up for lost time."

Jenny gave him a flippant little grin and shook her curly hair. She had gotten used to American GIs giving her a line and she didn't know John well enough yet to realize he was completely serious.

"My parents were Baptist missionaries here with the China Inland Mission. Mother died some years ago and father remarried. He's still with the mission. As you Americans say, 'I'm an old China hand.'"

"Oh, really. My folks were missionaries in India and I was born there, but they went home when I was about two and a half."

The pair spent the next hour or so discovering more things they had in common. Then John walked her home. The next two weeks were the happiest of John's life. He saw Jenny almost every day, sometimes twice a day, and dreamt of her each night. They took long walks along City Wall Boulevard, sipped tea in the nurses' sitting room at the Red Cross hospital, made fudge in the kitchen, attended church services and frequent parties and open houses given by the nurses for the American servicemen. Before the month was out they were "engaged to be engaged."

"Don't tell anybody else, because it's still a bit early," John cautioned his sister Betty at Bryan College back in the States, "but I have found the girl I expect to make my wife. Her name is Jenny, a lovely Scotch nurse in the British Red Cross, daughter of a Baptist missionary in the CIM in North China. I think she loves me, and I *know* I love her."

A radio message interrupted their mid-winter bliss. John was ordered to report to Kunming at once. The young couple had known they would be separated soon, for Jenny was being transferred to Simla, India, near where John had been born. It had only been a question of who would leave Changsha first. Her name was already on the waiting list for a flight to Kunming where another plane would fly her over the Hump.

On the last evening they were together, February 29, John gave her a poem he had written.

The other night I saw a single star
Gleaming through the rifted clouds,

138

A brief light twinkling down from far
Enveloped soon by thick'ning shrouds,

Reminding one of dreams that are no more,
Or visions brighter than our darkened sphere.
And though the star had gone, for many an hour
My heart was light, as if a friend were near.

A glimpse of thee, O bonnie Scottish flower
In this a darkened land and time,
Has roused my soul, not for this hour,
But forever, to love and cherish thee and thine.

Too short have been the days I've known thee;
If now we part, despite our wills,
Yet time will come when home I'll take thee
And we will roam the Highland hills.

"I'll cherish this for the rest of my life," Jenny sighed. Their time together was all the more precious because they were so aware of the uncertainty of the future.

The next morning they met at the airfield to say good-bye. The surrounding rice fields had turned a pale green with the promise of spring. Jenny looked lovely in the early sun with the wind ruffling her curls and blowing her skirt tightly against her body. John couldn't help but think what a beautiful bride she would make.

"I'll write you in Kunming," Jenny pledged, trying hard to be brave. "Maybe you'll still be there when I arrive."

John walked to his plane with a heavy heart. He had never known a parting could be so difficult. Just before he stepped in, he turned and gave her a little salute. She blew him a kiss, and tears flowed unbidden down her cheeks as she waved until the plane flew out of sight.

They both realized the chances of their seeing each other in Kunming were very faint. John never stayed in Kunming long, and the likelihood of Jenny getting a straight flight was almost nil. John prayed they might be together again soon, "if it be thy will."

At the intelligence conference Colonel Smith was conferring with Colonel Williams, General Chennault, and other key officers. They quickly brought John up to date.

Reports from the Chinese 10th Army indicated the enemy was massing a huge force in the Yellow River basin of northern Honan Province for a major offensive. The Chinese 10th was plagued by severe equipment shortages and low morale. Chennault feared they could never hold back the massive Jap forces, and if they broke through the lines and linked up with their comrades in the Yangtze Bulge, they would head south for Changsha. If Changsha fell, then Hengyang, Kweilin and the 14th's other critical eastern bases could be swept into enemy hands. Such an offensive could be a knockout blow to China.

"How many Japs?" John asked.

"We estimate a half million or more," Colonel Smith replied.

"I radioed Stilwell in Burma about the grave danger," Chennault told him. "He said his intelligence indicated that enemy troops in Honan did not have offensive capability and I was just crying wolf."

The General stopped and lit another cigarette. He took a long drag, then let the smoke curl out slowly as he contemplated his next words before confiding in his men. "I've cabled the President," he told them. "I begged him to cut through the military red tape and increase our tonnage."

"But could it get here in time?" Williams wondered.

"I don't know," the Big Tiger admitted. "That's why we must have some liaison teams in there to mark out the exact targets. We can't afford the luxury of wasting any ammo, and we have to cut the Jap supply lines."

"That means you, Birch," Colonel Smith said. He ran his finger along a war map and explained, "Your spotters have enabled us to hurt Jap ship movements on the Yangtze. Because of that, they seem to be using the north-south Pingham Railroad along here. We want you to take a couple of men and set up another network of spotters. Then we will have other teams working on air coordination. It's our only chance of holding them back."

John had so hoped he could remain in Kunming long enough to be with Jenny on her layover on the way to India, but the urgency of this mission was all too obvious. "When do I leave?" he asked.

"It'll take a few days to get your radios together. Much of our equipment has been diverted to Burma. By the time you're ready to go, we'll have a better assessment of the situation. So just hang tight."

While John was waiting at Kunming, an urgent radio message came from one of his Yangtze spotters. Another of the spotters had been discovered by the Japanese, shot, and quartered with a sword. He was the first of John's Chinese operatives to be caught.

"We've got to help his widow," John told Colonel Smith.

"What do you suggest?"

"Put $5,000 in the Changsha bank in her name. Let the other spotters know it's being done so they know we will take care of their families if anything should happen to them."

Colonel Smith thought a moment, nodded, and agreed to requisition the money.

While John lingered in Kunming, Jenny and three English friends got seats to Hengyang. She was closer, but still so far away. The nurses waited and waited until finally they were permitted on another transport going to Kweilin. Jenny thought there might be a possibility that John had left Kunming and returned to his field headquarters in Kweilin.

"Has Captain Birch been here?" she asked the first man she saw on the ground.

"Nope, haven't seen him. Colonel Smith is at Kunming, so he might be there."

There was still a chance. "I just have to get to Kunming," she pleaded with the officer making out flight schedules. "Sorry, Miss, but it might be a week or ten days before room is available. The military gets top priority, you know."

She knew all right. She also knew that even when she was scheduled, an officer toting a briefcase could show up and bump her off a flight at the last minute. She also knew John's feelings about these military bureaucrats who shuttled around China and India, often replacing cargo vitally needed by the 14th to fight the war. She said nothing, but returned to the Church Missionary Society's guest house where transient Britishers usually lodged in Kweilin.

There was no plane the next day or the next, but a couple of GIs offered to drive the group to Kunming in the back of a truck. Jenny longed to climb in and be on her way to John, but one of her friends was six months pregnant and could not consider such a rough trip. Nor would Jenny consider leaving her on the back side of the world without a medical escort.

A letter came from John. He was still in Kunming and fervently hoping she would arrive before his departure. She read over and over one paragraph that appeared to be a proposal.

> I expect to be poor in money and material possessions all my life, but to be rich in the joys that come from God's love, man's love and the world of nature. Please tell me if, in light of this, it lies beyond my power to make you happy. I think I know what your answer will be.

During the two interminable weeks she was grounded in Kweilin, Jenny wrote John in Kunming almost every day, even though she had no way of knowing if the letters were reaching him or not. When she finally landed in Kunming on March 23, she ran immediately to a phone and called Tiger Hostel Two.

"So sollee, Miss," a Chinese voice answered. "Captain Birch not here. No Amelicans here now. Call back later, please. Thank you."

The group took rickshas to the British consulate where they were given rooms. Jenny kept calling Tiger Two. She did locate one of John's pilot friends. "Captain Birch's whereabouts are always classified," he told her. "Only General Chennault and very few others would know, and they won't tell you."

Three agonizing days passed, and a fourth. "You might get a Hump flight tomorrow," she was told. She gave up hope of seeing John. He was likely a thousand miles up country spying on some Japanese installation.

Disconsolately she went into the dining room for lunch. She was pushing her food around with her chopsticks when she realized someone was standing near her table watching her. Glancing up, she saw John beaming down at her. He slid into the chair across from her and reached for her hand. "I just missed you in Kweilin," was all the explanation he could give her. "I'm leaving again tomorrow and will likely be gone for several weeks, so all we have is a few hours together."

"Oh, but that is so much better than not seeing you at all."

As always Jenny made John feel very young, and very much alive. Knowing how very dangerous his next mission would be made him savor each moment with her even more. Then, as they watched the sunset from atop a windswept hill near the airfield, he became very serious. Sensing his mood, she walked along beside him silently.

It was growing dark when she asked him, "What are you thinking?"

"Watching the sun drop down behind the Himalayas makes me think that you will be on the other side of the mountains when I return from my next mission. Just thinking of it makes me lonely."

"But you have a furlough coming. You can visit me in India," she tried to encourage him.

"The world is in such a mess," he murmured solemnly. "Should we bother to make plans for the future?"

She didn't press him any further, but sat next to him when he pulled her down onto an outcropping of rock. The moon had risen before he broke his melancholy silence. "Jenny, I have to say this. I've wandered away from the Lord. Meeting you has stirred up a new flame, a new love for God's work, but sometimes I still feel exactly like that despair expressed by Matthew Arnold as the 'melancholy, long, withdrawing roar' of the 'Sea of Faith.' "

"I understand, John," she replied softly, leaning her head against his shoulder. "I've wandered away, too. Maybe it's the war, being with people who have no concept of what Christianity really is. The living conditions make it difficult to have any time alone with the Lord."

"The war," John repeated with a sigh. "The war seems to stretch on forever. The bombing, the killing. Some men glory in war. I don't. I just want to get it over and get back into the work God called me to do."

"You will, John. You will."

"It will be different, though. I want to be on my own, not dependent on any mission board or denomination, just God. I want to preach the gospel, start churches. One thing I've learned during these years of violence is how to organize and handle men in the achievement of difficult tasks. I'd love to put that ability to work for the Lord."

John babbled on, pouring out his dreams and doubts to the girl sitting beside him. "In any case, I'm sure I'll always be poor and never have much to offer materially. You know how it is, being raised in a missionary family."

"Yes, I know. I was always afraid of being a missionary's wife. I saw my mother and father scraping and saving for me and vowed my life would be different. I would have plenty of money. Yet all along I knew deep in my heart that money wouldn't bring happiness. I always knew that even though there was never any money in our family, we were tremendously happy."

John slipped his arm around her and looked into her moonlit face. "With all I've told you, Jenny, would you still marry me?"

She nodded slowly, smiling. "Dear, sweet, John. I'd rather be poor with you than rich with anyone else in the world."

"What about the hardships on a pioneer mission post?"

" 'Whither thou goest, I will go,' " she quoted. "Even if it means living on a farm in Georgia." She laughed. "I don't know how to milk a cow, but I'm sure I could learn."

He let his arms fall around her waist and leaned toward her. Their lips met gently, then hungrily, as each reached out to the other. Then they knelt and prayed, John first.

"Lord, we have drifted away. Bring us back to a close walk with thee. Direct our lives as we go our separate ways, and if it be your will, bring us together again to be one..."

They stood up again, arm in arm, their faces shining with tears of happiness and hope, and walked down the hill to the jeep John had borrowed. He drove her back to the British consulate and said good night.

John lay awake a long time in his bunk, thinking, praying, pondering the commitment made with Jenny, wishing for a long heart-to-heart talk with his dear mother who was 10,000 miles away. At last he fell into a fitful sleep, first twisting his blankets tightly around his body, then flinging them aside. While it was still dark he gave up trying to rest and poured out his thoughts in a long letter home.

> China
> 31, March 1944
> Dear Mother,
> Last night I asked Jenny to be my wife. She is willing, so I guess we are engaged. I wish I could say there's not a doubt in my mind as to the rightness of our choice and not a cloud on the horizon of our future, but such is not the case. Never in my life have I been beset with so many devils of doubt and misgiving and fear — due partly to the dark and confused state of our time, and partly, I confess, to a remnant of selfish desire for freedom from the bonds (even though they be of love) of any woman. On the other hand, I love her and she feels the same way, though I still can't quite understand why.
> ... I must go soon on a secret mission; after that, I hope to get leave and see her in Simla, India. Wouldn't it be strange if I marry Jenny within a few miles of my birthplace! Doubtless the Buddhists would find their doctrine of "Wheel of Life" illustrated there!
> Please tell Father (re a letter I received from him long ago in Hangchow) that he can rest assured that in my case there will be preserved the Birch tradition that a virgin groom will take a virgin bride.
> Please pray, Mother-mine, that God will open the way to our marriage if it is his will, and that he will definitely block it if that meets with his directive will. Meanwhile, I'm looking for a diamond ring.
> I would rather you shared this letter with very few, please Mother. God bless you and give you peace and joy.
> Your loving son,
> John

He was shivering so that his hand was shaking, making the letter difficult to read. Nevertheless, he wrapped a blanket around himself and added more thoughts in a second letter:

> ... If she should shrink from a pioneer mission life, or from a lack of what this world considers material success, then I will go my way alone, even though I love her so much that all other women (except Mother) no longer exist for me, rather than pull her into a life she'll not enjoy. God's will be done.

By the time he finished this letter he was feeling hot and feverish with perspiration running down his back. He could no longer ignore the symptoms he had undergone numerous times in the past. Feeling extremely woozy, he made his way to the infirmary. The nurse on duty took his temperature. It was 104°. He was vaguely aware of being put to bed. A doctor came and John was given a dose of quinine.

The next couple of days were a blur. He thought Jenny was there at times, but couldn't be sure if he were dreaming or not. By the time he was feeling better, she was in India. His doubts concerning the wisdom of their marrying persisted, yet he was elated when he received a letter from her. The worry and vacillation over whether he had done the right thing in proposing seemed to affect him physically and his illness dragged on longer than usual.

Much of his time in bed was spent writing her long letters.

... I must confess that I still "walk after the flesh" many times, despite good intentions, and my wife will have to live with both my new spirit and my old Adam even while God may reckon old Adam as dead and gone! So, my feeling is often the same as yours: "so many chances for discord," etc. It is this uncertainty of and dissatisfaction with my own nature which makes it difficult to analyze and fix my attitude toward you. I *know* that I admire and like you; that you like me. I *think* that I am in love with you (and that I could *know* if we were together awhile) ... I believe our lives are in God's hands, and that "all things work together for good to them that love God," that both of us are willing for God to use our lives, whether separately or together, for man's good and his glory.

But there are still too many things about which I am not sure. Sometimes I envy the unlettered Chinese farmer boy whose life is complete with simple fulfilling of simple basic needs and appetites, almost wholly physical. Why are we so complex in our emotional and mental makeup?

Yes, I *do* know "Oh, What a Beautiful Morning!" A sergeant who bailed out of a B-29 in December taught it to me then! That's the way I felt this noon, when your two letters came. Since starting this letter, though, trying to discern our path in the half-ruined world of war makes me a little anxious and gloomy.

Keep me advised of any changes in your address. If I take a furlough in the summer, I want to know exactly where you are.

God keep you, dear!

Love,

John

Adding to John's frustration was the knowledge that he needed to be up in Honan setting up that intelligence net, but that wasn't the kind of undertaking that could be accomplished if he were weak and half-sick. He had to have patience to wait until his recovery was complete.

While he was waiting, a letter came from home saying the Donnelsons and Wellses had been repatriated in a prisoner exchange and were back in the United States. Mother Sweet, however, had died in the internment camp and was buried in the land she loved. John had so hoped to see her after the war, to tell her of his plans to go to the unreached peoples of Central Asia, but that would have to wait until heaven when they were together with other believers rejoicing in the presence of God.

While he reflected on Mother Sweet's passing, and his commitment to Jenny, more reports came indicating that the Yellow River buildup in Honan was increasing. Chennault was now virtually certain the Japs were getting set for the biggest offensive of the war in China. He sent his chief of staff, Brigadier General Edgar Glenn, to present the desperate need to Stilwell personally. Glenn landed at Stilwell's advance headquarters in Burma, only to be told that the theater commander was at the front line and could not be reached. Glenn waited a few days and then flew back to Kunming.

John finally wrote to Jenny that he did not feel the marriage was in God's plan. He just wasn't sure he had the right to ask any woman to endure the privation of existence in the wilds of Turkestan or perhaps Tibet. He couldn't be certain of Jenny, for he didn't know her well enough. The engagement had simply been entered into too quickly, although he could not silence his heart's affection.

He also wrote to his parents, explaining his decision:

> It seems now that she entered so deeply into my heart that I'll never be able to care for another woman, so I guess I'll return to my old creed — 1 Corinthians 7 ... Now, I can only ask him who knows the innermost thoughts of our hearts, and yet loves us, to forgive my wavering, to make Jenny happy and increasingly satisfied with the joys that Christ gives, and to make me stronger as a "good solider of Jesus Christ."

While sick and discouraged with himself, he addressed a special letter to his father, pouring out the agony of being torn between doubt and desire. His mother read the letter and was hurt that he had not shared this confidence with her. He tried to explain.

When I wrote it, I thought that what I had done would give you or any woman the impression that I hold lightly or even in contempt marriage, engagements, and even womanhood itself, — and that any words of explanation I might put in a letter would only intensify that impression. I was wrong ... Please understand that I was feeling disappointed with both Jenny and myself — mostly myself. Sick and tired, I longed for sympathy, understanding, and counsel from Father — from a man — from any man who might have known what it is to want a woman, yet to be unable to have her without surrendering too much of one's principles and plans.

It was now near the end of April. Rest and medication had won over the inner trauma, and he felt ready to go. John checked with Colonel Smith for last-minute instructions. Lieutenant William Drummond, the former art dealer from Peking, and Sergeant Eichenberry had already assembled all the equipment and were waiting for him in Lao Ho Kow, a town north of the Yangtze.

Colonel Smith reviewed their assignment and concluded, "You leave in the morning. Any questions?"

John didn't have any, but he hung around as if reluctant to leave. Finally Smith asked, "Is anything bothering you, John? Can I do something for you?"

"No, sir," John replied. "It's done now, though sometimes I wish it wasn't."

"What's done?"

"I've broken up with my fiancée."

Smith was quite surprised. "John, I didn't even know you had a fiancée."

"Jenny Campbell. A British Red Cross nurse. A beautiful brunette. Talked with a strong Scotch accent. So sweet. I really loved that girl, Colonel."

"Then why did you break the engagement?"

"Well, Colonel, maybe you can understand, since your folks were missionaries. I believe God is calling me to serve him as a missionary on a field where no other missionaries have ever gone. That would be no place for a woman."

"I suppose not, John."

"Colonel, I loved that woman. I still do. But I love God more. He has to be first in my life."

13

The Adventurer

*. . . If my hour to depart should strike, I am
ready to go, thanks to the merit of our Savior, the
Lord Jesus Christ.*

—John Birch, letter to parents,
May 1, 1944

John walked into the Little Tiger's Changsha headquarters on the
last day of April 1944. The fabled little Chinese warrior in the
black hip boots was as immaculate and polite as ever.

The two men discussed the ominous enemy build-up in Honan
north of the Bulge. "The dwarves have us, as you Americans say,
'over the barrel,'" the Little Tiger admitted. "A half million to 40,000.
How much help will we receive from the 14th Air Force?"

"General Chennault will do all he can," John assured him. "His
difficulty continues."

"Ah, yes," Marshall Yo murmured. "General Vinegar Joe."

John gave the Marshall an "ears only" briefing on his upcoming
mission. He trusted the Little Tiger implicitly, but could not be sure
of all his headquarters staff. When he finished, the Chinese general
courteously asked if he would be staying the night.

"Yes, I plan to visit a friend tonight and will leave early tomorrow
morning," John replied.

"Then your house will be ready," the Little Tiger promised.

The friend was Marj Tooker. After the trauma of the past month,
John looked forward to spending an evening beside her fire. He went
immediately to the Yale-in-China Hospital.

"If you don't mind eating with a couple of missionaries who are
visiting me, you are welcome for supper," she said.

"Three missionaries," John said pointing to himself.

"Oh, I forgot." Marj laughed. "Stay a few minutes and you can
walk me home and meet them."

John found the Australian couple to be most friendly, and the
fellowship around the table helped him forget for a little while the

impending enemy offensive that he knew would result in thousands of deaths and send hundreds of thousands of refugees fleeing westward. This time, he was almost certain, the Japs would take and hold Changsha.

After dinner the missionary couple graciously excused themselves and went to their room, leaving Marj and John alone. Marj put on a record of Pablo Casals, the great classical cellist, and soon the warm, vibrant tones were soothing John's frayed nerves.

"Is something going to happen?" Marj asked, a slight quiver in her voice betraying her concern.

"I'm afraid so," he confided. "I can't give you any details, but you should be ready to evacuate. Quickly."

"How much time do we have?"

"A month, maybe two. Just be ready. I'd help you, but I'll be away on another trip."

He had never volunteered to discuss his "trips" before. She didn't press him this time and changed the subject.

"Did Jenny and her friends get a flight over the Hump?"

John nodded.

They sat silently for a few moments, gazing into the fire, listening to the resonant sound of the music, allowing the tranquilizing effect to alleviate their fears. John seemed quite preoccupied. Marj guessed it was the war, or perhaps Jenny.

"I decided," John finally explained, "that it wouldn't be fair to ask Jenny to go where I'll be working after the war."

"You're still thinking of Tibet?" Marj asked, remembering previous conversations.

"Tibet or Turkestan. Neither is any place for a woman. No missionaries have been able to live in Tibet since William Simpson was martyred there in 1932. Turkestan is about the same. I couldn't expose a wife to that kind of danger and hardship, but that's where I'm going if Jesus doesn't come back first. To people who have never heard the gospel."

Marj listened quietly until John changed the subject again. They talked together until the logs turned to faintly glowing embers. Then John turned to leave and thought of something. He pulled three packs of cigarettes from his pocket. "I remembered you saying you were out. I wish you didn't smoke, but since you do I thought I'd be helpful."

Marj took the cigarettes. "Thanks. I'll think of you every time I smoke one. Will you write me?"

"When I get a free moment. Send my letters to Kunming. They'll eventually reach me from there."

John was reluctant to leave this comfortable haven and return to the stark realities of his life. Marj was a very special friend, even though he had never felt about her as he had Jenny. She was worldly, as Jenny was, for Jenny smoked and danced also, but he shared Marj's devotion to the Chinese. He imagined that if he ever got to know her better, they would find many more things in common. That was the problem with war. There was never time to get to know anyone. You met, felt drawn to one another, and then parted, possibly never to meet again.

The next morning John stepped aboard a sampan in a drenching rain. It was raining even harder when he got off the boat in Siangtan. He sloshed through the mud to the depot. The train to Hengyang was due in about an hour. From Hengyang he was to be flown to a small strip north of Changsha, where he would pick up guerrilla guides for the long journey that would end at Lao Ho Kow.

He was told the train would be hours, perhaps a day late. Nothing unusual about that. In the chaos that was Free China, it was fortunate that trains ran at all. He decided to walk over to the inn where he had spent the night several times on trips in and out of Changsha.

The wizened old housekeeper he had befriended on previous visits met him at the door, clucking sympathetically over his wet clothes and shoes. The Chinese insisted that he take a hot basin of water and a dry gown to clean up before taking a nap. While John slept, the man would take care of the wet clothing. John was glad to oblige, and when he awoke his clothes and shoes were beside his bed, neat and dry. His friend refused to take any money for the extra work.

While sitting around the inn, John wrote Marj a warm, philosophical letter, answering a question she had posed the night before: "What do you enjoy most?"

> I find joy in realizing and trying to share the love of Christ (although my life has been drying up somewhat in this field during the last year); in the glory of Nature... — a beautiful dawn makes me happy for hours. I feel exalted when hiking over the hills and along the clear rivers of Chekiang and Fukien — in the light that springs to the eyes of helpless people when they are given unexpected aid or sympathy; in the exercise of mind and body on a challenging job or strenuous play; in the feel of clean sheets on tired muscles; in longing for the future life with Christ, when all the ugly "former things have passed away" and given place to a "new heaven and new earth wherein dwelleth righteousness..." Three more things I really enjoy: sitting with my father on our porch on Sunday afternoon, watching the river flowing past down below and the cows grazing on the hills across the valley, and listening to his

philosophical remarks that slip out about once an hour; listening to classical music (about which I know almost nothing); hurrying forward to see what is around the next bend or over the next hill on a way I travel for the first time.

There was still no word about the train so John decided to write his parents, since he might be unable to get another letter to them for several weeks. He could write of his mission only in vague terms, yet he felt they needed some indication of the danger ahead — just in case.

My work is becoming more interesting and even promises a little danger and excitement in the near future. Beginning tomorrow I shall be unable to write you, so please don't be alarmed if there is a lapse in the arriving of my letters.

Please continue to remember me in your prayers; if my hour to depart should strike, I am ready to go, thanks to the merit of our Savior, the Lord Jesus Christ. But I hope that God will give me yet further time to live for him fruitfully here on this earth; I've *wasted so much of his time already*, living for self, that I really feel ashamed to ask for more.

He wrote several other letters, including one to Jenny in India. Then a coolie came to tell him that the train was coming. He hurried to the station. The next day he was far north of Changsha, heading toward enemy territory, where he would switch to a horse.

Traveling forty to fifty miles a day on horseback with an escort of guerrillas, he reached the Yangtze by May 6 and was in the Yellow River plains by May 10. He confirmed what other guerrillas had reported: a huge mass of Japanese troops bivouacking in the area. Time permitted only the marking out of a few targets for 14th Air Force planes to hit. It was more important to find where the Japanese were coming from and to locate their supply lines.

He rode toward the old north-south railroad right-of-way which paralleled the newer railroad further east. Even before reaching the roadbed, he heard the crunch-crunch of men walking. Dismounting and creeping closer, he watched line after line of enemy troops pouring down from the north. He moved back and raised the antenna of his portable radio to report this.

Crawling back to a spot near the right-of-way, he watched until the last column passed. Then he and his friends slipped across the opening and camped on the other side. About dawn another Jap army came by, marching in long columns. He radioed this information to headquarters, and by afternoon planes were hitting the columns.

Riding east, he soon reached the new railroad and heard the chug-chug-chug of a powerful locomotive. Down the tracks came a train of over a hundred cars loaded with armored vehicles, howitzers and other war equipment. He reported this back to Colonel Smith. There was absolutely no doubt that the enemy was planning the biggest offensive of the war in China.

There was one puzzle: Chinese Communist guerrillas were known to be active along the railway in the north. Why hadn't they interfered with the troop movement or at least warned their western allies of the Japanese route of march? Why, indeed, since they had such good contacts with Stilwell's political advisers, who had been praising the Communists as superior fighters to the Nationalist Chinese? Did they actually want the Japanese to defeat the Nationalist forces in East China? John could only surmise that this was so. He had long believed that the Chinese Communists were more interested in fighting their own Nationalist countrymen than the Japs and would try to take over once the Allies had won the war.

As a military man he could not solve the grave internal political problems of China. His job was to help defeat the Japanese invader. For the moment this required setting up a couple of Chinese observation teams on the railroad and equipping them with portable radios. Having done this, he left his horse with his guerrilla friends and hired a sampan to take him on a long trip down a northern tributary of the Yangtze to Lao Ho Kow where he was to meet Drummond and Eichenberry.

John always found water travel soothing and helpful in withdrawing from the rigors and horrors of fighting a war. Gliding down a river he could enjoy the beauties of creation and lapse into a peaceful state of relaxation. This, more than anything else, was his rest and recreation while in China and served to restore his mind and body for exhausting days and nights ahead.

He read his New Testament, slept on the deck, sunbathed, sometimes swam alongside the boat when the current slowed, or wrote letters which he kept in a watertight pouch and gave to the next pilot he met for mailing. One of the letters was to his sister, Betty:

> I'd love to share this scenery with you; a swift, clear river winding through towering green mountains, of which some still have snow on the peaks; sheer sandstone cliffs hanging over us, with flocks of little white goats high up on the rocks looking as though any minute they might topple over and come crashing down into the water; mountaineers' huts, made of gray stone, perched on the hillsides; small groves of bamboo and other trees that look like Lombardy poplars,

waving in the winds that sweep the mountainside; great gray rocks that look like elephants out in the river, splitting the stream into several roaring channels; foaming rapids that are miniature reproductions of the Yangtze gorges, and which give us thrills aplenty, as the boatmen fight to keep the sampan under control and off the rocks!

China's scenery always makes me think of the words in the second verse of *Greenland's Icy Mountains*: "Where every prospect pleases, and only Man is vile." I have been on this boat four days already and shall probably have two more — plenty of swimming and sunbathing. Wish I had someone besides these Chinese boatmen to share it with me! It's lots of fun, if you don't mind a few fleas and eating and sleeping with three or four rough-and-ready Chinese rivermen ...

It's awfully nice of you to want to write Jenny a letter, and of course it wasn't "too early." Now, however, it is possibly a little late, since I have "busted" things up pretty thoroughly. If you want it though, here is her address ... She is a splendid and capable girl, and I think both of you would be happy to have each other's friendship.

... Please tell George Stanley that now more than ever I congratulate him and Alice on finding so much happiness within the will of God. I wish George could be classified for combat duty, then sent over here! I have a selfish reason, of course, in wanting to see my own blood kin and hear news straight from home, but I have another reason. Since George feels called to spread the gospel, too, I'd like for him to have a look at China! If God would give me my own brother to be a partner someday in pioneer evangelistic work in West China, it's a happy man I'd be.

The rocking of this boat makes my writing even worse than usual; hope you can decipher it.

To his father he wrote a pensive thanks for counsel previously given about marriage.

Father, you were quite right in assuming that for a time any advice you might have sent me would have been disregarded. I think that time is past now. I regret very much that I never came to know you and your counsel better in the years I had at home.

I recently read an abridged version of Louis Tucker's biography, *Clerical Errors* in a 1943 (September) *Omnibook*. In it he describes his expressions of dying of ptomaine poisoning and his revival a few hours later. He never felt that he entered heaven itself — just got to see his own earthly father on the threshold of heaven, where they both enjoyed for a joyous instant perfect knowledge and understanding of each other — sort of a super-telepathy. Well, I look forward to really *knowing* you and Mother some day, even if we have to wait 'til Jesus takes us home.

John linked up with Drummond and Eichenberry on May 17. The trio was to establish a small forward base among Chinese guerrillas and proceed north to Shantung Province and set up an intelligence net of Chinese agents to provide target information for air strikes and aid in rescue operations of downed flight crews. Along the way they ran into a Chinese army of 100,000 men which had been trapped behind Japanese lines in a valley "pocket" for over a year. Like so many other valleys in mountainous China, this pocket had been bypassed by the Japanese who had invaded along natural land corridors. The valley was almond-shaped, about one hundred miles long and twenty miles wide at the mountainous southern end, and narrowing to a width of three miles of alluvial plains at the northern end. The broad Yellow River, which had changed course in 1938, poured through the heart of the pocket.

John immediately saw the pocket as a natural spot for a forward base in the heart of Japanese territory, a place for a central radio station in the northern intelligence net and secret airfields at each end. Used as refueling stops, the airfields could extend the strike range of bombers into Manchuria and even Japan. Crippled planes, unable to get home to bases in the south, could land safely here. Downed flight crews from all over north China could be brought to the fields by guerrillas and picked up by 14th Air Force planes.

He radioed his headquarters and got enthusiastic approval. Then he explained the idea to the commander of the "lost" army, General Wang, and received permission to proceed.

After helping Eichenberry and Drummond set up the station at a village called Shenchan, John took a squad of Chinese soldiers and scouted the pocket for sites for the airfields. He located the first one along a dry streambed near the river. He laid out a 3,500' runway himself, drawing on experience gained while surveying farmland during one summer in college.

Working under John's direction, thousands of soldiers swarmed over the streambed, digging and chopping away obstructions, leveling off humps with pick and shovel, and packing the runway with crushed rock and sand. They even built a crude terminal and a radio shack close to the runway. Then they made a second smaller field in a pasture near the village of Linchuan and called it the "Drill Field." All of the work on both runways cost the 14th Air Force not one cent.

The first plane in came to evacuate Sergeant Eichenberry, who was gravely ill from cholera. John was not feeling so well himself, but he spent every day supervising the building of the second airfield. While John worked at the airfield, Drummond manned the radio station, forwarding reports received from guerrillas about enemy operations in the north. A bonanza in intelligence was coming through, but the pilots of the 14th had their hands full with the new Japanese offensive that had been launched early in the summer.

The Little Tiger and his army valiantly tried to slow the advance, but they were pushed back by the sheer bulk of the offensive force. Colonel Smith threw every liaison team he could into the battle to set up air strikes, and General Chennault sent every plane he could gas up — 150 out of 1400 — into the fray. Fourteen pilots slaughtered thousands of enemy troops in the open. One strafing run, called in by Private John Shimondle, a radio operator, took care of 7,500 enemy soldiers on a treeless marsh.

There was no stemming the Nippon tide. By June 6, the day Allied troops were landing on Normandy's beaches in France, the enemy horde was halfway to Changsha. Marj Tooker and the Chinese doctors at the Yale-in-China Hospital began discharging their patients and prepared to evacuate.

General Stilwell chose that day to pop out of the Burma jungle and fly to Chungking. He left his Chinese army still fighting to open a road into China.

He had to stop in Kunming to refuel. Chennault was waiting there to brief him on the new offensive. He stepped off the plane and announced to the 14th's commander, "I'll give you thirty minutes, so make your briefing quick."

Chennault was boiling mad, but he held his temper and tried to impress on his superior just how desperate the situation was. "We're going to lose all our airfields in East China if we don't act immediately," he said.

"Well, Claire, what do you recommend?" Stilwell asked laconically.

"That you issue an order mobilizing all Allied resources in the China-Burma-India theater. I'm sure the Generalissimo will back you up."

"Oh, from what you say, it's too late for that. I doubt if anything can halt the enemy offensive."

Chennault could not believe what he was hearing, even from Stilwell. He was writing off eastern China. He begged Stilwell to reconsider, but Vinegar Joe would not call for the mobilization. He did agree to give the 14th more gas, but prohibited truck shipments of fuel overland from Kunming to Kweilin and Hengyang. This prevented the 14th from striking Hangkow, from which supplies were coming to advancing enemy troops.

Two days later Stilwell gave in a little more and declared an emergency. But he continued to deny Chennault's request for troops from other areas to reinforce the Chinese Ninth Army.

On June 18 Changsha fell. Ten days later the enemy blitz overran the Hengyang airfield and began battering Hengyang City. Now outnumbered forty to one, the Little Tiger's retreating soldiers fought back tenaciously.

Pilots of the 14th concentrated on the enemy's long supply line, which was strung out to the Bulge. They cut the line and probably could have turned the fortunes of battle if they had not run out of gas. Chennault disobeyed a standing order and dipped into reserves, but for five days all planes were grounded while the enemy repaired the damage that had been done.

Though denied further American arms by Stilwell, the brave defenders of Hengyang held out for forty-nine days. Hardly a word was written in the American press about the astounding resistance of the Chinese Ninth. China war correspondents, at Stilwell's behest, were in Burma.

After Hengyang was captured the remnants of Marshall Yo's army fell back to Liuchow, the southernmost of the 14th's eastern bases. They held out as long as they could before escaping into the countryside, where they continued to harass the enemy.

It was not a total defeat for the overall war effort. The 14th Air Force and Marshall Yo's army had tied up a huge Jap army for over five months and inflicted heavy losses. Had the East China cities and airfields been taken in half this time, the enemy could have thrown additional support into the critical Pacific, where the strategic situation was changing in favor of the Allies. Allied troops were now swarming over Guam. B-29 Super-fortresses pounded Japan and U.S. ships swept the Jap Navy from Leyte Gulf.

The 14th, as well as the Chinese Army, had paid dearly for this action. Over half of the pilots in the 23rd Fighter Wing, the unit to which John belonged, were dead. Survivors from this and other wings were bitter about Stilwell's foot-dragging. They were even more bitter after the war when it was disclosed that Stilwell had withheld help because he had wanted Chiang Kai-shek to lose face and be forced to give Stilwell unconditional command of the Chinese armies.

For John, it had been the longest, hottest, most miserable summer of his life. His only lift had come in late July when a guerrilla courier came through the lines bringing a bag of mail. There was a letter from Jenny. The batch also included letters from his mother, sister, brothers and an envelope of notes from members of the Benevolence Baptist Church on the occasion of the church's annual

Homecoming. He felt certain the Benevolence packet was his mother's idea. He wrote in response:

> "The warm, homey notes brought tears to my eyes — and I don't cry easily these days.
> I was picked up at one of our secret northern airfields on 8 August and flown to Kunming. The specific reason was to receive the Legion of Merit for my participation in the battle of Changteh in 1943. It was for a very ordinary job I did last fall.

John was also suffering from another attack of malaria. "We need every man we can get," General Chennault told him, "but if you'll take it, you can have a 60-day furlough. I recommend you go home, spend some time with your family, and unwind."

"That sounds great, sir, but no thank you. I'd be taking the place of someone who has a wife and kids. When the war is won, I'll take that furlough."

"Then get some rest here," the Big Tiger ordered.

While John "rested" at Kunming, a showdown loomed over the military command mess in China. Major General Patrick Hurley came as an emissary from President Roosevelt to pressure Chiang Kai-shek into giving Stilwell command of all the Chinese armies. Faced with cutoff of American aid, Chiang reluctantly told Hurley he would go along, but before this could be announced an ultimatum came from Washington demanding that Chiang do what he was already willing to do. There were suspicions that Stilwell had drafted the message and sent it to friends in the War Department, who persuaded Roosevelt to sign it and return it to China. In any case, Stilwell over-played his hand by personally delivering the cable to the Generalissimo — "to break the Peanut's face," he wrote in his diary. Backed into a corner, Chiang reneged and said he would never work with Stilwell again.

John flew back to the secret base in Anhwei Province, his body rested, but more heartsick than when he had come to Kunming over two months before. He felt that many of his friends had died needlessly because of Stilwell's obstinate refusal to help the 14th Air Force and the Little Tiger's army defend eastern China.

The day after John left Kunming, Stilwell was recalled to Washington by the U.S. War Department and Lieutenant General Albert C. Wedemeyer appointed in his place. Wedemeyer was a tall, rangy, open-faced West Pointer with broad experience in planning war strategy. He dissolved the ice of mistrust and established a warm cooperative rapport with both Chiang and Chennault. He pledged to give the 14th Air Force all the support possible and, in another move that pleased Chennault immensely, sent Stilwell's pro-Communist political advisers packing.

With added fuel and other supplies, the 14th took a "second wind" and began hitting Jap installations from north China to deep into Indo-China. Chennault was enthusiastically behind John's idea to use the secret pocket as a base for intelligence in north China. Three tons of radio equipment and supplies were delivered to Anhwei.

John did not stay in the pocket long. He took a squad of General Wang's soldiers and radios and headed north. As always, he carried his New Testament and a supply of gospel tracts. Since joining the service there had been few Sundays when he hadn't preached either to an American group or a Chinese congregation.

He returned to the base a couple of weeks later, looking leaner and having lengthened the intelligence net. Early in November one of his Chinese agents radioed that he had discovered an American flight crew. They had bailed out of a B-29 in June and had been hiding in the mountains ever since. They were now being brought to the base in the Yellow River pocket, the operative said.

The men practically threw their arms around John and Lieutenant Drummond. "You guys are the first Americans we've seen in almost six months," one said. John remembered meeting another crew that had been almost as glad to see an American. That was Jimmy Doolittle's bunch. A lot had happened in the two and a half years since then.

Drummond radioed for a pickup plane, and Colonel Smith promised to send a C-47 transport on November 15. That day they took the B-29 crew out to the field built on the old riverbed. By the time they reached the field the sky was black and threatening a downpour.

Chinese friends had prepared a feast for the Americans in a nearby house on the day of their departure. The heavy rain that was now falling spoiled the joy of the occasion. It appeared impossible that the plane could land. When a plane was due in, the *modus operandi* was to run out to the radio shack near the end of the runway every hour, listen for engine noise and transmit a code signal until word came from Kunming that the plane wasn't coming.

They were enjoying roasted goat meat when John looked at his watch. "It's time to go," he shouted and grabbed a slicker.

"Stay here, Captain," one of the men called. "Nobody's coming in this storm."

"Probably not," John yelled back, "but we haven't heard otherwise from Kunming."

About twenty minutes later they heard engine noise and broke for the airfield. The B-29 crew jumped on the Chinese ponies.

Drummond tried to run on foot, but got stuck in the mud. One of the flyers was thrown from his horse, but somehow he and the others managed to reach the plane despite the mud and pea-soup weather.

By the time Drummond got there, the plane had taken off. John was standing beside the runway holding a portable direction finder and a carton of cigarettes.

"How did you get the plane down?" Drummond gasped when they were back in a shelter.

"The Lord must have been with me, Bill. When I got out here, I saw the wind had blown the roof off the radio shack and the rain was pouring in on the equipment. I was tuning in the radio when I heard engine noise. I ran over to the runway but couldn't see ten feet in front of me. Fortunately I had this finder. I got a fix on the plane and talked the pilot down. Then when the B-29 crew got on, I ran ahead of the plane and directed the pilot down the runway. They got airborne right over my head."

John handed Drummond the carton of cigarettes. "For you. The pilot said this was his last run in China and he wouldn't be needing them.

"Now, let's get back to that goat meat."

14

The Prophet

Often I feel these barren years are my
apprenticeship, God-given, and that a message is
being formed within me that will one day burn
its way into the souls of many.

—John Birch, letter to sister Betty,
March 22, 1945

The approaching Christmas season made John feel very depressed. He was daydreaming about the last holiday season he had spent at Birchwood, when suddenly the thought came to him, *All my brothers and my sister are now grown up. They're not the kids I left behind. If I did see them, I'd have to get to know them all over again.*

The severity of the winter season did nothing to brighten his spirits. It had been weeks since a plane had been able to land in the pocket, which meant no mail from the outside world. At times it was hard to realize there was any other world than this war-torn nation he had adopted.

"I should have taken that furlough the General offered me," he told himself. "I could be at Birchwood right now, laughing and singing and teasing with my family, smelling Mother's baking, philosophizing with Father." He shook his head as he realized he was talking aloud. *This isolation is really getting to me*, he thought. The memories of home had brought a stinging sensation to his eyes.

I made the right decision, he assured himself. *I could have taken the place of some man who hasn't seen his children for years, perhaps he is now seeing his child for the very first time.*

In this melancholy mood John sat down to write home. He wasn't looking forward to his fifth Christmas in China, and couldn't keep negative feelings from creeping into his letter.

> I sometimes find myself dropping to a "hardshell Baptist" frame of mind regarding the spiritual condition and destiny of men, so I guess you'd better keep on remembering me in your prayers. The Lord has

cared for me thus far, far more faithfully than I have served him this past year. Sometimes I become so disgusted with my own attitudes and those in the men around me that I wonder why the Lord even tolerates us, let alone protects and prospers our lives and work, as he unmistakably does. I'm afraid I don't yet know the full meaning of grace.

A gentle knock came at the door. "Bey Shang We, General Wang invites you to a party," the Chinese noncom announced gleefully. The title "Bey Shang We" meant literally "Birch Captain." Spoken in Mandarin, it indicated high stature.

John was deeply touched at the General's thoughtfulness and happily accepted the invitation. When he arrived at the General's house, he found Wang and his top officers awaiting his arrival. Bill Drummond was already there, having been relieved at the radio station by a Chinese operator. There was even a Chinese soldier dressed as Santa Claus.

"Bey Shang We! Merry Christmas!" the General shouted. He raised a *mao tai* glass and offered the traditional toast of friendship. "*Kan pei.*" John was respectfully offered a glass of tea, which he clinked against Wang's glass. After half a dozen such toasts General Wang announced, "Bey Shang We will now teach us some of his American Christmas songs."

John cupped his ear toward the door. "Shhhh, I think the enemy is nearby." The Chinese fell instantly silent and some reached for their weapons. John crept toward the door, then suddenly turned around and began singing "Jingle Bells" at the top of his voice. Everyone broke into laughter, and the General shouted, "All of us, sing with Bey Shang We."

A few moments later there were sounds at the door. A bedraggled American flyer, wearing the Flying Tiger insignia of the 14th Air Force, and two guerrillas burst in. The flyer looked completely dazed. He stood there blinking his eyes and shaking his head as if he didn't believe what he was seeing. Bailing out far behind enemy lines, then stepping into a party with two Americans and a bunch of Chinese officers singing a Christmas song was beyond comprehension.

After a few minutes of adjusting to the situation, Lieutenant T.J. Gribbs explained that he had been forced to drop out of his squadron by a leak in his gas line. Realizing he was lost, he had attempted a landing about ten miles from Linchuan. One pass had been enough to convince him it was impossible to land in such terrain, so he climbed to a safe altitude and bailed out. The guerrillas had found him wandering around and brought him to the base.

A week later John heard the sound of a Chinese army column approaching his house. He opened the door and beheld a large group of men carrying pieces of a wrecked plane. "We've brought your airplane," the commander announced proudly. It was the remains of Gribbs' P-40.

Birch, Drummond and Gribbs sifted through the wreckage, hoping to salvage something useful. The best they could find was the rubber-tired tail wheel. It could go on a new wheelbarrow.

General Wang saw more possibilities in the wreckage. He had his metalsmith melt down the aluminum fuselage and make two American-sized bath tubs which he presented to John and Bill Drummond with grand eloquence. Neither had enjoyed the luxury of such a bath for months.

For days after the delivery of the plane, Chinese came to look at the wreckage. A "General Chow," who was from another area, asked if the pilot had been badly hurt in coming down. John realized the man had probably never seen a parachute and thought all planes landed in this condition.

"The pilot was not hurt at all," John told the old warlord with a straight face. He then called Gribbs into the yard so the general could see for himself. "Amazing! Amazing!" he chortled. John never did explain.

On another occasion John told a group of Chinese officers that Drummond was almost deaf. When Drummond came near them, they began shouting. John, standing to one side, almost fell over laughing, while Drummond tried to convince them that he could hear as well as anyone. Such levity helped make bearable the long gray days in the isolated pocket.

Throughout the war many missionaries had remained in the rural towns of north China which the Japanese had not bothered to occupy. Most of them were elderly Dutch, British and Americans who had been in China over thirty years. They felt China was their home and saw no reason to leave. However, the Japanese troop movements of the summer and fall of 1944 had put their lives in great jeopardy. Some who lived in the Anhwei area heard about the secret American airfields and sent word to John through guerrillas, asking to be rescued. "Sure, come on," John replied. "We'll get you out somehow."

The first of the missionaries began arriving at the field on the old riverbed in late December. They joined Gribbs and four or five other flyers who had also been brought to the fields by guerrillas. Lieutenant Drummond was there with them, waiting for the first break in the weather.

John put in a call to his C.O. at headquarters, only to be informed Colonel Smith had been called to Washington. He then found it extremely difficult to find a sympathetic ear in Kunming. "Captain, we aren't running a ferry service for lost missionaries," he was told. "You haven't got enough airmen to justify sending a transport now. We need every plane we've got for military business."

John explained that the missionaries and airmen were living in cramped quarters not large enough for an ordinary family. "They're running out of food and fuel down at the airfield. Can't you do something?"

"The priority isn't high enough, Captain. They'll have to wait a few weeks."

Compounding the problem was the daily arrival of still more missionaries. A worried Drummond radioed from the airfield, "Harvey's Restaurant is absolutely jammed. Please don't send any more customers."

John used the more powerful set at the radio station to talk to Kunming again. "Look, it's not just people I've got up here. I've got a pouch of valuable intelligence that is needed by General Chennault. Get us a plane up here on the first clear day." He sounded so urgent that the plane was promised. He did have intelligence, but it could have waited a few weeks.

In mid-January the weather turned favorable. John climbed on the back of a pony and rode out to the airfield fifty miles away. By the time he got there, more snow had fallen. The runway cutting across the white expanse would be invisible from the air. The plane would be unable to land and would return to Kunming. There was no telling when he could get another one.

He put the problem to General Wang. "No difficulty, Bey Shang We," he said. "How many men with shovels do you need?"

John figured eight hundred would be enough. They swarmed onto the field and within hours had the runway clear. The plane landed safely and the fliers and all but one of the missionaries squeezed on board. The plane was too overloaded to take on that last man, so he had to wait for another month.

While the passengers had been boarding, the pilot passed along some disturbing information to John. "The word is that you field intelligence guys are going to be transferred to OSS. That's why Colonel Smith is in Washington. You'll probably be hearing from him soon."

John had been afraid this was going to happen. The last time he was in Kunming he had seen two planeloads of OSS majors and captains arrive from India. The briefcases they carried were enough to turn off any Flying Tiger, and John was no exception.

He knew Colonel Smith had had disagreements with them. For one thing, they thought the Chinese radio operatives should each be paid $150 a month instead of the $10 they were continuing to receive. "We're not buying them as the Japanese do," Colonel Smith had said. "We're paying their expenses and giving them an opportunity to help us get the Japs out of their country."

Now Colonel Smith was in Washington making a deal with the OSS. The more John thought about it, the madder he got. "Their ideas that worked in Europe won't work over here," he fumed to Drummond. "The Chinese are unique. It's an entirely different culture.

"They'll just mess up our field intelligence net that has worked so well. I can't understand how they can think loyalty can be bought. That's ridiculous. Well, I'm not going to roll over and play dead, and I'm not going to join their outfit."

John was still hot under the collar when the radiogram came under the name of General Chennault confirming the prediction of the pilot. "This will mean more personnel and supplies," he promised, "enabling you to do a better job for the war effort."

John stomped the floor in anger. He fired back his response. "No! Would rather be buck private in 14th than full colonel in OSS and have access to 'Wild Bill' Donovan's slush funds." He knew the coded message would be copied at theater headquarters in Chungking. Every OSS agent in China would soon know how he felt about them. He didn't care.

Shortly after sending the angry message, John was ordered to move back into Honan Province where the enemy had mounted a drive toward the large western city of Sian. The 14th Air Force air coordination teams were dropped ahead of the Japs at a designated meeting place. John's mission was to train them for combat.

For the next few weeks he worked eighteen to twenty hours a day, showing them how to mark targets and call in air strikes, positioning them in critical areas. When the last team was in place, he collapsed from exhaustion. Chinese soldiers carried him to the nearest emergency airfield at Ankang where the 14th Air Force medic immediately put him in the infirmary. Besides having another attack of malaria, he had contracted typhus.

Two weeks of medication and vitamins, plus bed rest, did wonders. He was ready to get back to his base in the Anhwei Pocket, but the doctor insisted he remain for a few more days.

One evening as he lay in his bed trying to read in the light of a flickering candle, a young lieutenant stopped to see him.

"Captain Birch, I'm Bill Miller with OSS."

John frowned and motioned for Miller, a recent graduate of West Point, to take a chair.

"Captain, I heard about you in Washington. Everybody in OSS has heard of you."

"Yeah, they've heard what I told Chennault about transfer to your outfit."

"Yes, we heard that. But before we left Washington we were told about the great job you've done out here."

"I've done what I could," John mumbled, uncertain of Miller's mission.

Miller soon explained. "I've been assigned as an escape and evasion agent at Foyuang in the Anhwei Pocket where you've been working."

"That's about fifty miles from Linchuan," John noted.

"Well, I hope we can be good neighbors."

"There's no reason why not. I'll help you all I can," John pledged. "While your house is getting fixed up, you may want to stay at my place." In spite of all he had heard about OSS men, John liked Miller. He was also beginning to be sorry he had sent the radiogram.

The two talked the rest of the evening, then Miller came back the next day for more briefing. When shoptalk lagged, John asked Miller if he was a Christian.

"From what I've heard about you, I anticipated that question. I'm a pretty good Catholic."

"But are you a Christian?" John pressed. "Have you accepted Christ as your personal Savior. No church will save you."

"I know that, John, and I do believe in Christ. He's my Savior."

"Well, praise the Lord," John exclaimed. "You know when I came to China, I couldn't see anybody saved and going to heaven except people who believed exactly as I do. I still believe the same way, but know now that it's one's relationship to Christ that counts."

"That's right," Miller agreed.

"I've met some fine Catholic missionaries," John continued. "I had to admire their dedication, priests and nuns who for the sake of the Chinese people would give up marriage and live very humbly. Not that I believe celibacy is required for a minister, although in my case it seems to be the best course.

"I have more in common with the Catholic Church than I do with some Protestants. Catholics believe in the virgin birth of Christ and his resurrection. You Catholics take the Bible to be God's inspired Word, which many Protestants don't."

"I should recruit you for the priesthood," Miller teased.

John shook his head. "You add a lot of church tradition that I could never accept: Mary, the Pope, the doctrine of transubstantiation, the idea that works are necessary for salvation.

I could never be a Catholic, Bill, until the Catholic Church accepts the Bible fundamentals of the faith. But we can still be friends."

"Right. Good friends, I hope," Miller added.

In a couple of days Miller got a plane into the pocket. John stayed on for further recuperation, then was called to Kunming where Colonel Smith tried to talk him into transferring to OSS. John remained obstinate.

"Look, Birch, I love the 14th as much as you do," Smith said. "There isn't another outfit to which I would rather belong."

"You betrayed us," John said sharply, suddenly realizing he had touched a sensitive nerve.

"Captain, watch your tongue. We've got a war to fight, a war in which we have to obey orders. Try to get it through your head that I'm following orders. I'll tell you something. When I came back from Washington with the news about transferring to OSS, nobody would speak to me. They wouldn't even pass me the salt at the table. But they've had time to think it over and everyone is going along but you."

"Sir, you're wasting your breath. You can bust me or do whatever you want. I'm not joining that establishment of incompetents. No, wait, I don't mean that entirely. Some seem to know what they're doing. Bill Miller, for instance. But from what I've heard, some are over here just to play cops and robbers."

"That's not for me to judge. All right, I believe you," Smith signed. "Will you at least cooperate with OSS if I can persuade them to let you remain in the 14th?"

"I'll help any way I can. You have my word, sir."

Colonel Smith talked to the top OSS man and explained John's refusal. "There's not another American in China more stubborn than Captain John Birch — unless it's General Chennault. Let him stay on the 14th roster and be on detached duty to OSS. He'll do anything you want."

"Very well, Colonel," the OSS officer agreed. "We'll try it. But keep it quiet."

General Chennault requested to see John. "I know how you feel about the OSS," the Big Tiger said. "I don't care much for them myself. But as a personal favor to me, will you stay on with the other 14th Air Force Men who are working with OSS?"

John said he would cooperate so long as he wasn't formally transferred.

"One more thing, John. How about taking a furlough first? You need a rest. Then come back and help us finish the war. I can have you on the next plane for India," he offered.

India. Jenny. The thoughts raced through his mind, but he didn't hesitate. "Sir, I've thought of a furlough, but the war can't last much longer. I intend to stay until the last Jap is out of China."

"Okay, John. I know you too well to try to get you to change your mind, but take it easy, will you? I want you to come out of this war alive. I've had enough dead heroes."

The evening before John was due to return to the Anhwei Pocket, he had another long talk with his C.O.

"Colonel, this war will be over soon, but it won't be the end of the fighting," John predicted. "As soon as the Japs surrender, the Commies will go all-out to take over China. Why can't the fancy-pants in our government see that? And they won't stop in China. They intend to take over the world. We'll be fighting them in the Battle of Armageddon."

Smith listened, saying little, letting John wind down. Finally he looked at his watch. "Better get some sleep, John. I'm going to bed."

Japan's fortunes of war were fading fast. In the Pacific, American troops had conquered Iwo Jima at great cost and were now pushing across Okinawa. B-29s were pounding Japanese cities daily.

In China, the 14th Air Force ruled the area from the Great Wall to Indo-China. No enemy ship could move along the coast or on the Yangtze without being attacked. On land, enemy troops were in retreat. Thanks largely to the ten air coordination teams John had trained in Honan, the Japs had been driven back from Sian. A land supply route had been opened through Burma, although most tonnage was still coming in over the Hump. All of this was a tribute to the leadership of General Wedemeyer who had brought in a new era of cooperation and goodwill between Chiang Kai-shek and the American military in China.

Unlike Stilwell, whose mind had been poisoned by his advisers, Wedemeyer saw the Chinese Communists as revolutionary opportunists, preying upon the tragedy of China. He noted that they had never fought a single battle of consequence against the Japanese, but instead "played the role of jackal or hyena against the wounded and suffering Chinese elephant that would not submit to his enemy." Their main concern, Wedemeyer felt, had not been fighting the Japanese, but occupying territory which the Nationalists abandoned in retreat. Wedemeyer, to the great delight of Chiang Kai-shek, absolutely refused to tolerate Communist fellow-travelers in his headquarters.

Amidst all the good news John heard disquieting rumors of a reorganization of air forces. Such a reorganization of the American military command in China would greatly reduce General Chennault's power and prestige.

The 10th Air Force was coming from India to China under the command of General Charles Stone III, successor to General Bissell. It would have headquarters in Kunming. Chennault's 14th Air Force was to be moved to Chengtu, north of the Yangtze. Here at the end of the longest supply line in the world, the 14th would be reduced to a one-base operation.

General George Stratemeyer was being brought in as overall commander of air forces in China and air advisor to General Wedemeyer. General Chennault felt this was a terrible setback, a humiliation. He had been fighting in China for seven years and neither Stone nor Stratemeyer had served a day in the country.

Actually Wedemeyer had, upon hearing of the reorganization plans, suggested to Generals Marshall and Arnold that Chennault be promoted to Lieutenant General and made Air Commander in China. But Marshall and Arnold had not forgotten the vendetta between Generals Bissell and Chennault, and favoring Bissell, they rejected Chennault for the position and appointed Stratemeyer. They were also influenced by friends of Stilwell who had told them the mess in China before Wedemeyer took over was Chennault's fault.

General Wedemeyer informed Chennault of what was about to happen, noting that his suggestion to Arnold and Marshall had been overruled and that he had no choice but to obey orders. It was not yet known what Chennault would do, but there was speculation that he would bow out rather than submit to the obvious snubbing by Arnold and Marshall and the moving of the 14th's headquarters from Kunming to Chengtu.

John saw no reason not to believe the military grapevine. The Washington establishment, influenced by Chennault's enemies, Bissell and Stilwell, had been out to get Chennault since the war began. John was further upset because he felt he had also been demoted. He had been in sole charge of American spy operations from the Anhwei Pocket, which he had discovered and set up. Now there were three bases, including his own, and he was one of three officers reporting to a new C.O., Major Gus Krause.

Jim Hart, one of the new OSS operatives and a former Louisville, Kentucky newspaperman, tried to assure John he hadn't been demoted. "Intelligence has been expanded to include more than that of value to the air force," he told Birch. John still felt maligned.

The next mail brought more disappointment. The folks were talking about selling the recently rebuilt Birchwood, the cattle and the farm equipment and moving to a smaller place. "George Stanley is already in the service," his father wrote. "Herbert and Robert are booked for the Navy within a month. None of them want to farm."

John couldn't blame his parents, but the dream of at least returning for a visit to Birchwood had often eased the weariness of war. He was tired of the suffering and dying, the petty military squabbles, the coarse profanity and bawdiness of the men about him. He yearned to return to the peace of Birchwood, sit at the supper table and hear his father read the Bible, plant bare feet in red Georgia clay, feel the grass whipping against his ankles as he ran through the meadow, swim in the cool river and haul a wiggling channel catfish onto the bank. Now they were selling the old place.

While reflecting on cherished memories of the past and aspirations for the future, he penned a short essay which he titled "War-weary Farmer."

I should like to find the existence of what my father called "plain living and high thinking."

I want some fields and hills, woodlands and streams I can call my own. I want to spend my strength in making the fields green and the cattle fat, so that I may give sustenance to my loved ones, and aid to those neighbors who suffer misfortune. I do not want a life of monotonous paper shuffling or of trafficking with money-mad traders.

I want only enough of science to enable a fruitful husbandry of the land with simple tools, a time for leisure, and the guarding of my family's health. I do not care to be absorbed in the endless examinings of force and space and matter, which I believe can only slowly lead to God.

I do not want a hectic hurrying from place to place on whizzing machines or busy streets. I do not want an elbowing through crowds of impatient strangers who have time neither to think their own thoughts nor to know real friendship. I want to live slowly, to relax with my family before a glowing fireplace, to welcome the visits of my neighbors, to worship God, to enjoy a book, to lie on a shaded grassy bank and watch the clouds sail across the blue.

I want to love a wife who prefers a rural peace to urban excitement, one who would rather climb a hilltop to watch a sunset with me than to take a taxi to any Broadway play. I want a woman who is not afraid of bearing children, and who is able to rear them with a love for home and the soil, and the fear of God.

I want of Government only protection against the violence and injustices of evil or selfish men.

I want to reach the sunset of life sound in body and mind, flanked by strong sons and grandsons, enjoying the friendship and respect of my neighbors, surrounded by fertile fields and sleek cattle, and retaining my boyhood faith in him who promised a life to come.

Where can I find this world? Would its anachronism doom it to ridicule or loneliness? Is there yet a place for such simple ways in my own America? Or must I seek a vale in Turkestan where peaceful flocks still graze on quiet hills?

John was still brooding when a letter came from his sister Betty asking his plans for the future. He answered:

I have pondered and prayed over this a lot, and I know that if I survive the war I shall never escape the call to serve Christ. I am unsure of the place; it may be West China, or Georgia, or a television station on some mountain peak ... I may write books (on the side).

I shall probably run at least one stock ranch — perhaps in Chinese Turkestan — for Chinese farming co-ops. I expect thus to find support for missionary activities by the increase God gives from my herds and fields. In these dark days I see all human or part-human institutions as unreliable, even churches which are now being led by the Holy Spirit! Somehow I want to stand alone between a strife-torn earth and wrath-darkened heavens and thunder out, late in time, a call to repentance and belated trust in Christ during the lust-ridden years which will follow this war! Often in these days I feel that these barren years are my apprenticeship, God-given, and that a message is being formed, by him, within me that will one day burn its way out and across man's barriers, into the souls of many. I know that God is preparing me (has prepared, in some respects) to stand privation, pain, isolation, fatigue, physical danger, etc., to what end? This I trust him to show me in his own time.

When John wrote this, Japan was already trying to surrender through Soviet intermediaries, but the Soviets, for reasons of their own, were slow in passing this news on to the American government. General MacArthur had advised President Roosevelt that the Japanese were making unofficial peace overtures. Roosevelt, only weeks away from death and functioning through advisors, cracked that MacArthur was a good general and a poor diplomat.

John didn't know about the high-level plotting by Communists, both Soviet and Chinese, and their American sympathizers in the closing weeks of the war. He did know that Communists further up the Yellow River in Honan Province had broken the river dikes, allowing an ocean of floodwater to inundate crops in the Nationalist-held Anhwei Pocket. Chinese farmers in the area had anticipated one of the best harvests in years. Now their families would be in danger of starvation.

John did know the Chinese Communists were moving into positions behind the retreating Japanese. He tried to convince his OSS colleagues of the nefarious Communist plans. He told Captain James Hart, "The Commies are dodging around now so that when peace comes they'll be able to kill their brothers who are loyal to the Generalissimo. I keep telling people this," he sighed, "but sometimes I feel like a sparrow twittering in a tree at a tornado forming in the distance."

The war between the Allies and the Axis was over in Europe on May 8. While America rejoiced, the Soviets moved rapidly in Eastern Europe to capitalize on concessions made foolishly by Churchill and Roosevelt at the Yalta and Tehran summit conferences. With her peace feelers ignored, Japan continued to fight.

John, a lowly captain, was aware of only what was happening in China. Yet in all of his fulminations against communism, he believed that politics, diplomacy and war could provide no permanent solutions. On the U.S. Independence Day he wrote in one of his last letters home:

> One last word — for public consumption — and I mean this with all my heart. There is only one real problem in the world with all its complicated evils, and there is only one answer, amidst the maze of futile plans. Here is the problem and the answer: "The wages of sin is death, *but the free gift of God is eternal life through Jesus Christ our Lord*" (Romans 6:23).

Four days later he received in code the announcement that General Chennault had requested retirement and relief from active duty for reasons of ill health. The Old Man might be half-deaf, but John knew it was the Chinese way for saving face. Stilwell had gotten his revenge. The American general who had fought the longest and hardest for victory in China would be denied his role in the celebration that would come at the war's end. It was small consolation to John that Chennault was given a hero's send-off by cheering Chinese in city after city, and was awarded the Distinguished Service Cross by General Wedemeyer.

On August 6 the electrifying news came that a U.S. bomber had dropped an atom bomb on Hiroshima, Japan, resulting in unbelievable destruction. Surrender was expected shortly.

Bill Miller, whose radio was not as powerful as John's, risked a telephone call in the antiquated Chinese phone system and got through to John at Linchuan.

"What confirmation is there of the big news?" he asked.

"Chungking just called, ordering me to stand by to move north." John replied. "It's the real McCoy."

"What are the Japs going to do about it?"

"That remains to be seen, Bill. All we can do is stand by and hope for the best when the movement order comes. I'll talk to you again at ten in the morning."

On August 8, the Russians entered the Asian War and invaded Manchuria. They met little opposition. On August 9, a second atomic bomb was dropped on Nagasaki. Japan opened peace negotiations. John and the other Americans at his outpost waited eagerly for President Truman's announcement of the end of hostilities. On August 12, a Sunday, John held his usual weekly worship service at the post, "especially thanking God for bringing us to the eve of victory." Every man attended except the radio operator who had to stand by for a message.

Monday, August 13, John received a letter from George Stanley in which his young brother had groused, "At best this or any other war is just beating our heads against the wall ... All fighting and winning is temporary only."

John replied:

I will admit that much of what we rightly "render unto Caesar" is of temporary nature, because it is all in the present life. But many of these temporary things are of high importance and enjoined by God (i.e., the execution of wrath upon evildoers by human government). To me it is of utmost importance to gain the temporary opportunity to preach Christ's gospel!

Have you ever seen a humble Chinese brother who was beheaded because he preached Christ rather than the Emperor of Japan? I have. To me it is of high importance that peace-loving Chinese peasants be allowed to live out their lives in peace!

Have you ever seen Chinese girls after Japs machine-gunned them? I have. Have you ever watched a Jap soldier steal the pitifully few grains of rice belonging to a large family of starving children? I have.

I want peace, but not that purchased by tolerance of such evils as I saw Japan spreading across this part of the world! Without much military training or knowledge, except by observation of fights between Japs and guerrillas in Chekiang, I tried to volunteer as a private but they made me a Second Lieutenant instead. Since that day, I have tried, as wholeheartedly as I could, to serve the flag that had protected me all my life.

If you had ever lived one day under the shadow of the Jap secret police, you would thank God that America had enough "suckers" (as you call them) to redden the sands of Tarawa or drop flaming death through the China skies, that there were enough "suckers" to stop the Imperial navy at Midway and the Jap bombers over Kunming.

As John was writing his kid brother the dissertation on patriotism, the radio man rushed into his room. John then wrote:

The word has just come over the radio that Japan has unconditionally surrendered! Praise God from whom all blessings flow. No, brother of mine, we did not vainly beat our heads against a wall; we cut our hands smashing the teeth of a monstrous mouth that was devouring, and that rapidly, the lives, land, liberty, and happiness of poor helpless human beings in many parts of the world. And now that mouth, even though it be temporarily, is *closed!* Yes, George, liberty is worth the price.

Goodnight and love to all.
John

15

The Sacrifice

*They [the Communists] are getting ready to start
the real war. After China they'll go for Korea. ...
Sooner or later we'll have to fight them.*

—John Birch to Lt. Bill Drummond,
August 20, 1945

Now that the peace was won, the Soviets and the Chinese
Communists moved rapidly to make quick gains. Soviet troops
rolled across Manchuria, meeting little opposition and capturing
huge quantities of weaponry which they would later turn over to their
Chinese comrades.

The Chinese Communists were already moving to exploit the
inevitable chaos and confusion. The Communist plan in China was
to push into Japanese-occupied areas ahead of the Nationalists and
Americans and take over all the territory and arms they could. This
strategy required disruption of communications, airfields and
railroad lines to prevent Nationalist and American officers from
getting there first and receiving the surrender of the Japanese
leaders.

General Wedemeyer was quite aware of Communist intentions.
Shortly before the Japanese surrender, he had received a warning
from the War Department to prepare for sudden Jap collapse. He
was directed to rescue immediately American, British, Dutch and
other Allied prisoners held by the Japanese to prevent a wholesale
slaughter of prisoners as had taken place in the Philippines.

Wedemeyer prepared orders for American OSS teams to get to
the Japanese bases as quickly as possible and arrange for surrender
to the proper authorities. John and Bill Miller were both expecting
orders to move since the first A-bomb drop. They knew of the
Communist threat. Red guerrillas had been all around the Anhwei
Pocket, sabotaging Nationalist facilities. Some had been caught
almost on Miller's doorstep.

Although official U.S. policy viewed the Communist movement as an internal problem the Chinese would have to solve for themselves, the American military had been on the scene long enough to realize the potential danger to peace in China. Wedemeyer and the OSS men were determined to keep the Communists from taking advantage of the end-of-the-war confusion.

When John and Miller kept their morning radio schedule on August 19, they learned that both were bound for the same city, Suchow, where a large Japanese headquarters facility and airfield was located. In the euphoria of knowing that the war was over, they disregarded code and talked openly about how they would get there.

"I'm taking a junk down the Yellow to Pengpu and I'll catch the train north to Suchow from there," Miller said. "Why not come with me?"

"Too risky," John responded. "I hear the Commies are on both banks of the river downstream. They could shoot you and nobody would ever find your body. I'm hoping for a plane to fly us in. Be better if you go with me."

"Nah, I'll take may chances on getting to Pengpu. What if you don't get the plane?"

"I've got an alternative route figured out."

The plane didn't come and John was due to leave the next day, Monday, August 20. That evening Jim Hart, who was living in the same house, stopped by John's room for a visit. Hart was going in a different direction.

There were only three rickety chairs and a bed in John's room. His musette bag with his personal effects lay in a corner. A single dress uniform hung in a closet. John lived very sparingly. At about 135 pounds he was fifteen pounds thinner than usual. He also appeared extremely tired and nervous. As he talked, he kept running his fingers through his russet hair.

Hart knew the plane had not come and asked, "How are you getting to Suchow?"

"I'm going overland to Kweiteh on the Lunghai railroad and get the east train. Suchow is only ninety-five miles from there."

"The Commies may already be on that railroad," Hart warned. "If it were me, I'd go with Miller down the Yellow and take the north train to Suchow."

John repeated what he had told Miller earlier. "Too risky. I prefer my way. If Commies are on the Lunghai, I don't think they'll give Americans any trouble. Not if we're on a train."

"Well, they are on the move, that's for sure," Hart grumbled. "They're grabbing every rifle they can get and trying to take over every base they can from the Japs, claiming they are the legitimate government of China."

"They're getting ready to start the real war," John declared. "After China they'll go for Korea. I've had Korean agents tell me that Communists are already in their country fomenting trouble. Our air force should dump an atom bomb on their capital in Yenan. Sooner or later we'll have to fight them."

"Well, let's hope it doesn't work out that way."

"It's going to be that way," John insisted. "The Bible predicts that a world dictator will arise in the last days, the Antichrist. He'll be a Communist, perhaps Mao Tse-tung."

Hart tried to change the subject, but John, not usually so loquacious, was all wound up. He kept talking about the inevitable conflict between Marxism and Christianity and how it was impossible for the two ideologies to coexist. He compared communism to the Ku Klux Klan. "Anyone who uses any means to justify his end soon comes to violence. The time then comes when people have to close their eyes or fight it. It was that way with the Nazis and the Shintos. Now it will be the Communists."

"Yeah, but you'll be going home soon," Bill offered.

"Yes, but I'll be back."

"You got a girl back in Georgia, John?"

"No. I was engaged to a Scottish nurse down in Changsha, but I decided it would be best if we didn't marry."

Hart said good night around midnight. In the wee hours he woke to see a light shining under John's door. He walked over, thinking his colleague might be ill, and saw John bent over his Bible.

The next morning John assembled his party. They included three other Americans: Lieutenant Laird Ogle, a specialist in morale intelligence; Sergeant Albert C. Meyers, a radio technician; and Albert Grimes, a civilian OSS operative skilled in counterespionage. Grimes wore a 14th Air Force captain's uniform and was second in command. Assisting the uniformed Americans were five Chinese officers and two Japanese-speaking Koreans who went along as interpreters. The group of eleven carried twenty-seven pieces of baggage and three radios. One of the Chinese, Lieutenant Tung Fu-Kuan, was assigned as John's aide.

They left about 1 p.m., trekked northward to a town on the Yellow River and took a junk for a day's journey northeast to another point on the river. They again turned north, walking all night until they reached Kweiteh on the Lunghai Railroad about noon. Here they were received courteously by a Japanese commander who assured them they would be well received in Suchow. However, he warned that Communist guerrillas were causing trouble along the railroad to the east.

The group spent Wednesday and Thursday nights at Kweiteh, then proceeded with two Chinese who had been collaborating with the Japanese, General Peng and his orderly Lei Yu-chi-ing. General Peng was to escort them to his counterpart, the puppet General Ho in Suchow. It was understood that John was still in command of the mission.

They boarded an eastbound train at Kweiteh the next morning. John still believed the Communists would not interdict an American mission on a main railroad line traveling under direct orders of General Wedemeyer.

They encountered no delay for the first forty-five miles, then the train halted at Tangshan station. After a few minutes of waiting, John sent the Koreans to ask the Japanese station-master what was the holdup. The Koreans reported back that the line had been sabotaged ahead and Communists, Japanese and Chinese puppet troops were also fighting in the area. Until the line was repaired and things calmed, the train would remain at Tangshan.

They discussed what to do. Ogle proposed that the four Americans go on alone and try to get through to Suchow. General Peng thought they should all wait in Tangshan, but if the Americans insisted on continuing on, then it was his duty as their escort to accompany them.

"We'll all go," John decided and sent the Koreans to commandeer the locomotive and its crew along with a baggage car. Within an hour they had transferred their equipment and were rolling again.

They only went ten miles before the engineer stopped. They got out and discovered that several rails had been ripped up and carried away. Because a village was nearby and the next station was only a mile ahead, John ordered the baggage unloaded and told the crew to take the locomotive and car back to Tangshan.

"Ogle and I will go into the village and hire coolies to help with our baggage," John said. "The rest of you stay here."

They found only frightened women and children and a Portuguese Catholic priest. "Horrible! Horrible!" the priest exclaimed in Chinese. "The Communists came last night and killed many of the men. The others are still hiding. The Communists desecrated my church and wrecked our mission dispensary. Come and see," he entreated.

John sympathized with him, but explained it was urgent that they move on. He and Ogle hurried back to the railroad and found a Japanese patrol had arrived on a handcar bringing replacement rails. Some of the Jap soldiers were pounding the new rails in place.

Others had taken up defensive positions on both sides of the railroad as if they expected trouble. At John's request, the patrol commander directed his men to move the handcar over the break and load in the group's baggage. He and his men then escorted them to the station where a large supply train was guarded by a garrison of about six hundred Japanese troops.

"Who are you and what is your business?" the commanding officer demanded of John.

John identified himself and his men to his former enemy, but refused to give any details of the mission. "In your position," he told the Japanese officer, "you have no right to ask any such question."

Darkness was now falling fast. The officer suggested the group spend the night in the village. "We will watch your baggage," he promised.

"No, it would be safer to remain here," John said.

"As you wish, Captain. I will have provisions made for eating and sleeping."

The night passed without incident. The group left the next morning, taking turns pumping the loaded handcar. The sun climbed rapidly in a clear sky and by 10 a.m. they were sweating profusely in the summer heat.

They noticed houses all along the right-of-way, but saw few people. No one waved or came out to greet them. Then, coming to a crossroad, they spotted six Chinese workmen.

John hailed them in Chinese. "We will pay you good wages to pump the handcar to the next station," he offered.

"No, cannot," one answered. "We ourselves just escape from Communists. Advise you be on close watch. They are short journey ahead."

A mile or so on they ran into about three hundred armed Communists. "Lieutenant Tung and I will speak with them," John declared.

As John and his aide walked forward, some of the Communists circled in back of the group. John was still in full uniform. The Flying Tigers insignia was known all over China. Tung wore a Chinese uniform with khaki shorts.

"I am Captain Birch, proceeding under orders from General Wedemeyer on an intelligence mission to Suchow," John announced. "This is my assistant, Lieutenant Tung. May we see your man in charge?"

"I will take you to him," one of the Communists replied. "But first you must please disarm."

"No," John replied firmly. "We are allies. We must respect each other."

"Then you cannot see our responsible man. You may speak with our second man."

"I must see your commanding officer."

The man argued some more, then gave in and took John and Tung to a Chinese who he said was the C.O. John again presented himself and Tung. Instead of giving his name, the Communist officer rudely demanded that his men be allowed to examine the group's equipment and take for their own use whatever they might want.

"No," John declared with set jaw. "This is the property of the United States government. It is not for anyone's personal use."

"We can take it if we wish, Captain. Our soldiers have your men surrounded."

John had never before been so challenged by a supposed ally. His eyes hardened, his back stiffened. "You will not take it. If you try to use force, you can expect serious reprisals. My government does not deal lightly with thieves. Now move out and let us be on our way."

Tung passed John his sidearm.

The next Communists they came upon were ripping up track and cutting down telephone poles. Tung went forward and negotiated their passage quickly, but John was seething with anger as his men struggled to pull the heavy handcar over the broken places.

"They call themselves friends of the people. They say in their propaganda that they want to rebuild China. Well, look at them now. Bandits! That's all they are."

They passed through another bunch of Communists successfully, then around 2 p.m. came to a break in the tracks just short of the next station, Hwang Kao. Tung spoke quickly. "I will run ahead and see the man in charge."

John helped his men get the heavy handcar and their baggage across the broken place. The men groaned and complained and kept wiping sweat from their faces. "Bandits! They're nothing but bandits!" John repeated.

Just after they got the handcar back on the rails, two U.S. P-51 fighters flew directly over, heading in the direction of Suchow. The men waved and tried to attract the pilots' attention, but were unsuccessful.

A few minutes later they reached the outskirts of Hwang Kao. Ahead, on the left side of the tracks, was a mud parapet. About twenty armed men were moving around behind it. John motioned for his party to keep going. By the time they reached the parapet, the soldiers were in firing positions with rifles pointed at them.

Tung, who had gone ahead, had entered the railroad station and found it bristling with hostile-looking Communist soldiers. "We are on a mission to Suchow for the American commander in China,

General Wedemeyer," he called. "May I speak with your responsible man, please?"

The Communists before him exchanged suspicious glances. Finally one said, "I will take you." He led Tung outside the station to a nearby house and indicated an officer standing near a window with other soldiers.

As Tung approached, he saw soldiers pointing down the track at his friends and heard whispers: "Here come more spies. We had better disarm them."

Someone then said in a loud voice, directed at Tung, "Lock him up. Surround and disarm the others."

Tung held up his hand in caution. "My friends, the war is over and we have no more enemies. The Americans have helped us very much. I am with Captain Birch's party as you can see. We are bound for Suchow, under orders to inspect the airfield. If you disarm the Americans, you may cause a serious misunderstanding between China and America."

The man who had been pointed out to Tung as being in charge came over. "We will send a man with you to meet your friends." Then Tung overheard the officer say to a subordinate, "Take your gun along. If anything happens, kill this man first and then kill the rest."

Tung pretended not to hear. "What shall I say is your name, sir?" he asked the officer.

"You don't have to ask my name. By the time you get there you will find out."

Accompanied by the Communist soldier, Tung started walking back to meet his companions, who had stopped at the parapet. "My surname is Mao," the soldier now disclosed to Tung. "My family name is of no importance to you." When they reached the group John said, "Who are you? Another bandit?"

General Peng and Albert Grimes both stepped beside John. "Easy," Grimes murmured. "Don't push him." John appeared to relax.

"Are they going to let us pass?" John asked Tung.

Tung repeated to John what he had overheard, including the intention to disarm them. John stepped closer to the Communist who had said his name was Mao. "So you wish to disarm us."

"Easy, John," Grimes cautioned again.

This time John paid no attention. "Americans have liberated the whole world, and you want to stop us and disarm us! Are you bandits? Are you the responsible man? Must we give our guns to you?"

"No, I am not the responsible one. Since you are unwilling to be disarmed, you may proceed. We will not be liable for anything that happens to you." This was spoken in the nature and tone of a threat.

Both John and Tung received the distinct impression that the Communists would let them pass and then shoot them in their backs.

"Take us to your responsible man," John demanded.

At this moment a second Communist officer came up and acted as if he were in charge. The Americans noticed that he was wearing a leather belt with a shoulder strap, the type usually reserved for formal occasions. "No!" he declared, gesturing for the soldier who had accompanied Tung to leave.

"I'm not going any further," Ogle and Grimes heard John say. "I must find out what division these men belong to and see who is their C.O."

General Peng tugged at Tung's sleeve. "Please persuade Captain Birch to be more tactful."

"Very well," the Communist with the dress uniform belt said to John. "You may see our responsible man. Come with me."

"Let Grimes and me go with you," Ogle requested of John.

"No, stay with the others and the equipment."

As they walked along, Tung maneuvered close to John and passed along General Peng's plea. "Never mind," John replied, "you don't know my feelings. I want to find out how they intend to treat Americans. I don't mind if they kill me. If they do, they will be finished. America will punish them with atom bombs."

They entered a house where several other soldiers were lounging about. "Wait here," the officer requested, indicating a bed they could sit on.

They sat on the bed for a while without talking. The officer and the soldiers remained in the house without drawing their guns. Finally John became impatient and broke the silence. "Who really is your responsible man? Will you or won't you let me see him? You have already delayed us over an hour and a half."

The officer wearing the belt looked coldly at John. "Have patience, Captain. We must report in order of rank."

Fearing worse trouble, Tung said, "Please hurry, sir, as we are on an official mission. After we see your responsible man we can proceed."

"All right. We will escort you to the 3rd Garrison Headquarters. Follow this man."

John and Tung stood up and stepped through the door after the man appointed. He led them to the house where Tung had been taken the first time. No one was there. They stepped back outside and asked a soldier, who said, "He is at the north gate."

They went there and found no one. "So sorry, but we now go back where we came from," their escort said. "Please follow me."

As they walked about, twenty armed soldiers moved up along their flanks. The sweat was rolling down John's back. He was hungry and thirsty and running out of patience. Tung, who was still unarmed, kept watching him apprehensively as they walked.

John had almost been at the end of his physical tether when he left Linchuan. The long trip, the debilitating heat, the frustrations and delays by the trouble-making Communists were bringing him close to the breaking point. For three years he had given himself without reserve to free China from the yoke of oppression. Now some of those for whose freedom he had fought were treating him and his men like enemies. More than that, they were insulting his country by such rudeness and disrespect.

The resentment and frustration that had been building up boiled over. John reached and grabbed their guide by the back of his collar. "What are you people? If I say bandits, you don't look like bandits. You are worse than bandits."

The man did not reply.

Tung, alarmed, tried to cool the situation. "Don't take the captain seriously. He is only joking."

They walked a few steps further when a voice called, "Come. Here is our leader."

They turned and saw that it was the officer with the belt again. Tung saluted, but the salute was not returned.

The officer ordered in a swearing, haughty manner, "Load your guns and disarm him first." He was speaking of John, for Tung had remained unarmed all the time.

Tung saw that soldiers had nearly encircled John and were making motions to get his gun. "Wait a minute, please. If you want to disarm him, I will get the gun for you; otherwise a serious misunderstanding may develop."

The officer suddenly pointed at Tung. "Shoot him first."

One of the soldiers fired. A dumdum rifle bullet hit Tung in the right thigh, a few inches above the knee.

"Shoot the American," the officer ordered.

The soldier lifted his rifle, then hesitated.

"Go on, shoot him. It is an order."

He fired, hitting John in the upper left thigh. Tung, dazed, heard another shot fired, though he could not tell how much time had elapsed. He then heard a voice saying, "Bring him along," and John answering, "I'm hit in the leg. I can't walk."

At this time Tung lost consciousness. Later — he could not tell how long — he heard a man say, "This man is not dead yet." A rifle butt crashed across Tung's nose. Again came the voice, "He is not dead yet." Then another voice, "This is enough for him." A pause. "We cannot leave the bodies here." Once more Tung slipped back into merciful oblivion.

While this tragedy was unfolding, the others in the group had been permitted to move up to the station. They were no longer covered and there was some friendly fraternization.

Ogle went into the courtyard to buy fruit. Grimes asked about a better handcar and was given one. Soldiers even helped them transfer their baggage. While this was being done, General Peng's orderly, Lei, took their canteens and went looking for boiled water.

The tenseness had eased since they heard the first shot. Then about fifty or sixty armed soldiers quickly moved up and trained a machine gun on them.

An officer stepped forward. "Who is in charge here?"

"In Captain Birch's absence, I am," Grimes replied.

"Lead your men into the village."

Grimes, the only American besides John who spoke Chinese, refused. "Captain Birch ordered us to watch our equipment," he said.

General Peng, who had put down his sidearm, opened his palms in a pleading gesture. "Don't shoot, don't shoot, we'll talk!"

"Disarm all of them," the Communist ordered.

Soldiers moved among them in disorderly fashion and removed their guns. Then Ogle appeared. "Give us your gun," the officer demanded of him. Ogle looked around, as if to ask, "Why should I?"

"Better let them have it," Grimes counseled. "They've got our weapons." Ogle then complied.

"All of you, let's go," the officer announced and the soldiers began prodding the travelers with their bayonets. They set off at a fast pace. From behind them they heard noises, indicating that bags were being broken open. After covering a short distance, they were lined up against a wall.

Grimes tried to reason with the officer in charge. "Look, we're all allies and friends fighting for the same cause. Why not let us go on our way?"

"Shut up!" came the response. "Do not talk further in English or Chinese or we will kill you." At this time the Communists bound their hands behind their backs and emptied their pockets.

They heard two more shots. Grimes and Ogle now believed that the Communists intended to kill all of them.

The hum of plane motors was heard. The two P-51s were coming back. Quickly they were jammed against houses in an obvious effort to keep from being seen. After the planes passed, they were told to start marching again.

A mile or so outside of the village, Lei, General Peng's orderly, joined them. He was not bound and was freely conversing with the

Communist soldiers. Grimes overheard the Chinese word for "kill" several times, but was unable to determine whether John and Tung had been killed, or whether the remainder of the group was to be killed.

They entered another village and were taken into a small house, left bound and warned once more not to talk. When their guards moved away, General Peng whispered to Grimes, "It would be better if you do not admit any official relations between us."

Peng was called out for interrogation, then Grimes. The questioners wanted to know who they were, where they were going and what their mission was. Grimes told them the truth.

"Your Captain Birch," the interrogators told Grimes, "displayed a very bad temper and provoked our soldiers by his statements and attitude."

Grimes was then lectured about the Communist cause and warned that the Communists would brook no interference in the pursuit of victory. They also attacked the Nationalist Government and accused the Americans in China of being Chiang Kai-shek's agents.

"May I correct you on one point," Grimes interjected. "American army personnel came to China only to fight the Japs. We are not allowed to participate in any way in Chinese political issues."

"That is what you say," the interrogator declared. "You will see to it that your men will cause no trouble and do exactly as you are told."

Grimes was then taken back and allowed to talk to his companions. He told Ogle and Sergeant Meyers, "I believe John and Tung are either dead or seriously wounded."

"I think so too," Ogle said. "As I was coming back with the fruit, I saw three villagers running across the courtyard with their hands pressed to their heads. They had seen something they didn't want to see."

Ogle thought about this a minute. Then he said, "Ask permission for me to be taken to John. We can't leave him and Tung without knowing their condition."

"It'd be useless to ask," Grimes replied. "They wouldn't grant the request and by asking we would jeopardize all our lives."

When Ogle persisted, Grimes reminded him that in John's absence he was in charge, adding, "The situation is still far too tense to make any request of any sort."

A little further on, the orderly, Lei, whispered that he knew the fate of Captain Birch and Lieutenant Tung. "While I was getting water I heard shots. I ran to the window and saw the soldiers slashing at Captain Birch's face with bayonets and knives. I must believe the Lieutenant is dead also."

While this travesty was happening to John and his group, Lieutenant Bill Miller was also having problems. Miller had left the Anhwei Pocket with his group, feeling completely confident that he would beat John to Suchow. When he was delayed on the north-south railroad by Communist sabotage he was deflated, for that was just what John had predicted would happen. He finally arrived in Suchow on August 29 riding a Japanese armored train. Fully expecting to find John waiting with an I-told-you-so grin, he was surprised when he stepped off the train into the damp night air to be greeted by the Japanese stationmaster with the words, "You are the first American I have talked to since before the war."

Instead of being elated to find he had chosen the better route, Miller felt a pang of concern. The stationmaster invited him to have a cup of tea, and while they were exchanging polite amenities his host casually asked if he had heard about the murder of an American army captain by Communists. "I understand it was a very brutal murder," he added.

A cold shiver ran up Miller's spine as he thought, *That could have been John.*

"The Captain's Chinese name was Bey Shang We," the stationmaster continued. "Did you know him?"

Miller's ashen face and shocked expression answered the question even before he muttered numbly, "He was my friend. My very good friend. We talked every day on the radio."

"I am very sorry."

"What happened?" Miller pressed the Japanese. It seemed difficult to accept the fact that John was dead. His faith in God had been so strong, it had always made him seem rather invincible.

"I don't know much about it," came the kind reply. "The incident occurred about thirty miles west of here, in Hwang Kao. I understand the Captain's face was mutilated beyond recognition. His Chinese aide survived and was brought to the Suchow Hospital. Perhaps you could learn more from him."

Miller rushed to the hospital where he found Tung burning up with a 106-degree temperature. "We couldn't save his leg," a Chinese doctor explained solicitously. "It was gangrenous and infected from a large wound caused by a dumdum bullet."

Miller shuddered. Dumdums were outlawed under the Hague Rules of War.

"He also received severe blows to the head. We had to remove one eye. You can see that he is in very bad condition, but perhaps he will be able to tell you something."

Miller moved a chair close to Tung's bed and introduced himself through an interpreter.

"Poor Bey Shang We," the feverish Chinese moaned. "Poor Bey Shang We."

"How did it happen? Can you tell me, Lieutenant? It will help in bringing his murderers to justice."

"Yes, yes," Tung replied, "I will tell you all I can remember. We left Linchuan on Monday, August 20..."

Miller took rapid notes as Tung talked with amazing coherence.

"... I heard a third shot, then someone said, 'We can't leave the bodies here.' I sensed Bey Shang We's body being moved first. Then I felt them pick me up by the arms and legs and carry me off to a trench where I was thrown next to him.

"I must have fainted again, as the next thing I remember was a voice saying, 'We can't leave these bodies in the open air: their spirits will haunt us at night.' I recognized that these were farmers speaking.

" 'We had better bury them now,' one said.

" 'I am not dead yet,' I pleaded. 'If you can't rescue me, then kill me here.'

" 'Shhh,' one whispered. 'The Communists are still around. We will come back when they have gone.'

"I lay there beside Bey Shang We's cold body. After dark the farmers returned and moved me to a bomb shelter. Someone gently took off my bloody clothes and covered me. Then a small boy brought hot tea which renewed my strength.

"The next people I saw were Japanese soldiers. When I told them who I was, they departed without a word. The next morning more Jap soldiers came by. They remembered me as being in Bey Shang We's group that had stayed with their garrison two nights before. After giving me food and medical attention they left.

"That's all I remember," Tung whispered in a weakening voice. "Poor Bey Shang We. I tried to help him. If he had only acted more calmly, he might be alive now."

"What happened to the others in your party?" Miller gently pressed.

"I never saw them after we were shot."

Miller left Tung in the care of the Chinese doctor and went to the hospital morgue, where John's body lay wrapped in yards of white silk. He took a quick look at the face. He had looked upon mutilated faces before, but this was his friend. Shuddering, he located the teeth and saw that a bridge in front was missing. John had worn a bridge. The body build was also John's. When he saw the photographs taken before the body was wrapped, he was certain this was his friend.

It seemed so bitterly unfair that John, who had gone through so much danger throughout the war, should die like this after the peace had been won. He had risked his life many times fighting the enemy, and now he lay there grotesquely mutilated by the Chinese he had loved so much.

Miller resolved to find out as much as he could so the men who had perpetrated this hideous crime would be brought to justice.

Further investigation disclosed that John's body had been rolled in a mat and partially covered with dirt by the superstitious farmers. There was evidence from the Chinese autopsy report that after being hit in the thigh, John had been shot in the back of the head at close range. His feet had been bound together at the ankles and the hands tied together behind his back — the usual position for Chinese execution. This indicated that after the original wound he had been bound and forced to kneel for execution.

General Mori, the Japanese commander at Suchow, had refused to surrender to Chinese Communists and was waiting for a Nationalist representative to arrive. He offered Miller the use of his powerful radio to send a message to General Wedemeyer's headquarters in Chungking.

"Captain Birch was not only a brave man, but an important officer in the American army," Miller told General Mori. "He deserves a suitable funeral."

The little Japanese commander bowed. "I am at your service, Lieutenant."

"Captain Birch was a Christian. Do you know of Christian missionaries in Suchow?"

"There is a Catholic cathedral here and some Italian Jesuit fathers. We allowed them to stay since Italy was our ally."

Miller, the Italian Jesuits, General Mori and other officers and Chinese puppet officials who had governed Suchow under the Japanese planned John's funeral together. Two American pilots had died in crash-landings at the Suchow airport and the group decided to incorporate their funerals with John's.

At the appointed hour the entire Japanese high command in Suchow, twenty high-ranking officers, Chinese officials and other leading citizens marched solemnly with Lieutenant Miller into the towering Catholic cathedral for a requiem high mass.

Following the mass, a mournful Japanese military band led a procession through the streets of the city. Twenty-four Chinese coolies carried the flag-draped coffins to the burial site on a wooded slope of the Hung-lung Mountain overlooking the south side of Suchow.

The three American officers were to be interred in side-by-side crypts, with John in the center. At the graveside a Chinese Protestant minister performed the final rites, followed by Latin prayers from the priests. As the coffins were eased into their final resting places, a Japanese drummer beat a sad farewell while the crowd of dignitaries, Confucianists, Buddhists, Shintoists, Catholics and a few Protestants stood in respectful silence. Then at the command of a Japanese officer, three rifle salutes were sounded and the masons began cementing the stones in place. After the crypts were secured, the workmen stenciled vital statistics at the front of each vault, adding below John's name and date of death:

CAPTAIN JOHN M. BIRCH
AUGUST 25, 1945

HE DIED FOR THE CAUSE OF
RIGHTEOUSNESS

16

Afterword

Truth crushed to earth shall rise again:
Th' eternal years of God are hers;
But Error, wounded, writhes in pain,
And dies among his worshippers.

—William Cullen Bryant,
"The Battle Field"

That Captain John M. Birch had been brutally murdered by Chinese Communists was well known among his military colleagues in China. But even though the war was officially over, news from China was still subject to censorship by American officials who did not want the Birch family and other Americans to know what had happened. The reason would later become obvious: These deluded Americans favored the Communists in their attempt to unseat Chiang Kai-Shek's Nationalist government and take over China by revolutionary force. If Americans learned that China's so-called "agrarian reformers" had murdered one of the war's greatest heroes, public opinion might swing in favor of the Nationalists. The future of China was at stake. These censors who valued Communist ideology more than truth wanted China to be a Marxist nation.

Most Americans in China were not naive about the plans of Mao's reformers. Among them was General Albert Wedemeyer, commander of American forces there. Wedemeyer, who had not known John Birch personally, was infuriated when he heard of John's murder, the abuse and wounding of Lieutenant Tung and the capture of other members of the party. In Wedemeyer's patriotic mind, the atrocities amounted to direct hostile action by Mao's forces against the United States of America.

Wedemeyer was already in a stew when he got news of the atrocities in Hwang Kao. This was not the first time Americans had been attacked by Communists in recent weeks. On May 28 two U.S. officers, two enlisted men and a Chinese had parachuted into North

China and been captured by Communist forces. Wedemeyer's letter demanding their immediate release had gone unanswered. Then, near the time of the incident at Hwang Kao, a group of American Marines had been fired on while pushing a handcar along a railroad track. Now an American officer and war hero, John Birch, had been murdered.

Wedemeyer learned that Mao and Chou En-Lai were at that moment in American Ambassador Pat Hurley's office. He called the Ambassador. "I've just heard that the Communists have murdered one of my men. Can I come over and speak to Mao and Chou?"

When Wedemeyer arrived, Hurley saw that he was very angry. Hurley was under orders from President Truman to seek a reconciliation between the Chinese Nationalists and the Communists. "Mr. Chairman," he now hastened to say to Mao, "General Wedemeyer is your friend. He is understandably upset because one of his men was killed."

"No, I am not his friend," Wedemeyer said in an aside to Hurley.

The American commander got right to the point. "Mr. Mao, I've just received a message that one of my officers, a Captain John Birch, was killed by some of your men near Suchow. A Chinese officer was wounded, and three other Americans and some Chinese and Korean soldiers were taken captive."

Because Mao did not speak English, Chou interpreted for him. "The Chairman regrets that your Captain Birch has been killed. He extends his sympathy to the family."

"Mr. Mao," Wedemeyer continued firmly, "I demand an investigation of this matter. I want to know what happened. I want the guilty people punished. I don't want it to happen again."

When Chou translated this, Mao nodded gravely. "The Chairman will ask our senior military commander, General Chu Teh, to conduct a most thorough investigation," Chou translated. "If a crime has been committed, you may be assured the criminals will be punished."

"Tell Mr. Mao I will hold him personally responsible to see that this promise is carried out," Wedemeyer replied.

Wedemeyer returned to his office and dictated two memoranda. He sent one to Chiang Kai-shek requesting "an immediate and thorough investigation of this serious incident." The other went to Mao, spelling out sharply these demands:

"That you immediately conduct an investigation and submit a report to this Headquarters by 14 September relative to the true facts of the 28 May and 25 August incidents.

That immediate steps be taken to release the American personnel involved.

That you inform this Headquarters as to what steps are being taken by you to preclude similar unfortunate occurrences involving U.S. personnel.

It is not always feasible or possible to furnish advance information to commanders in remote areas within China when U.S. personnel are operating against the common enemy. It is my position, however, that U.S. personnel are entitled at all times to fullest cooperation everywhere in China in conducting their legitimate operations. I have been directed by my government to use whatever force I deem necessary in order to insure that U.S. personnel and property may proceed on legitimate missions without interference.

The American commander warned Mao that:

the U.S. Government and the American people [will view] the capture of the four men on 28 May and the hostilities against the Birch mission on 25 August as being of the gravest importance ... and will require consequences.

Mao acted quickly. Within a week the Americans captured on May 28 were released. General Chu Teh, Mao's military commander, reported that Ogle, Grimes and Meyers were being given "safe escort" to an airfield for evacuation. However, it was two months before the three were permitted to fly back to Chungking.

Mao's spokesman denied any criminal responsibility for the death of Captain Birch and the wounding of Lieutenant Tung. The Communist general ignored Wedemeyer's contention that American soldiers were "entitled at all times to fullest cooperation everywhere in China" and that it wasn't "always feasible or possible" to give advance notice of their whereabouts.

Mao insisted his soldiers had not known the Birch party was coming along the railroad. He maintained that the Japanese were still fighting around Huang Kao on the day the incident occurred and gave an entirely different narration of the incident from what Tung had given Miller:

During this tense period, two sentries of the rear guard ... discovered two armed persons, a foreigner and a Chinese, coming from the enemy direction toward them. They were immediately challenged by the sentries to halt and be recognized, but they did not obey the order, pulled out their arms, and dashed forward to the place where deputy battalion commander Chang was, cursing while advancing.

This obvious whitewashing of the incident in no way satisfied Wedemeyer. He ordered OSS investigators to follow up on Miller's questioning of Tung. The Chinese officer, now rapidly improving, doggedly stuck by his story. Comparisons of transcripts gave absolutely no indication that he was lying. Grimes, Ogle and Meyers, were interrogated after their release and confirmed everything up to the time when John and Tung left them. They related the Chinese orderly's eyewitness account of John's murder.

Wedemeyer gave all of his correspondence and transcripts of the interviews to Lieutenant Colonel Jeremiah O'Connor, Deputy Judge Advocate of the China War Theater. On November 13, Judge O'Connor presented a formal report of his findings, making these salient points:

> The presence of the Birch party had not been announced in the area, and the Communists were still in battle action. Therefore "it was entirely proper for them to hold Birch and Tung until satisfied that they were friendly." The Communists were "to a degree properly resentful at being termed 'bandits.'" However, the actions taken by the Chinese Communist Army personnel fell short of according the rights and privileges due even to enemy prisoners of war and constituted murder. The shooting was done maliciously ... The killing was completely without justification.
>
> Captain Birch and Lieutenant Tung, at the time of the shooting, were surrounded by more than twenty armed soldiers. The assumption that Birch (who of the two alone was armed) would have attempted gunplay seems entirely unwarranted and therefore the reply from the Communists seems worthy only of disbelief.
>
> Unlawful dumdum bullets were used, which expand or flatten easily in the human body.
>
> The statement of the second officer to 'shoot him [Tung] first' seems clearly to indicate the total lack of necessity for quick action if Birch had made any menacing gesture. Further, it appears that the soldier who was ordered to shoot hesitated at first and had to be ordered a second time. Tung states that neither he nor Birch at any time attempted to use their weapons.
>
> Birch had resided in China prior to the war and had had much intelligence experience, apparently with a very fine record. Ordinarily it would be assumed that he would know how to proceed in operations like the one during which he was killed.
>
> Birch was in the full uniform of the United States and clearly entitled to the minimum protection due to soldiers or organized army forces.
>
> Birch and Tung were given 'the runaround' after asking to see the commanding officer. ... The Communists were not interested in showing anything but hostility to members of friendly forces.
>
> Birch was struck in the leg first, which was presumably sufficient if the purpose was merely to assist in disarming him. Apparently the

purpose went beyond that when the second shot was fired and he was
bayonetted.

... There is a distinct probability that Birch's face was mutilated in
order to prevent identification of the body.

It is strange that the Communist reply does not take a stronger
attitude in view of the allegation that Birch and Tung drew guns and
threatened the Communists.

Lieutenant Tung was badly beaten as he lay upon the ground, after
being wounded by a bullet. His face was bashed in by a rifle butt, which
resulted in permanent blindness in his right eye. This treatment is added
evidence of the use of maliciously excessive force and the fact that the
Communists' conduct was of reprehensible nature.

The Communists had identified the man responsible for John
Birch's murder as a deputy battalion commander named Chiang, but
refused to admit guilt. The Chinese Nationalist government sent
three telegrams asking that the Communists turn over Chiang and
any others involved "so they can be court-martialed." The
Communists did not respond.

General Wedemeyer wrote Chiang Kai-shek two letters,
demanding punishment of the guilty Communists. Chiang did not
respond to these letters, dated 4 December 1945, and 28 February
1946. In any case, there was nothing the Nationalists could do.

Over six months had now elapsed. Early in March 1946,
Wedemeyer sent the file to his superiors in Washington. The War
Department stamped it SECRET and placed it under lock and key.
By this time President Truman had disbanded the OSS, naively
assuming the U.S. was no longer in need of an international
intelligence service. Any files which the OSS might have had on the
John Birch case were transferred to the War or State Departments.

Apparently none of John Birch's files, including the Wedemeyer
investigation of his murder, was made available to the White House,
the Senate, or to Congress.

The Knowland speech given in the Senate in 1950 was read by a
candy manufacturer and conservative political analyst named Robert
Welch. In 1954 Welch published his slim biography of John Birch. The
book caused a mild sensation. *The Saturday Evening Post*, for example,
editorialized:

Amazingly, there were in Washington responsible officials who
were willing to suppress news of the murder of an American officer,
apparently to prevent the American people from rising in their wrath
and veto further appeasement of communism. Not a great deal can be

said for the judgment, discretion and reliability of those responsible for suppressing the tragic and revealing story of Captain John Birch.

In 1958 Welch organized an anti-communist society to "promote less government, more responsibility, and a better world," which he named in John Birch's honor, with the consent of John's parents. The controversy that erupted over the John Birch Society triggered a spate of media stories about the real John Birch. In trying to discredit the Birch Society many writers tried to tarnish the heroism of its namesake. Some gave the impression that John was more responsible for his own death than his executioners.

A few of John's old wartime associates sought to defend him as a genuine hero. Jim Hart, who had known him at Linchuan, tried to publish a new biography and had to be content with two installments in a men's adventure magazine (*Saga*, July and August, 1961). None of these writers had access to the secret file which remained hidden to public eyes for so many years after the war ended.

Finally, in 1972, Samuel J. Archibald, a journalism professor, forced the declassification of the John Birch file through the Freedom of Information Act. However, release of the file was held up until after President Nixon's news-making trip to China. Archibald loaned his copy to Wesley McCune, then director of Group-Research Inc., a Washington-based organization which monitored the activities of political conservatives. McCune wrote an article for the *Washington Post* titled, "John Birch: Did He Seek Death?" McCune suggested that John had been primarily responsible for his own death. This understandably upset the Birch family and many of John's military associates. Bill Miller responded: "John Birch could only have saved his own life by humiliating himself and his country before the Chinese Communists."

When we began researching this biography we were unable to locate a copy of the file in U.S. Army or Air Force archives. General Wedemeyer tried to obtain a copy for us from highly placed friends without success. Wedemeyer then graciously loaned us his personal copy after we had interviewed him for this book.

Most of the leading figures of the World War II - China era are dead. Generals Wedemeyer and Doolittle are deceased. General Stilwell died of stomach cancer in 1946. Mao Tse-tung, Chou En-Lai and Chiang Kai-shek have also passed on.

General Chennault succumbed to lung cancer in 1958. Colonel Wilfred Smith, John's C.O., who was an important source for this book, visited Chennault when he was dying. "Son, I want to tell you something," the Old Man rasped. "I never knew how you and the boys did what you did, but I appreciated everything." Recalling the emotional reunion, Smith said, "That was better than the Medal of Honor. That was thanks from the Tiger."

Shortly before his death Chennault received a phone call from the White House informing him that Congress and the President of the United States had conferred on him the third star of a lieutenant general. President Dwight D. Eisenhower extended his personal congratulations.

Some of John Birch's officer colleagues are still living. At last word, Jesse Williams was living in Texas, Malcolm Rosholt in Wisconsin, Arthur Hopkins in Florida, Paul Frillman in New York and Bill Miller in the Virgin Islands. Jim Hart died in 1977, his dream of publishing a book about John Birch unfilled.

John's missionary pal Oscar Wells lives with his wife in Bethany, Oklahoma. Fred Donnelson died in 1974. J. Frank Norris passed on in 1952.

John's friend, Marjorie Tooker, resides in Vermont. She helped with our research. Jenny Campbell, an assumed name to protect her privacy, was last known to be living in England. Both Marjorie and Jenny made trips to see the Birch family in Georgia after the war. Jenny never married. She continued to correspond with one of John's aunts and reportedly said that if John had survived the war, they would have married.

All of John's siblings are still alive. All, except George Stanley, were interviewed by us for this book. Robert and his wife Jenae, the keeper of John's war papers and letters, kindly provided us access to the confidential materials. John's well-marked Bible was stolen from sister Betty's car in Atlanta.

Ethel Birch longed to write a book about her son. After the war she solicited letters and personal interviews from all of those close to John in China. These recollections, given when the memory of John was still fresh in the minds of his friends, along with the journal kept by Mrs. Birch during her travels, were generously made available to us by the family.

In January, 1977, Mrs. Birch suffered a stroke. Her husband, George, remained with her day and night until she slipped away on September 2. Before she was hospitalized Robert had assured her, "Don't worry, Mother. If the Lord is ready for you, you'll be seeing John before too long."

Tears rolled down her face. "I know, Son. I'll see him face to face." At her funeral they sang her favorite hymn, "Face to Face" which had been written by her father's only sister.

We talked with George Birch in Macon. He was then living by himself a few blocks from sons Robert and Ellis. An oversized portrait of John in military uniform stared down at us from a living room wall. John's medals, awarded by General Chennault and the Chinese National Government, hung beside the portrait.

Mr. Birch lived with his daughter Betty in North Carolina for six years until his death three months short of his 100th birthday in 1992.

Our research sources included the Yale-in-China Association, the John Birch Society, PO Box 8040, Appleton, WI 54913, the Baptist Fellowship, Overseas Missionary Fellowship (formerly the China Inland Mission), the Library of Congress, the Chattanooga-Hamilton County Bicentennial Library, Bryan College's Ironside Memorial Library and the Mercer University Library. Drs. Dozier Cade and Theodore Mercer gave special assistance. Cade, then director of the School of Journalism at the University of Tennessee, was the official interrogator of Lieutenant Tung, John Birch's critially wounded aide. Mercer, then president of Bryan College in Dayton, Tennessee, first challenged us to look into the intriguing life of John Birch and provided introductions to members of John Birch's family.

John Birch is known today mainly by the Society which bears his name. Few other tokens of his life exist. A World War II casualty monument stands at the top of Coleman Hill Park (a municipal park) overlooking downtown Macon, Georgia. John's name is on the bronze plaque thereon, along with the names of other Macon men who lost their lives while serving with the Armed Forces. He is further honored by a plaque on the sanctuary of the First Southern Methodist Church of Macon. It was built on land given by his family, taken from a tract purchased with the money John sent home monthly. A building at the First Baptist Church of Fort Worth, where J. Frank Norris was pastor, is named The John Birch Hall. A small street in a housing development in a suburb of Boston is also named for him.

The rolling hills in south Georgia that John Birch loved so much are still in the family. His father had held on to the property tenaciously until his death. The 600 acres are now owned by John's brothers. A few stone walls covered with cudzo are all that remain of the home that burned while John was in China. But the land — the land that John dreamed of while writing his essay *War Weary Farmer* — remains.

And China?

His grave monument and the marker erected at the Hwang Kao railroad station where he was killed have undoubtedly been destroyed, but surely there are many Chinese who still remember Bey Shang We.

Index

H

I

J

K

L

200

M

N

O

P

R

S

Y

Please send me:

___

The Secret File on John Birch by James & Marti Hefley
_____ Copies at $12.95 = _____

___

We Can Change America... and here's how! by Darylann
Whitemarsh. For Americans who want to change the direction
our country is going. Step-by-step instructions and
illustrations that are geared to the individual.
_____ Copies at $9.95 = _____

___

"Mama, it ain't over 'til the pink marble comes!" by Sandee
Williams with Jeanne Todd. The story of Dorothy Williams as she
helps her family cope with her diagnosis and death from cancer.
_____ Copies at $9.95 = _____

___

Escape from America by Wallace Henley. A spine-chilling novel
of suspense and intrigue that warns of what America could become.
_____ Copies at $8.95 = _____

___

When Evil Strikes by Lila Wold Shelburne. Despite
seemingly impossible circumstances, Romans 8:28 is
validated in this powerful story that reads like fiction.
_____ Copies at $9.95 = _____

___

In His Steps Today by Marti Hefley. The novel that asks the
question "What would Jesus do if he were living today?" A best
seller that is fiction with a challenge.
_____ Copies at $7.95 = _____

___

On The 8th Day... *God Laughed,* Gene Perret with Terry Perret
Martin. Arranged alphabetically by topic, this collection of 900 jokes
by Bob Hope's head writer is a belly buster.
_____ Copies at $5.95 _____

___

*Please add $2.00 postage and handling for first book,
plus .50 for each additional book.*
Shipping & Handling _____
MO residents add sales tax _____

TOTAL ENCLOSED (Check or money order)_____

Name _____

Address _____

City_____State____ Zip _____ Phone_____
MAIL TO HANNIBAL BOOKS, 921 Center, Hannibal, MO 63401.
Satisfaction guaranteed. Credit card orders call 1-800-747-0738
during regular business hours.

Country Classics from Hannibal Books

Way Back in the Hills, by James C. Hefley. Colorful autobiography of the author's growing-up-years in the Ozark mountains.

_____ Copies at $4.99 = _____

Way Back When by James C. Hefley. Relive the "good ol' days" when the first white settlers made their way deep into the Ozark mountains.

_____ Copies at $5.95 = _____

Way Back in the Ozarks, by Howard Jean Hefley & James C. Hefley. Stories of a boy named "Monk," his dog & his coon.

_____ Copies at $5.95 = _____

Way Back in the Ozarks, Book 2 by Howard Jean Hefley & James C. Hefley. "Ozark Monk" relives the tale of Danny Boy.

_____ Copies at $5.95 = _____

Way Back in the Ozarks, VHS VIDEO TAPE Meet "Ozark Monk" as he entertains you with stories from his first book. Filmed on location.

_____ Copies at $15.95 = _____

Way Back in the "Korn"fields by James C. Hefley. You'll hoot and holler, guffaw and grin at over 900 jokes with a decidedly country flavor. Arranged alphabetically by topic.

_____ Copies at $5.95 = _____

In Care of the Conductor, by Jim Rogers. A young boy grows up during the depression in Newton County, Mississippi

_____ Copies at $5.95 = _____

Please add $2.00 postage and handling for first book, plus $.50 for each additional book.

Shipping & Handling _____

MO residents add sales tax _____

TOTAL ENCLOSED _____

Name _____

Address _____

City_____State____ Zip _____ Phone _____

MAIL TO HANNIBAL BOOKS, 921 Center, Hannibal, MO 63401. Satisfaction guaranteed. Credit card orders call 1-800-747-0738 during regular business hours.